Empath and Psychic abilities

The survival path for highly sensitive people: Practice meditation to discover the power of your mind with intuition, telepathy, aura reading and clairvoyance. Open your third eye and find a connection with your spirit guide.

D1721358

Tara Brakh

Empath

Table of Contents

Empath

///

Empath

Psychic Abilities Guide

Empath

Empath

Empath

Survival guide to understand empathy gift. Discover the potential of highly sensitivity to protect yourself from negative energy. learn how evolve your emotion in relationship and self- confidence.

Tara Brakh

Empath

Introduction

What Is an Empath?

An "empath" is someone with an extrasensory ability to sense and/or feel the emotions of others, such as a telepathic faculty. This can be useful for understanding others and helping people in need, but it also has its drawbacks. Many people don't like being around an empathetic person because they believe that their emotions can distract them from their own lives.

How to Deal with an Empath?

Although there are numerous means to help yourself cope with being around an empathic person, they're not easy or quick fixes. For thing, you have to be ready to talk about your feelings with the empath, which can be emotionally challenging. The good news is that once you're both feeling comfortable with the topic, you can usually work out a compromise where one of you does the interpreting for the other so that both of you end up feeling better.

What Causes Empathy?

Empathy has been around for centuries. It's hard to say when or where empathy was first developed, but ancient Greek philosophers, like Socrates and Aristotle, thought that it was inborn in everyone. People who had a hard time carrying on conversations because all they could think about was themselves were seen as highly empathetic by their peers and neighbors.

Many people believe that empathy is down to the way your brain is wired. In general, we use our senses (like sight and hearing) to interpret what's going on around us, so if someone's upset, you can usually tell by looking at them or listening to their speech. According to this view, emotions are the same way. When you feel sad or angry, it's because something in your environment has affected your senses in a negative way.

When Are Emotions Connected?

In the past 20 years, researchers have found that there are many levels of empathy. At the most basic level, you can feel what others are feeling by looking at their facial expressions and listening to their tone of voice. But when emotions get more complicated, they make a connection in several areas in the brain. This is why you may start to feel a wave of sadness as soon as you hear about someone's loss, but not when you hear about someone's gain.

How to Try out an Empath's Skills?

If you're eager to try out empathy but are afraid of upsetting the other person, there are ways you can try to help without being intrusive. For example, if someone comes up to you and the first thing that they say is "I'm so pissed off," then stop what you're doing and listen. Also, if someone's angry or upset with something that's happened recently, take a moment to listen and then help them come up with solutions.

Is Empathy Defined?

You may feel anxious reading this book because it makes it sound like empaths are just accident-prone people who fail at everything they do. But let's be clear: There's a big difference between empathy and sympathy. Sympathy is when you feel sorry for someone's situation, and empaths can definitely do that, but empathy is more about being able to relate to a person's emotions or feelings. So, empaths and non-empaths both experience emotions—they just experience them in different ways.

Empaths Can Find It Hard to Make Friends

Having this characteristic can make social situations confusing for you, especially if you're really worried about upsetting the other person by getting too close. This "getting close" part is where things get tricky because it doesn't always mean that two people are going to automatically like each other.

This book will not only teach you about what empathy is all about but how it can help you as an empath and how to better understand yourself when it comes to empathizing with the people around you.

Empath

What Is an Empath?

The hallmark of an empath is the ability to feel, absorb, and understand people's emotions—and, to some extent, the people's thoughts. However, using this general statement as a basis for determining one's likelihood of being an empath is not enough. You also have to examine if you or the person you evaluate possesses the following main traits of empathic individuals.

Extremely Sensitive

Sensitivity among empaths comes in two forms. First, their sense of smell and hearing tends to be more acute than normal people. They can easily get overwhelmed by strong odors, loud noises, and people who talk incessantly.

Second, their sensitive nature makes them easily affected by the words and emotions of other people. They are inherently good

Empath

listeners, but sometimes to a fault. Their openness towards others leaves them vulnerable to being taken advantage of or being hurt by the people around them.

Highly Intuitive

Through intuition, empaths can find out who would be ideal companions for them. Listening to their guts allows them to avoid being stuck with energy vampires and toxic people. However, trusting their intuition takes time and practice, even though empaths typically possess this trait upon birth.

Caring

Empaths generally have a soft spot for those who are in need. Seeing scenes of misery and helplessness tug at their heartstrings. However, instead of just finding ways to help out, empaths feel others' suffering and pain as if they were their own.

For empaths, caring is not simply reaching out to a homeless man who is starving and thirsty. They would feel the ache and distress of that man intensely, causing them to feel upset even if they were fine just a moment ago. That is why empaths try to make others feel better, whether they will get something back in return or not.

Emotionally Absorptive

An empath's emotions are only as good as the emotions of those around them. If their companions feel happy and motivated, the empath would absorb these positive vibes and adapt to similar feelings. However, if the people nearby feel despondent, the empath's emotions would reflect the same mood.

Introverted

Because of their sensitive and absorbent nature, empaths prefer to be alone or be with a small group. Even if the empath is on the more extroverted side of the spectrum, they impose limits on how many parties and social gatherings they would go to and how long they will stay there.

Overwhelmed by Intimacy

Too much intimacy with another person can be challenging for empaths. Because they tend to absorb the feelings of those around them, most empaths fear that they will be influenced too much by their partner, causing loss of their identity eventually. They can be in a healthy intimate relationship as long as their partner is willing to understand their needs and compromise along the way.

Attuned with Nature

Everyday life can be exhausting for empaths. They have to deal with the different emotions and demands of the people around them. As such, they relish time spent out in nature where they can be alone and regain their focus and energy. Hiking, camping, or going to the beach are some of the outdoor activities that many empaths enjoy doing.

Being an empath can be a curse or a gift, depending on how one would look at it. Examining people's traits with this special ability provides good points for either side of the argument. Therefore, it is now in the hands of the empaths themselves how they will make the most out of the positive traits and the negative traits associated with empathy.

Empath

General Types of Empaths

Being an empath is like being an artist. While art is fundamentally about self-expression, it takes many forms, such as painting, sculpture, dance, and the like. The same can be said for empaths. Although the fundamental reality of being an empath remains fairly the same, there are several different types of empaths that a person can be. We will talk about 6 different types of empaths, showing which qualities are unique to each. With this information, you will be able to identify the exact form of empathy you possess and how it can apply to your day-to-day life.

Emotional Empath

Emotional empaths are the most common type of empath and the most basic. This is the variation that most people identify with when they think of the term "empath." As an emotional empath, you will be able to sense the emotions of those around you, thereby knowing what a person is feeling regardless of their outward appearance. The ease with which you can sense others' emotions can be both a blessing and a curse. Although it can be a good thing to know what another person is truly feeling, the truth is that you can sense the emotions of others as easily as you sense your own feelings. This can make it difficult to differentiate between the two at times, causing a fair amount of emotional confusion as a result.

To say that you can sense other people's emotions may actually be understating your experience somewhat. The fact is that you cannot only sense how others are feeling, but you can share those feelings as well. Again, this can cause significant confusion concerning your actual emotional state. You will probably experience mood swings as a result of how others are feeling, and this can make you seem unstable in extreme cases. Subsequently, it is important to develop the ability to differentiate between the emotions of others and your own feelings. This will help you stay true to your emotional state regardless of the environment you are in. Additionally, by remaining detached, you can be more beneficial when helping those around you since you aren't allowing your own energies to be altered or drained by their emotional experience.

Physical/Medical Empath

The second type of empath is physical/medical empath. If you possess this type of empathy, you will be able to sense another person's physical health and well-being. Essentially, the experience is the same as with emotional empathy; however, instead of being able to tap into another person's emotional state, you can tap into their physiological state. One way this takes shape is that you get an image or a sense of "something wrong." For example, if someone has a chronic illness, such as diabetes, the word "diabetes" might appear in your mind, seemingly out of nowhere. Alternatively, you might actually be able to feel the symptoms of another person the same way an emotional empath can feel another person's emotions. This can be very distressing if you don't know what is going on since you may experience numerous symptoms throughout any given day, even though you are in perfect health yourself.

Geomantic Empath

Geomantic empaths are those who can sense the energy of a place, landscape, or environment. If you have ever experienced a strong emotional response to being in a place, you might be a geomantic empath. However, this is only true in the case that the environment is relatively free of people. After all, if there are many people in

Empath

an area, you might actually be picking up on their energies, which is what an emotional empath would do. Geomantic empaths, in contrast, feel the energy of an environment that is relatively deserted, meaning they are feeling the energy of the place, not of other people.

One example of this can be seen in nature. As a geomantic empath, you will feel a deeper sadness anytime you witness trees being cut down or patches of natural land being developed for human use. The sorrow you feel for such an event would be similar to the sorrow an average person would feel for a tragedy in which numerous lives were lost. Essentially, as a geomantic empath, you identify all life as equally sacred, and the fact that you feel the energy of natural environments only strengthens that fact.

Plant Empath

One of the things that most empaths discover at some point in their lives is that the energy that flows through humans is very much the same as the energy that flows through all of nature. Therefore, it will be no surprise to discover that there is an actual form of empathy that specifically focuses on plants. If this form describes you, then you are a plant empath. Like a physical/medical empath, you can sense and identify the physical well-being of those around you. However, in this case, instead of people, it's all about the plants around you. This means you have an intuitive green thumb!

As a plant empath, you can feel the actual needs of the plants you come into contact with. To the outsider, this can seem as though you are keenly observant, capable of discerning a plant's health by even the subtlest of signs. However, the truth is that you only find those signs because you know what to look for. This can make you very capable of working in places as parks, nurseries, or for any type of landscaping company.

Animal Empath

Most empaths feel a closer bond to nature, resulting in them having more plants and animals in their lives. However, an animal empath takes this bond to a whole new level. Much like a plant empath, animal empaths can sense the condition and needs of any animal they come into contact with. One of the main differences between plants and animals, however, is the depth of communication that can occur between animals and animal empaths. While plants can communicate needs and conditions, animals can communicate feelings, thoughts, and even desires. Make no mistake, just because an animal can't express its thoughts with the spoken word doesn't mean that those thoughts don't exist.

Claircognizant/Intuitive Empath

Finally, there is the type of empath known as the claircognizant/ intuitive empath. These empaths are capable of not only sensing the emotions of other people but of actually perceiving other people on an intuitive level. This means that they can receive information from another person just by being around them. Scientific studies have demonstrated the possibility of this phenomenon, specifically as it relates to the actual nature of thoughts. It turns out that thoughts are comprised of energy, making it possible for them to be perceived much the same way that emotions are. The single difference is that claircognizant/intuitive empaths seem to pick up on energies of a more conscious nature, such as thoughts, intentions, and personality traits.

Empath

The main advantage that claircognizant/intuitive empaths have is that they can perceive a person's true identity quickly and easily. This means that they know what a person is like regardless of outward appearance or even their emotional state. Subsequently, they can get the most accurate first impressions of people. In more extreme cases, claircognizant/intuitive empaths can all but read another person's mind, making them virtually telepathic. Unfortunately, this level of perception can easily lead to sensory overload. It is recommended, therefore, that claircognizant/intuitive empaths develop the ability to 'turn off' their abilities at will to allow them the ability to recharge their batteries. Additionally, it is advised that they carefully choose the company they keep, ensuring that they spend time with people they can trust and feel comfortable around.

Gift of Being an Empath and How to Turn It into a Super Power

Your empath ability is a superpower. I love watching superhero movies because I like to see how superheroes use their superpowers. Some superpowers you can learn through extensive training, but others you are born with. Empaths are born with their gift, and this is what makes them unique; no one can learn how to be an empath. But in superhero movies, no one starts operating in the full strength of their gift right away; they've got to go through a period of training to perfect it. For example, the great martial arts expert Shang-Chi is an extraordinary hand-to-hand fighter. There are not many that can compare to him in the Marvel Universe. He trained Spider-Man and helped him develop a technique called Spider-Fu. Domino's luck power was more passive until she started training with Shang-Chi and developed it further. So, what am I saying? Don't feel discouraged if you feel that your empath gift is more of a burden than a blessing. It's only because you haven't developed it fully and turned it into your superpower yet. Some empaths are lucky enough to have been raised with empath parents who passed on their gift to their children and trained them in it. If you are not one of those people, you might want to consider looking for a mentor like Shang-Chi to train you. But the reality is that mentors are difficult to come by, so you can train yourself to become the powerful empath warrior you were created to be. Here are some tips to get you started:

Trust Your Intuition

People either live in their heads and make decisions based on logic, or they are guided by their intuition and seem to get it right every time. Intuition, also referred to as "your gut feeling," is an inborn ability to acquire knowledge about a particular situation without conscious effort and reasoning. When you ignore your gut feeling and do the wrong thing, it's only when you are faced with the same consequences that you will recall you had a bad feeling about it before going ahead. The good news is that you can avoid this outcome by practicing these steps:

Practice Mindfulness

Mindfulness trains you to become more attentive to the things that are taking place within your external and internal environment. As mentioned, meditation helps you become still by quieting the mind. But mindfulness techniques will help you tune in to yourself and the world through making a conscious effort to focus and notice things. Again, practice makes perfect, so incorporate mindfulness into your daily routine. Experts suggest that ten minutes a day will make a significant difference. Since empaths are such emotional people, the "naming your emotions" mindfulness technique is a good place to start because it will help you determine what you are feeling, especially when the emotion doesn't come from you. For example:

- When you feel an emotion, close your eyes and focus on it.

- Without passing judgment, give the emotion a name.

Often, we confuse our emotions; besides, feeling upset is not the same as being frustrated, sad, or angry.

Give It a Try

Sometimes, just thinking about something isn't enough, and you won't know whether something is good for you unless you give it a try. For example, let's say you are thinking about becoming a professional gardener because you like plants. Go ahead and take a garden design course because you might find that because, even though you like plants, you don't enjoy working outside in the cold or on the hard landscaping tasks that come with it. If you need to make a decision and are not sure what to do, give it a try and see how you feel.

Use Your Body as a Pendulum

You may have heard of using a crystal or a pendulum on a chain as a dowsing tool to look for lost objects or to gather the information we need. However, using our bodies as the pendulum or crystal is much more effective because it puts us in tune with our inner being. Using your body as a pendulum involves asking your higher self a question and then waiting for your body to tilt in a forward or a backward motion. The first step is to determine how your higher self communicates with you by centering your body and asking yourself the direction for "Yes," and "No," and then paying attention to the direction that your body moves. Your body will either tilt forwards for "Yes" or backward for "No." Using your body as a pendulum takes a while to master, so you will need a lot of practice to get it right.

Use Wisdom Cards

When you are not sure about something or someone, use wisdom cards. They are also known as power animal cards and energy cards. Some people also use color cards, image cards, idea cards, or goddess cards. Use whatever card set feels right for you. There are several ways to consult cards, but the simplest way is to shuffle the card set and think of the confusion, doubt, or question you want clarity on. Position the cards, so they are facing downwards, and allow your hand to move over the cards. Your hand will naturally want to stop somewhere, so chose a card and reflect on what it says or shows. You can either take the meaning on the card literally or as a metaphor, a symbol, an image, or a story related to the question you've asked.

Pay Attention to Synchronicities

Jungian psychology and esoteric wisdom have long held that every coincidence carries a meaning and provides guidance as they correspond to our inner experiences and emotional states. Some people refer to them as nods and winks from the universe, letting us know, if we pay attention, that we are on the right track. You might have days when you see the same sequence of numbers such as 22:22, 44:44, or 11:11 in different locations that have no relation to the other. You might run into the same person (whether you know them or not) three times in the same week. You might go through a period when everything seems to point in the direction of a certain city. We all have coincidences in our lives, but most of us don't pay attention to them. Once you start paying attention to synchronicities, you will find it easier to tune into your gut feeling because the signs will confirm how you are feeling.

Make a Commitment

Your inner wisdom is more powerful than you can imagine. After practicing the above techniques, decide that you are no longer going to question your intuition, trust that it is right every time, and follow it. You can start by using your intuition to guide you with the decisions that are not so important and then work your way up. Don't worry if you're not right all the time; the idea is to get familiar with the feeling when you are right, then you will always know when something is wrong.

How to Improve Your Psychic Ability

Unless you were raised in a household where highly sensitive traits were the norm, there is a good chance you were encouraged to suppress your psychic abilities. In general, adults don't take children seriously but see them as tiny beings who don't have any experience in the world. A sensitive child is often told to stop being silly. Seeing ghosts is considered a figment of their imagination, and talking to Grandpa, who died before you were born, is definitely impossible. However, the reality is that, in general, children are very in tune with the spiritual world because they are more sensitive. In most cases, their world is perfect, full of clouds and rainbows. As a result, children feel more, hear more, and see more. The creator gave us these survival instincts to help us move through the world safely. Through the conditioning we receive as children, we start to believe that intuition and emotions have no real importance in a world where most people are struggling to pay bills and survive. So, we turn our noses up at mediums, clairvoyants, and anyone else who has psychic abilities. Besides, we accept that the most important aspect of our reality is the physical world. But not to worry cosmic warriors, with a bit of practice, you can fully revive your psychic abilities.

Scan Your Environment

Practicing environmental scans is a great way to cultivate your psychic abilities. To do this, move into the center of a room. From here, you can either move around the area or scan it with your eyes and pay attention to the scents, sounds, and sights. Which areas do you find most appealing? Which areas do you find the least appealing? Explore everything from the furniture and windows to the corners. How does the energy coming from these places make you feel? You will find this exercise a bit strange, to begin with, especially if you are in a room with other people, but just do it discreetly, and no one will notice what's going on. Practice environmental scans in cars, subways, parks, offices, and bars. Anywhere you go, perform an environmental scan. The idea is to train yourself to become aware of your surroundings so you can quickly tune into the subtle shifts in energy. Eventually, you will be able to use this skill to access memories and future events.

Access Your Subconscious

It is normal to protect ourselves from information overload. There is so much going on in the world that we can't afford to absorb everything, so whether consciously or unconsciously, we create boundaries to protect ourselves. Nevertheless, the most effective way of tapping into your psychic ability is through the subconscious (unconscious mind), and one way to access it is through dreams. When we are free from psychological constraints, we can effortlessly move between spaces. Dreams are a gateway to the unseen world, and the more familiar we become with the subconscious world, the more in tune we become with our psychic powers. You can connect with your dreams by keeping a pen and paper by your bed, and as soon as you awake from a dream, write it down. You will soon start to realize how connected the physical and the spiritual world really are.

Tune into Energy

When empaths get bad vibes from people, they tune out because they can sometimes live in a fantasy world where everyone is good, and when that fantasy is interrupted with negative vibes, it's disturbing for them. But tuning in to a person's negative energy can help strengthen your skills. Delve deeper into the energy of the new people you meet by looking beyond how they speak and the way they look. Instead, get your information about them by tuning into their energy. You might be asking, "Well, how is this possible?" When you are in the person's presence, pay attention to their energy and see what you pick up. Start a conversation with them on the topic of what you can sense and see whether your instincts were correct.

Empath

Empath Effects

Downsides of Being an Empath

Downside 1: Picking Other People's Emotions

The ability to feel other people's emotions may be pretty unique. Like most other things in life, there are both positives and negatives to handling other people's emotions. It is not the fact that you are directly experiencing the feelings of those around you that makes it a negative thing. It is the inability to pick and choose what you feel that makes it potentially dangerous, and this can be energy-sapping—both emotionally and psychologically—making you end up battling with pain and confusion. Whenever you are around people who suffer from anxiety, depression, fear, sadness, or stress, you tend to experience the same with the sufferers—without being able to control it. It is the "right here" kind of thing that can make the empaths experience devastating sometimes.

Empath

Downside 2: High Tendency to Feel Overwhelmed

In addition to lacking control over the feelings empaths pick up, they can also become easily overwhelmed by tragic news, heavy noises, bright lights, strong smells, coarse fabrics, blasting sirens, and busy or crowded environments. Looks like a lot of things to avoid? Intimate relationships can also be overwhelming when empaths tend to mirror the energy in that relationship, especially when their partners do not live up to their expectations. They can also be overwhelmed by their partner's needs. Also, empath parents often feel overwhelmed and exhausted from the demands of child-rearing because they tend to absorb their children's feelings and pain, especially during their formative years. For empaths, this tendency can make being a spouse or a parent exhausting.

Downside 3: You Become Overloaded

You should also consult your tendency to become an overload of emotions and information. First, your listening abilities make you prone to bearing the whole world on your shoulders as everyone tends to "offload" their problems and worries on you, and you tend to bottle them all up. While being a problem solver and counselor to others, you are also likely to build up a shield for yourself by not letting others on your thoughts and feelings, thereby causing you to bear more emotions than you should.

In the same vein, empaths are always on the eternal look for knowledge and answers to their many unanswered questions. They tend to know many things and many people, which can lead to information overload. The disadvantage of being overload with information is that you may end up being overwhelmed. You may also find it challenging to make decisions, and in most complex cases, you may experience a brain fog. As an empath, your ability to feel love and compassion for others is always on a different level.

Downside 4: You Are Prone to Lose Your Sense of Self

People who do not understand empaths have unnecessarily tagged them as being "overly sensitive," "too emotional," or "extremely compassionate," and in many cases have prescribed how they should live and behave because they are seen as "not being in charge." Intuitively, empaths also tend to reflect other people's behavior around them without the intention to do the same, which is disadvantageous because they tend to lose their true selves in the process.

Are you worried about these demerits? You don't have to! Be rest assured that all these downsides can be effectively managed or avoided however the case may be. Interestingly, the upsides to being an empath outweigh the downsides, and they reflect the innumerable prospects of developing and embracing your gift.

The Upside of Being an Empath

What is it that they say about looking at the bright side of things?

Upside 1: Picking Up the Feelings of Others

Yes! You read right. Seeing that the central trait of empaths is their ability to pick up the emotion of others, it sure has a lot to tell on why there is both a positive and a negative side to it. The likelihood to mirror the emotions of others is an excellent side to empathy. This trait can help improve intimate and distant relationships because empaths can see from their perspective and understand them better. The empath is uniquely designed to have the ability to detect and deeply experience the feelings of others. This trait can be highly beneficial in your workplace; you could sense if your coworkers feel inadequate. You can pick up on that intuitively, faster than an average person, and offer support. The same would work for an anxious date; you could sense how they feel and help get them along with you very well. You possess the unique ability to relate to others deeply and unconventionally.

Upside 2: The Tendency to Be Loving and Compassionate

You possess traits that help you better identify with other people and their feelings and emotions, including those you'd usually disagree with. Many people may find it challenging to understand the feelings of others even when they explain how they feel, but an empath cannot relate to this. An empath can easily resonate with knowing what it is like to walk in other people's shoes.

The gift of compassion is an innate ability in empaths. When you learn to "take charge" of your nature, you will realize that you have a lot of good to offer both for yourself and your loved ones.

Empaths find themselves giving meaning to being in other people's shoes, allowing them to find a familiar place with people in and peaceful way. This trait can also make you a good leader. No wonder why we were able to identify earlier that it is believed that several great leaders were empaths in their times.

Upside 3: Tendency to Feel Good About Yourself

The exhausting and overwhelming situations empaths face may place them at their lowest and may feel more inadequate than usual.

Bad side? The best news is that they tend to be in their highest and feel even higher highs. Being an empath, being in your lowest could signal an allowance for your soaring highs. You see, you have the innate power to feel good, which can even last for a lifetime.

Upside 4: The Empath and His Creative Abilities

Empaths happen to make a majority of the most creative, innovative, intelligent, and witty people we've got in the world. If you are an empath, you may always want to consider gaining relevance or earning an income following creative pursuits. Empaths are usually an embodiment of valuable and innovative ideas. These empath's creativity is often expressed through dance, acting, painting, music, creative writing, drawing, spiritual exercises, and bodily movements. Empaths have the sixth sense to deeply appreciate good music, works of art, paintings and sculptures, and other creative works. You can also easily give meaning to the emotions of the makers of those imaginative works. You are drawn by the raw beauty and emotion denoted through a paintbrush and clay as an artist. Similarly, a music piece speaks to you on a visceral level. Empaths will also suit as perfect storytellers due to their imaginative and creative nature.

Upside 5: You Could Fit in for a Lie Detector

Being an empath gives you the capacity to detect lies, even with the seemingly little white lies. You can quickly figure out when your partner says they are okay when they are not. Interestingly, you cannot be easily deceived or cajoled. Whether or not you will consider this as something beneficial to have, I believe detectives or investigators who are empaths will find their job much more manageable.

Empath

Upside 6: You Have Deep Passion for Things, and That's Alright!

Empaths usually exhibit passion and deep-seated love for people, babies, animals, or nature with a driven commitment to help or improve them. The good side to being passionate about these things is that you can channel this passion for living a rewarding and fulfilling life. It explains why most empaths are often tireless teachers, volunteers, as well as caretakers for our environment, pets, and wildlife. Many empaths can sacrifice their time to help others, even at the expense of payment and accolades. Empaths are passionate and dedicated to activities they are drawn to, and they can efficiently channel that passion as a drive to enjoy life and their choice of work. Passions are usually the drive for empaths who tend to stay committed to what they love doing, and they may even get lost in such involvement.

Deal with Your Anxiety

Controlled Breathing

The first exercise we'll cover is called "natural breathing." This is breathing that is focused on the abdominal region of the body. This exercise is one that can be adopted as your general manner of breathing throughout every day unless you're doing some sort of physical activity that exerts the body. By utilizing this practice throughout your day, your body will get the oxygen it needs, and the exhalation of carbon dioxide will be closely regulated where it ought to be.

As you utilize this method, you will be slowly taking in a normal amount of air through your nose until your lungs are filled, then exhale evenly. The first time you give this a shot, you might want to put one hand on your stomach, as well as one on your chest. This will allow you to feel that the hand on your stomach will rise while the one on your chest stays level. This is your indication that you're breathing with the lower part of your lungs. As you continue to focus on this even rhythm of breathing, a sense of calm should begin to take over.

Natural Breathing

1.   Put one of your hands on your stomach, then the other one on your chest.

2.   With a gentle and slow rhythm, inhale a normal, comfortable amount of air through your nose, taking care to fill only your lower lungs. This means that the hand on your stomach should rise while the hand on your chest remains level.

3.   Exhale without much force, just allowing the breath to leave your body.

4.   Continue breathing in this way with a relaxed approach, concentrating on your breath and not the things that have bothered you.

This pattern is sort of the stark contrast to the reflexive response of hyperventilating or breathing too fast and too shallowly to do the body any good in times of stress.

The second breathing technique is a more calming breath that sort of takes the reins, takes over your thinking, and stops the hyperventilation in its tracks. This is a great tactic to use in times when you're feeling a sense of panic or heavy anxiety. This method of breathing is one of the quicker ways to rein in hyperventilation and to bring you back around to that calmer, more collected frame of mind and physical state.

Calming Breathing

1.   Put one of your hands on your stomach, then the other one on your chest.

2.   Through your nose, take a long, slow breath to fill your lower lungs first, then your upper lungs. You'll feel your hand on your stomach rise, then the hand on your chest.

3.   To the count of three, hold your breath.

4.   Through a small opening in your lips, slowly release the breath and feel the muscles relax in your chest and abdomen.

5.   Relax the muscles in your face, jaw, and your shoulders to relieve stress and pressure.

In addition to being a great tactic for releasing you from the grips of hyperventilation, this is a great exercise that can help you exercise calmness throughout your day. At several points when it's convenient for you, take the time to do this exercise. You can do this in times when tension rises, when work gets stressful, or even when you simply have a moment to yourself.

This exercise can be a great way to become comfortable and familiar with this process so that, if you find yourself hyperventilating due to anxiety or stress, you will have this tactic under your belt and ready to use it to bring you back around to even ground.

The more familiar you get yourself with this process during times of calm, the more readily you will be able to remember and use it during times of panic or high tension. Waiting for an emergency to strike before you prepare for it will set you up for a much more difficult time getting through it.

Question Your Thought Patterns

Ask yourself if you're in the middle of a negative thought pattern that could be destructive to you if you continue on with it. Ask yourself if the thought pattern is helpful or if it's harmful. Is it one that should be permitted to continue because it will lead you to a better result, or is it one that will only hurt you if it's allowed to continue?

Simply by questioning the type of thought pattern you're dealing with, you interrupt it. Interrupting a thought pattern is the best starting point for changing its course and putting the mind onto a track that will yield better results.

Aromatherapy

Between incense, candles, essential oils, and so many others, there is no shortage of ways to introduce aromas into your life that will help you to feel less stressed, feel happy, and get some quality relaxation time into your day.

Take a little bit of time and breathe in those smells, close your eyes, and allow yourself to take the time to get the benefits from those aromas. Aromatherapy can be a hobby in its own right if you're interested in making candles, blending essential oils, and more.

Take a Walk

Taking a walk is a great exercise because it's light, it doesn't exhaust you, it gives you time to think, it gives you fresh air, and it gives you just a little burst of endorphins that you can use to help you get through periods of stress, sadness, anxiety, or other negative emotions.

Bonus points if you take your walk right after a meal, as this helps with digestion in the evenings and can lead to a much sounder, more restful sleep!

Do Yoga

Yoga can help in relaxing you, stretching you out, keeping you from being tense, and centering your mind. If you don't like doing the classroom thing, there are plenty of instructional videos and publications that will teach you how to do the poses in the comfort of your own home.

It is recommended that you try your poses with someone who knows how to teach them the first time around, so they can tell you if the things that you're doing are proper form or if you need to adjust for safety.

Write It Out

No matter what you're feeling, you can always write it down to process it. You can even type it out if that is something you prefer to do to save paper, your hand muscles, and time. Going through your emotions at the pace it takes to write them out can help you go through all the parts of what you're feeling, lay them out in a way that makes sense, and also understand the ramifications of everything you're dealing with.

Empath

Light Stretching and Muscle Relaxation

If you're feeling stressed or anxious, take some time to loosen all your muscles. Relax your shoulders, unclench your jaw, sit up straight, unclench your hips or glutes, and just let the muscles fall into a more comfortable position. Stretch your arms and joints light until you feel just slightly rubbery, then allow yourself to get back into your work once you're feeling better

Oxytocin Pressure Point

There is a pressure point in your hand, just between the thumb and forefinger, that will release oxytocin when pressed. Without exerting so much pressure that you hurt yourself, grip the thicker, soft flesh between your thumb and finger with the opposing thumb and forefinger, and press.

Do this for a few seconds while breathing deeply and slowly, then refocus on what you're doing. You should feel a little bit of relief.

Adjust Your Posture

Check the way you're sitting in your chair or standing at your desk. If you find yourself hunching over or in an odd position, make adjustments so that you're sitting up straight. Your chin is parallel to the desk surface, and your arms aren't extended too far from your body in order to complete your tasks. Relax your muscles and get back to it.

Spend Time in Nature

Taking a walk along a body of water, spending time in the woods, or spending time with animals are all great ways to bring yourself back down to Earth, so to speak. It can be so easy to get so tied up in the things that we need to do each day that we simply forget the world around us.

People who are highly sensitive will generally find the properties of nature to be very restorative, and they will find a good deal of peace in the great outdoors.

Cope with the Hypothetical Worst-Case Scenario

If something, in particular, is worrying you, think about what the worst possible outcome for it could be. Tell yourself that this is simply an exercise in the hypothetical, that none of it will come to pass in the immediate term, and try to think about all the aspects of that outcome that would negatively affect you.

How could you cope with those things? What things would you do to bring your life back into the realm of normalcy and regularity? Could you do it?

Often showing ourselves that we will be okay in any possible event is the way to cool down the anxiety response. Things will turn out okay, and you will be fine.

Take a Break to Center Yourself

For some, this could mean a brief meditation. For others, this could simply mean pulling yourself out of whatever thought process has your brain all wrapped up, coming into the "here and now," and working on the situation that is currently in front of you.

Once you feel that your attention has pulled away from that other situation that isn't right in front of you, go back into the tasks that need your immediate attention with all the attention you now have.

Empath

You will find things to go along much more smoothly when you make this effort and when you are very purposeful about what you do with all the attention, you have to offer.

Take a Hot Bath

This one might sound cliché to you, but it's miraculous how much this can do. It's a very relaxing environment that you make for yourself when you take a bath, the water is very warm and relaxing, and you can add things to the water, such as bath bombs, Epsom salts, essential oils (make sure they're fit for skin contact), and more to help you relax and enjoy while you recuperate and recover with the help of the warmth and the additives in the water.

How to Control Empathic Abilities

An empath is not created but born. This trait is just as much a part of you as your DNA. You cannot learn to be an empath. You are born one, or you're not. However, you can learn how to manage and use this skill.

The dictionary definition of empathy is a person's ability to feel, perceive, and recognize another person's emotions. All of us have this ability to a certain extent since it's part of being human.

We can understand the way other people feel. For the empath, though, it's a different matter entirely. Emotions of others are literally shared and taken on as the empath's own.

Empathy Is Not Sympathy

Empathy is a different thing than sympathy. Sympathy is the reaction we take when we know another person is going through something difficult. We may feel sorry for them, which is still our feeling and not theirs. This is not related to the empath experience, which feels the other person's pain in a literal sense.

Learning to Handle Emotional Input

People will, and often do, share their negative emotions with you without being asked. They broadcast them in a way that you cannot ignore. You must either handle their pain or suffer yourself.

Since this flow of input often cannot be shut off at will, learning how to handle it the right way will keep you from going crazy.

Selective Ignorance

Selective ignorance can be your greatest asset as an empath. This means erecting a protective shield around yourself and keeping out other people's emotions. This mental shield can help you select when you want to notice other's feelings or not.

Ask Your Mind for Help

These types of techniques are not only imagination. When you ask your mind to help you, it will. Ask yours to help you be more selective with what you allow into it.

Knowing Yourself

Knowing yourself deeply and being able to recognize your own internal states of being is a must.

This will help you easily decipher which feelings are yours and which are not. The better you get at this, the easier it will be to discard the feelings you don't want to deal with.

When you aren't aware of what you're feeling and thinking, you can't tell up from down. Make it a habit to monitor what's going on inside of you until you can do this at will any time.

Constructing Healthy Limits

You have the ability to heal and help when someone else is suffering, but this doesn't mean you have to do so, or even that you should.

Many times, people are suffering for a specific reason. They might need to learn something or handle something better.

When you instantly try to take away the pain from people who have made mistakes, you might be holding them back from learning something important.

Cleansing Your Emotional Body

Empaths draw emotions and feelings to them like a magnet. If you don't take the time to clean this out every so often, the stress will continue to build.

Eventually, it can drive you crazy or seriously detract from your happiness. If you don't take the time to cleanse your emotional body every once in a while, you can become anxious, neurotic, depressed, narcissistic, or worse. This isn't an exaggeration!

This can be done by meditating regularly, going back to your light shield, and staying conscious of what you're feeling at all times.

When you are in this deeply aware and conscious state of mind, you will know what to do to solve your problems.

Limit Negative Influences

Negative feelings, whether they are someone else's or your own, should be limited or avoided when possible. It's easy to get lost in this side of things without being able to find a way out.

In extreme cases, this can feel as though everyone disrespects you, as though you're always under attack, or that you cannot relax. This will eventually make you vulnerable.

Keep Positive Friends Around

Empath

The first thing you can do is to surround yourself with positive people who make you feel good and empowered. You should also cut out negative influences and spend as little time with those who drag you down or make you feel stressed out.

Of course, you don't always have a choice about who you will spend time with. But this just makes it all the more important to take advantage of the times you can choose. Choose wisely! As an empath, you are more impressionable to people's influence.

Can Empath Turn You Distant and Cold?

Many empaths are considered distant and cold to other people. This can happen for a couple of different reasons. The first one being that some empaths are actually distant and cold, having shut off emotional input from the outside world.

Emotional Disconnection

When an empath doesn't have any knowledge or guidance on their true nature, this can happen quite easily. They shut off their ability to empathize as a form of self-defense.

The Controlled Empath

The second category of a distant and cold empath is the controlled, trained empath.

Outwardly, they might look like someone who is emotionally disconnected, but on the inside, there's something else happening. These types have developed a more logical way to view life in defense of feeling too much.

On the outside, they appear emotionless, but they just have a lot of discipline mentally. If this type of empath isn't careful, they might grow distant from the people around them.

Standing Up for Yourself

Don't allow people to use you as a place to vent. Almost every empath knows that unless they consciously put up boundaries, they will be the ones that people come to with their complaints or negative feelings.

This is because people sense that you will understand and have the ability to make them feel better. Even strangers might start telling you all of their most personal problems, hoping that you will help them.

Saying "No" Sometimes

Of course, you do have this ability, but letting this happen to you without putting up boundaries will run you into the ground, eventually.

The shielding techniques we talked about doing help, but you also have to know how to say, "No."

You Can't Help Everyone

An important realization every empath must have to live a healthy life is that you cannot help everyone. Actually, more people are beyond your help than you probably think.

Once you realize and accept this, it can be very freeing for you.

Empath

How can you tell the difference? Of course, you still want to help people because you thrive on being the nurturing type and, on some level, are meant for this.

But you need to know how to discern those who can be helped from those who cannot. Let's look at this in greater detail:

Helping People Type 1

This type can be helped and lays all of their issues out there. They have already attempted to handle their problems in their own way in a logical way and are venting to you to get some peace of mind.

They want to be listened to so they can hear themselves and find their own answers.

This is the type that you should be able to actually help in a meaningful and lasting way. In addition, helping them will not drain you, but will give you energy.

Helping People Type 2

This type is, unfortunately, a lot more common than the first. They will be very upset over some issue.

Instead of attempting to look for reasonable answers in a logical fashion, they will be seeking distraction from their own inner turmoil.

Oftentimes, they have their issue buried deep inside and want to put it onto you. Although this feels good for them, it can harm you, so be cautious.

With type 2, in this type of interaction, what has happened is that they have dropped off a heavy load they were carrying.

But they didn't do anything to fix the issue that caused it in the first place.

They will perpetually create problems, find temporary relief by putting them onto someone else, and then move on to repeat this cycle.

Learn how to recognize this type and avoid them. You cannot help them, with the exception of a situation where you can help them face their issues in a healthy way.

Empath

How to Control Your Emotions

Living as an empath is like being on a constant emotional roller coaster. One minute you are fine, and the next, your head is spinning in a whirlwind of thoughts and feelings, and you are not quite sure where they came from. The good news is that it is possible to control your emotions. You don't need to live in a state of constant turmoil. Here are a few tips to assist you.

Don't Expect Everyone to Live up to Your Expectations

As an empath, you've got strong feelings. You can tune in to what people are thinking by reading their reactions, and this can sometimes send your mind into overdrive. You spend every waking moment going over the details of the conversation, and you end up concluding how the person feels about you. Nine times out of ten, your brain will trick you into believing that they don't really like you or that they didn't really agree with what you were saying. You might also feel disappointed that the person you were speaking to didn't feel the same level of compassion as you. But you have to remember that first, you are a highly sensitive person, so things are going to affect you more than they are going to affect others. And second, people are always going to have different opinions—what overwhelms your heart may not overwhelm somebody else's.

We live in a fallen world; nothing is perfect here, and it never will be. Ideally, everyone should be kind and loving to one another, but as you know, that's simply not the case. You only have to turn on the TV or open a newspaper to see how much evil takes place in the world every day. It would be magnificent for you if everyone was an empath if everyone had the emotional capacity to shoulder the burdens of others, but this is simply not the case. You have no power over the way other people think, and there is no point in wasting your energy trying to change it. When you conclude that, in general, people are not going to share the same level of compassion as you, it will make your life a lot easier because you won't spend so much time living in disappointment. You will be able to brush things off and keep moving.

Not everyone is going to agree with you. In fact, some of your friends and family are going to make decisions that are in direct conflict with yours. You will decide to go one way, and they will decide to go another, and there is absolutely nothing wrong with this. When it happens (because it will), let it go. Everyone is entitled to their own opinions and has their own life decisions to make, whether you agree with them or not. You might feel in your spirit that a friend is making the wrong choice, so unless they ask you to intervene, leave them to it. Some people will have to learn the hard way, and the consequence is the best teacher. When you try to convince others to do something that is against their will, you waste a lot of energy. Situations like this leave you feeling drained and exhausted.

Not forcing your expectations on others is one of the most important life lessons I have learned. It's a waste of time, parallel to speaking Chinese to a man who only speaks English—they will never understand! And that's ok. When it comes to your expectations, the only person you should be concerned about living up to them is you.

Have Your Tool Kit with You at All Times?

There are plenty of tools available for empaths to use in everyday situations. To make life easier for yourself, you should have them ready and available to use at all times. If you are sensitive to temperature, light, or sound, and you know you have to leave the house, make sure you take what you need with you. If you drive, I would advise that you keep a spare set of these items in the car, so you don't have to worry about packing them every time you leave the house.

If you are sensitive to loud noise, carry noise-canceling headphones. If you don't have a pair already, you can buy small discreet earbuds that you can wear in any environment. Carry a sweater, cardigan, or t-shirt in case the temperature changes. Empaths can find it distressing when they are too hot or too cold.

Preparation is your best defense against protecting your energy. You will experience less anxiety when you know that you have everything you need just in case of an emergency.

Set Limits with Technology Use

Empath

Empaths may love technology more than anyone else. Since they like to isolate themselves, it allows them to communicate without being present in social situations. But it also has its downsides. When you are constantly available online, it gives energy vampires easy access to you, and that is definitely something you want to avoid. Also, people can post the most distressing and heartbreaking news on social media. In recent years, several violent deaths and suicides have been posted online.

Sometimes energy vampires are not people, but the platforms that you are constantly scrolling. Do you ever feel drained after looking through your Instagram or Facebook feed? You can absorb negative energy when you spend too much time online.

Setting limits or abstaining from social media for a while can promote mental clarity and restore energy levels. Set yourself a technology time limit of 30 minutes to 1 hour per day. This is just enough time to do what you need to do without getting sucked into all the drama that takes place online.

How to Restore Your Energy

One of the negative effects of being an empath is a constant loss of energy. You can avoid this when you need to. But a natural part of being an empath is opening your energy fields for the greater good, which will leave you feeling drained. The healing process no longer solely involves medicine and therapy; people seeking help now have a range of options to choose from. Here are a few practical techniques that can assist you in maintaining balance and restoring your energy levels:

Acupuncture

Empaths often suffer from digestive issues and lower back pain because of the negative energy they carry in these areas. Acupuncture is an ancient Chinese treatment, and one of the many ways in which it works is through balancing vital energy. It involves inserting needles into certain parts of the body to promote the free flow of energy. Acupuncture improves the circulation of oxygen and blood throughout the body, which promotes energy production at the cellular level. Additionally, acupuncture improves the digestive function, which is vital to providing essential nutrients that support energy production to the body.

You may have heard of the term "chi." Ancient Chinese practitioners use it to refer to a person's energy or balance. Acupuncture treatment is deeply relaxing. It brings the body's system back into alignment creating a healthy balance that enables energy levels to recover and rebuild themselves.

Your Mantra

Empaths possess the unique ability to read people with precision and accuracy. However, they find it difficult to understand their own emotions. Mantras are short powerful statements that remind you of your life's direction. They are more than inspirational quotes that provoke people to take action. They are powerful words that call what you want into your reality. Some empaths will not engage in social activities or spend time with people unless they have repeated their mantra. Here are some powerful mantras that you might want to consider using:

- "I control where my energy goes, and I will not allow others to take it from me."

Empath

- "I have the confidence to express what I need and defend myself when necessary."

- "I will disassociate myself from toxic situations without feeling ashamed."

Once you have chosen your mantra(s), get into the habit of saying them every day. You might feel a bit strange saying them at first because, in reality, you don't actually believe the words that are coming out of your mouth. But the more you say them, the more you will start to believe them, and they will eventually become a part of your core belief system.

I love mantras because you have full control over what you say. Spend some time defining your own mantras.

Palliative Care

Palliative care is also known as "supportive care." It is treatment, support, and care for terminally ill patients. The aim is to improve their quality of life by being as active and healthy as possible in the time they have left. It can involve:

- Managing painful physical symptoms

- Psychological, spiritual, and emotional support

- Support for family and friends

Ok, so you are probably thinking that being an empath is not a terminal illness, and, "How is palliative care going to help me?" Well, another aspect of palliative care is palliative arts, which involves engaging in purposeful activities to add meaning and enrich life.

This type of therapy involves patients dealing with their emotions through activities such as sculpting, painting, writing poetry, and listening to music. This enables them to focus on their negative emotions by expressing them in a positive light. Since empaths are typically creative people, this is a great way to relieve some of the tension associated with being a highly sensitive person. Empaths also find it difficult to express negative emotions to others, so this is another way of releasing energy that does not benefit you without the fear of being judged.

Change your thought process. Your thoughts dictate your actions, so if you want to change the way you react to certain situations, you are going to have to change the way you think.

Empath

Develop Your Chakras Balancing

Exercises for Balancing the Chakras

To rebalance the chakras (centers of spiritual power in the body) we will begin with a practice of opening the energy channels of the hands. This will serve to prepare the body to better feel the subsequent positions and generate a sense of well-being that invites you to continue. Each exercise should be done with great care, paying attention to the breath, which is an integral part of them. Never bring yourself to the threshold of pain. The sensation to be felt during the practice must be of pleasant relaxation and stretching. If a position causes discomfort, stop immediately and try again another day. Remember, the objective of these exercises is to restore balance and well-being, not to challenge yourself!

Over time, you will feel the need to stretch more intensely because this will give you pleasure, and you will be able to do it without damaging your body. Learn to think of your body not as an enemy to fight and win but as your home that you must take care of with respect and love. The results will not be long in coming!

Exercise for Energy and Awareness

1.   Sit comfortably, taking care to keep your back straight and your shoulders open and down.

2.   Place your hands facing each other, with your left thumb touching the palm of your right hand.

3.   Focus on the area where your thumb touches your hand.

4.   Relax and feel a warm current at that point.

5.   Feel the flow of energy.

6.   Move your hands apart and bring them together 3 times.

7.   Feel the energy flowing between the two hands.

8.   You should feel it as a slight tingling, or a sensation of warm air between the two hands.

9.   Imagine that between your hands a ball of warm and vibrant light is being created, and you can feel it in shades of orange and yellow, so focus on it.

10.   You should get to feel a pulsation passing through your hands.

11.   Let it also pass through your arms, reaching your shoulders.

12.   Feel this pulsation passing through your whole body and invigorating it.

Opening the Chakras of the Hands

1.   Rub your hands vigorously for 30 seconds.

2.   Place your palms against each other, and feel the energy current. Repeat 3 times

3.   Open and close your hands into fists 30 times quickly, then bring your arms forward with your palms facing up, and absorb the energy from outside while imagining it filling your whole body.

The opening of the chakras of the hands has the advantage that it can be practiced at any time of day. It takes no time but a minute, but gives a priceless feeling of energy. Look at the following description of the chakras:

- Little finger = heart chakra

- Ring finger = third eye chakra

- Middle = solar plexus chakra

- Index finger = throat chakra

- Thumb = sacral chakra

- Wrist joint = root chakra

- Center of palm= crown chakra.

The fingers have a close connection to the chakras, as they have within them the opening points of the affected meridians.

The hands can also tell the balance state of your body. The right channel carries the active physical and mental energy, and the left channel carries the passive emotional and receptive energy. It is like the Sun and Moon, when the two energies are in balance, you feel physically and mentally right. You can 'feel' the state of balance of these two energies by putting your hands together palm to palm. You can try to feel which of the two sides is warmer and try to rebalance.

Too hot means too high of an energy level to rebalance with the opposite side. To restore balance, you must bring up the energy of the opposite side, and push down the energy of the hot side.

Below are the steps for rebalancing:

- Place the warmer cupped hand facing the other.

- Imagine lifting the energy from the root chakra, as if it were water, up to the third eye chakra.

- Invert the cupped hand and push down the energy of the warm side to the level of the root chakra.

- Repeat seven times until both hands are cool.

Balancing the Muladhara Chakra

All exercises, in this case, yoga "asanas" (poses), designed to unlock and rebalance the first chakra, mostly affect the pelvis and hip area. They bring a great feeling of stability and make the joints elastic and the muscles flexible.

Uttanasana

"Uttanasana" is a yoga asana that stretches the muscles at the back of the thigh in the back of the legs. This exercise can help unlock the first chakra, increasing the flexibility of the legs. Contracted muscles denote a sense of insecurity and instability that can lead to nervousness, anxiety, and fear. Keep the abdominal muscles actively engaged the entire time to help support the lower back. Hold this position for 20 to 30 seconds, then slowly return to a standing position.

Janu Slrsàsana

This asana helps rebalance the root chakra. This pose can instill calmness and the ability to slow down and root yourself in one place. This can be especially helpful if you are constantly in a hurry, unable to make a decision.

Sit on a small pillow if you are experiencing lower back pain or tension in your hips. Inhaling, bend your left knee to bring your left foot toward your perineum to touch your inner thigh. Keeping your back straight, raise your arms above your head and reach towards your right leg, without bending your back. Do not worry if you are not able to reach the foot; rather, stretch forward comfortably. Hold the position for 20 to 30 seconds before rising and repeating with the other leg.

Supta Virasana

This asana gives a sense of peace and tranquility to your body and mind. Perform this exercise whenever you feel restless, stressed, tired, or at the end of a long day.

Empath

Start on your knees on the floor with your legs folded under your body, sitting on your heels. Your big toes should be touching. Extend your knees the size of your pelvis. Stretch forward until your forehead touches the floor or on a pillow placed in front of you. Inhale and exhale deeply in this position for 5 to 10 times.

Savàsana

This asana brings a sense of security and peace. On a physical level, it slims the hips, and flattens the abdomen if you take care to seek contact with the ground in the lumbar area. If it is difficult, you can put a pillow under the head. Lie on the floor, making the spine adhere to the ground, with the legs slightly apart, and the arms along the body with the palms facing up. Close your eyes, relax all the muscles of your body from the feet up to the head. During the inhalation, contract all the muscles of your body and let them go in the exhalation for 10 breaths, then remain listening and continuing to breathe slowly and consciously.

Balancing the Svadhisthana Chakra

Water is the element associated with the second chakra. Psychologically, water is the metaphor and symbol for emotions. The second chakra deals with basic emotions or "gut feelings," such as fear, anger, and joy, as well as basic emotions that are often unexpressed. The second chakra governs the kidneys, the reproductive system, and the bladder. A blockage of the second chakra results in the feeling of immobility as well as the blockage of creativity, movement, and carefree living.

Gomukhasana

It is an asana that unlocks the tension of the second chakra, as well as relieving physical blocks of the neck, shoulders, and arms—typical of stress. It is so powerful that it proves to be decisive in cases of fibromyalgia.

Baddha Konasana

This asana is a very powerful way to release tension in the hip and groin areas. Bring the soles of your feet together to form a triangle. Bring your feet as close to the perineum as is comfortable. Hold the position for a few minutes, sending the "prana" (breath control) towards the chakra.

Upavistha Konasana

This asana works on the inner and back sides of the thighs. Through pressure on the belly, the 'intestines are properly massaged and the pelvic area is relaxed.

Balancing the Manipura Chakra

Opening the third chakra can help you develop a healthy sense of self-worth, stand up for yourself better, grow as a leader, achieve goals, and create the life you want.

Urdhva Dhanurasana

1. Lie supine (belly up) on a yoga mat. Bend your knees so that your lower legs are perpendicular to the floor, and place your feet shoulder-width apart. Lift your pelvis and extend your hips. Place your hands just above your shoulders. Press your palms down evenly, and arch the pelvis upward.

2.   Contract your adductor muscles to push your knees toward each other and turn your thighs inward. Ease the body by pushing the top of the head down onto the mat.

3.   Open the chest upward.

4.   Having mastered this position, press your hands to the floor and extend your elbows to lift your torso while straightening your knees.

Benefits of Chakra Healing

1.   Greater Health and Well-Being

Chakras are the pillars of energy and life centers that transmit life force to various parts of the body through the "nadis" (energy channels). This is similar to how we want to keep arteries clean, functional, and clear so that our blood can flow to all organs through them without obstruction.

There are several reasons for blockages in the chakras, such as negative emotions, fears, incorrect lifestyles, and other dismissive habits. Chakras have a direct impact on an individual's physical, mental, emotional, and spiritual well-being. Balancing of the chakras is done through the unlocking of the chakras with the "rock crystal spiritual surgery" treatment.

2.   Purification of the Chakras Is Beneficial for Spiritual Health

Like physical health, spiritual form is also very important for the human body to remain stable and calm in the modern world. Energy moves downward from the spiritual realms to the mental, emotional, and ultimately physical experience. Therefore, it is very important to deal with and resolve spiritual issues as they have powerful effects that are reflected in everything you do in all aspects of life. The chakras are the interface between the spiritual realms and the physical body that must be balanced to maintain balance in the human body.

3.   Removes Bad Energies Stored in the Body

Chakra balancing and purification will help you live a healthier lifestyle, not only in terms of a fit body but in terms of physical and mental fitness while also keeping your heart and mind fit. It will allow you to enjoy your relationships as well. Balanced chakras help release everyday toxins and debris from the body.

4.   Purifying the Chakras Instills Love and Joy in Your Life

Purifying the sacral chakra infuses love and joy into your life. The keywords or purpose of the Sacral Chakra are mentioned in literature as life energy and creativity.

Empath

Meditation Exercises

The spiritual clearing is a term used to portray particular conduct that empaths and sensitive individuals need to receive to keep their energy field clean from the negative contemplations and the negative feelings of others.

If you are an empath, you tend to detect and feel others' contemplations, feelings, and even their physical agony. Contingent upon the level of your empathic capacities, you may even be affected by your interpretation of those kinds of torment without knowing it. That is the reason energy mindfulness and establishing are fundamental elements and significant parts of energy clearing.

Energy Clearing Techniques

You can't change the way that you are an empath. This is how you are made at a soul level, and you can't change this spiritual blessing. A

Empath

few people talk about turning on and off being an empath, but this is somewhat deceptive because it is beyond the realm of imagination to expect to kill this capacity on and voluntarily. What you can do is be mindful. Being an empath is being the kind of person you are, and you are here to figure out how to utilize your empathic blessing as an amazing asset for your appearance and self-change.

How about we plunge into the most valuable spiritual clearing systems that are helpful as an empath:

Cutting the Cords

This is a significant task that empaths need to turn out to be adept at. Since you are so acceptable at connections and individuals to love you, they additionally remove your energy from you because your energy feels so great, healing, and cherishing. This happens because you permitted it without knowing.

At various times associations or etheric strings with relatives, companions, and darlings can, in any case, be available significantly after the relationship is finished. It's an ideal opportunity to cut the lines!

To cut strings, essentially, think about the individual with which you have had a relationship, and picture the rope being cut. Favor the individual and state the accompanying, "I currently discharge you in adoration and light."

There are further developed systems on the best way to cut ropes, yet this basic technique is as compelling. I assess that the more we need to convolute things, the more things get muddled. It's up to you! My recommendation is to make it basic and make it simple.

Be that as it may, do it and do it as regularly as you feel the need.

For instance, before nodding off every night, ask yourself: "Do I have any connections or lines with anybody that I met today?" If you discover something, discharge it and favor it.

Inquire a couple of days after the fact to ensure that the issue has been discharged. If you don't know or feel that the string is still there, get proficient assistance. I regularly discover ropes associated with one of the chakras or connected to the energy field:

1. Clearing Your Aura from Negative Thought Patterns

Your psychological body is continually interfacing with the psychological body of others, so you get contrary thoughts from others.

You likewise make your own thoughts, and a considerable lot of them may not be in arrangement with your most elevated sense of "great." Know about the accompanying kind of thoughts:

• Negative

• Redundant

• Repetitive

• Automatic

If you need to find out about your reasoning, examples convey a scratch pad with you and record all the thoughts that you have inside a 24-hour time span. You will be amazed by the fact that it is so difficult to monitor your thoughts!

Empath

At the point when your thoughts are certain, you adjust to positive vibrations, and you make healing, parity, and congruity. At the point when they are negative, they make obstruction and blockages.

Negative thought patterns can be bolstered for quite a long time, particularly when associated with a traumatic encounter.

They can be founded on feelings and desires for others. In any case, they can stall out in your psyche and happen again and again undetected until you begin to focus and effectively choose to watch your idea patterns.

Musings that are made out of dread, sadness, dread, fault, and outrage stay connected to your energy field and cause you to vibrate increasingly more in arrangement with these sorts of energies. After some time, they cause you to draw in these very encounters throughout your life.

These thought patterns vibrate inside you so that they catalyze a fell response at all the degrees of your energy bodies: Spiritual, mental, emotional, and physical. They cause you to draw in individuals, circumstances, and experiences that are in vibrational arrangement with them. It resembles a greeting for low energies to connect to your energy field.

To clear this example, take a gander at your life and check whether you are pulling in circumstances you don't care for. If you do, you are some ways or another, vibrating in arrangement with them without your cognizant mindfulness.

Your task is to check in with your energy field a few times during the day, particularly if you feel drained and discouraged, to check whether you have got or made any negative thought pattern, and intentionally let it go. These are the things that I typically state:

- "I am in control of my brain, my feelings, and my body."

- "I am a processor, amplifier, and transmitter of energy."

- "I process my energy to get the hang of it, enhancing the positive, and transmuting the negative."

As you state this, envision a silver-white light purging your energy field from any flotsam and jetsam of thought frames that are beginning to grab hold. This task will just take one moment to do.

The main thing I ask of you is to be steady!

2.   Adjusting Your Chakras

Chakra adjusting for empaths is an absolute necessity, and it's a day-by-day practice. Two times every day, morning, and night times, you have to take a couple of moments to wash down your chakras.

I like just to envision the accompanying meditation:

1.   Envision each chakra being purged, restimulated, and readjusted.

2.   Imagine the whole chakra framework like turning wheels while permitting negative energy out of the body and positive energy inside the body.

3.   With your brain eye, see and feel energy streaming and

circling in flawless parity and agreement.

3.   Make a Sacred Space

This is so significant for everybody, except particularly if you are an empath. A sacred space can be any area in your home where you can be without anyone else's input and see a spot as completely self-communicated.

This could be your craft room, your meditation room, or essentially your office. This spot must be yours and yours alone. Try not to impart this space to other people (truly, your children and pets can come in and out!). It doesn't need to be inside; it tends to be outside.

Be inventive with this, however, locate an exceptional spot for you to go at any rate once per day. If it is outlandish for you to make a genuine space, make one up in your mind and go there. You will be astonished by what you can make in your psyche.

A few people end up in the open country, others along the beach, a desert island, or a healing sanctuary; others see themselves on different planets, out in space, or a spaceship made altogether of light energy.

4.   Smearing Yourself and Your Environment

I love this part, and it is an absolute necessity, particularly when you feel down, tragic, or restless. Smirching your energy field and the earth truly assists with transmuting negative energies from your energy field.

Do this frequently, particularly if you have been in circumstances that caused you to feel out of synchrony with your emotional, mental, and physical body. Utilize white sage. Likewise, remember to smear your home routinely to keep the energy of your living space new and clean.

5. Interface with Nature

For anybody who feels overpowered by emotional pressure and mental anguish, nature gives the best type of energy healing accessible. It is my conviction that empaths are here right now to help the enthusiastic frequencies important to clean the planet.

Most negative thoughts and negative feelings are conveyed by people. In this way, if you are an empath, proceed to invest energy in nature alone at any rate once per day to energize, and you will permit nature to rinse you. Touching a tree can assist you with establishing and wipe out undesirable energies from your body.

Interfacing with creatures, blossoms, floods of water, and common scenes is the most relieving energy healing treatment you can get. What's more, it's free!

Sit on the ground with your back against the storage compartment of a tree or stroll around with exposed feet to drawn positive energies from the earth. This procedure is called establishing or earthling, and it will cause you to feel great.

6. Utilize Protective Stones

I don't accept that we should be continually worried about security since I accept that we are the main expert in our life. Accepting that we need consistent insurance can pull in the negative musings of debilitation, dread, and victimhood.

So as to ensure your energy field, you should know about your energy. I do accept that empaths need to discover approaches to keep themselves grounded and washed down constantly. This is, as I would like to think, the best type of assurance.

After the heart wall clearing, it's imperative to put a shield of security around the heart to keep it totally protected from negative structure energies and to keep it in a consistent arrangement with positive energies. When you have cleared your heart wall and set a shield of assurance, you should simply initiate your shield.

At the point when I work with individuals, I educate them on basic energy strategies that they can use to ensure their auric field. However, I don't advance the requirement for insurance as much as the requirement for energy mindfulness.

At the point when we are intentionally mindful of our energy, we can't fall casualties of others except if we permit it. Your energies should be continually moving in doing what we are here to do as empaths: Process, transmute and enhance energy. On the off chance that you are not doing this throughout the day, you will feel dormant energy. Regularly, this is the motivation behind why you fall back into the negative part of your blessing and feel the requirement for assurance.

Self-Care—Body and Mind

If you had told me that self-care would be one of the top reasons for my success in achieving everything I've ever wanted, I wouldn't have believed you. For most of my life, I had always expected someone to give me an answer or guidance, leading me to some solution outside of myself. I had developed an outward-facing perspective in which I learned to look to others' experiences to dictate how I felt.

Before I became aware of the term "empath," I really hadn't been taking great care of myself. Because I was born so sensitive to other's emotional states, from day one, I learned some interesting survival skills to manage my daily experience. My survival skill lessons first started with my family. This is, after all, where we first all learn how to be in relationships. Our parents provide the template for relationships as well as the attachment strategies we will spend the rest of our lives mirroring. But of course, again, I didn't know that it was the case at the time.

The first survival skill I learned as a child to mitigate the intensity of emotional information that was coming my way flowed like this:

- "If other people around me are happy, then I am okay."

- "If other people around me are sad, then I am not okay."

- "Therefore, for me to be okay, other people need to be happy."

- "It's up to me to make sure people are happy, so I am okay."

That's how I learned to use my empathic abilities to see what other people needed to feel happy. I also subconsciously allowed myself to energetically absorb negativity, doubt, fear, and worry—any of the negative emotions I sensed others would be feeling—in an attempt to help them get rid of their negative experience.

Years later, in my early twenties, when I finally learned the word "empath," I realized that I had, in fact, been operating like an emotional sponge. I would frequently have people tell me that I was like a dose of sunshine or that, when I walked into a room or a social situation, I was like an immediate vibe raiser. I had that effect naturally, but at the time, it was happening subconsciously at the expense of my own well-being because I had no idea I was operating with an underlying desire to help everyone else feel better so I could feel worthy of being happy.

Your Job Is Self-Care—A Practice for Life

Empaths are wired to be on high alert when it comes to emotional and energetic sensitivities. This intensity can come with similarly powerful weariness after a high degree of energy has been exhausted. As such, it's crucial for us, as empaths, to spend more time than the average person caring for our bodies and re-centering ourselves so we can exist in our optimal state of being. You might find that you quickly become drained, exhausted, or completely paralyzed at certain points along with your empath's experience—particularly after giving a lot of yourself, after absorbing energy from a crowd or from an intense relationship, or from intensely feeling a painful or even ecstatic experience going on around you. Self-care is not only the answer to protecting yourself from ongoing exhaustion and feeling drained, but it's also a practice for life that will support you in feeling grounded, knowing yourself more deeply than you've ever imagined, and truly accepting and celebrating yourself as the magical being that you are.

The best things I have ever learned and practiced in my entire journey toward becoming fully empowered in my empathic abilities and gifts are all grounded in self-care, no doubt about it. Since you are the most important person in your life, it's time for you to start treating yourself like that. Start now, and have fun with it. Self-care is meant to be a joyful, loving experience that you can be creative with and through which you can express yourself fully. One of the most empowering things you can ever learn and strive to embody in your life is to truly be the person who can give you everything you've ever needed. How can you do that for yourself now?

Self-Care Might Not Be Easy for You at First

It isn't as easy as you might think to really commit to self-care. Though it seems like it might be fun to start taking care of yourself, there's more to it for empaths. If you've learned to live your entire life for others, to help others feel good, and to look good to please others, when you finally start to look inward at your own relationship with yourself, it can at first be an uncomfortable and unpleasant experience.

You might find that once you actually ascertain where you stand on the self-care front, you really have no idea where to even begin. You might also realize that you've been living as though everything has been okay all along when in fact, this couldn't be further from the truth. You might see how many ways in which you've been allowing yourself to settle for less-than-optimal well-being to dim your light, play small, or fit in with whomever you find yourself surrounded by. Ask yourself this: What becomes possible for me when I finally start supporting myself in all the ways I truly desire? You might see how there is an underlying fear you've felt that if you really start taking care of yourself, you will shine at your full capacity, and then what? Will you be alone? Will people no longer understand you? Will you have to make some serious life changes?

That was the case for me. When I finally started looking inward, I didn't like what I found. It felt like I was meeting a stranger for the first time—and it wasn't a stranger I particularly wanted to spend time with. My whole life, I always strove to surround myself with other people. It was around others that I felt safe. When other people were around, especially if I could take care of them and help them feel happy, I felt like I had a purpose. However, once I was invited to be with myself and really take care of myself, I didn't even know what peace felt like.

In addition, simply becoming aware of my overactive mind, which was always operating on hyper-speed, was incredibly scary. I had numbed that effect with alcohol for close to a decade, but now my mind was activated in full force. Getting sober from mind-altering substances showed me how intense my thought patterns were and how loud my mind was, constantly berating me for various things I wasn't doing well enough. Finally, starting to listen to what was going on was overwhelming—to say the least. It's no wonder I had turned to drugs and drinking to mute the noise. How was everyone else living like this? Did everyone else have this same experience as well, with their mind constantly yelling at them? I felt confused and alone.

My first iteration of self-care started with hiring a life coach, who guided me through my first Reiki sessions as well as an immensely powerful guided meditation in which I met my inner child for the first time. She helped me get on a healthy eating plan, and I even did a cleanse protocol to reset my entire body and all its inherent systems. I experienced what it felt like for the first time to wake up early with a natural internal alarm clock and had some of the best sleep I had ever had in my life. I experienced optimal energy; I detoxified my life from unhealthy, exhausting relationships and obligations; I stopped doing everything for everyone else, and I really started intentionally cultivating a loving inner dialogue with myself. Because I fully invested in myself for the first time, I was enjoying the most incredible transformations in my life that I had ever experienced. I was awakening to my true power and purpose.

Learn to Love Being on Your Own

Being on your own, let alone choosing to be solo, may be extraordinarily challenging for you if you're an empath that has developed the coping mechanism of constantly surrounding yourself with other people to distract yourself from your own emotional experience. Going solo may tune you into that loud tape set on repeat, inundating you with an intense onslaught of emotional, energetic information. You might feel overwhelmed by how loud your mind is; it might even feel scary to really listen in and discern the conversations that have been going on in the background despite your best attempts at distraction. Trust me; I've been there.

Exercise: Amplify Your Self-Love

It's time to venture into the multiple layers in which love can manifest and be received, given, expressed, and shared. Remember, you are loved. But how are you tuning into this (divine) truth moment to moment?

This is the real work. This is presence. This is radical acceptance. This is power. When you operate from a space of love in which you simply know that you (and everyone else) are just that—love (reflecting one another, and so on)—you enter the realm of infinite possibility.

So, like everything else, it starts with you. It's an inside job. Here's your invitation to begin with a beautiful declaration of love for the most important person in your entire life: YOU. Your invitation is as follows:

1.   Write a letter to yourself and celebrate how much you love yourself. Now is the time to tell yourself all the things you wish you'd heard your whole life from others. Answer the following questions and be sure to communicate to yourself in a loving, caring, celebratory tone—like you are your own loudest, proudest cheerleader:

o   What are you most proud of about yourself?

o   What are your most unique gifts, talents, and abilities?

o   What do you love about yourself (your body, your mind, your spirit, your wisdom)?

o   What are you grateful for about yourself and your life?

2.   Once your letter is complete, what's next? You have a few choices:

o   You can hide it away and take it out sometime in the future to re-read (time-capsule style).

o   You can read it out loud to someone you care about so he or she can witness you in your beautiful glory.

o   If you really want to stretch, ask someone you love to read the letter to you as though he or she is saying all the things to you— simply reading your letter aloud so you can fully receive the love.

Empath

Affirmations for Empath

You can meditate in your head or speak each affirmation aloud. You can even sing them or choose what feels best for you and is appropriate for your situation.

If you feel that negative thoughts are covering your mind while doing your affirmations, just try to relax, focus on your breath, dismiss them, and continue.

To amplify the positive effects of these guided meditations, I recommend doing these exercises daily. However, don't criticize yourself if you don't have time to do your affirmations for a day or even a week. Let's do some affirmations together!

Guided Meditation 1

- "I deserve to feel the love I give."

Empath

- "It is OK to have boundaries."

- "I don't have to fix everyone. I don't have to fix everything."

- "I release all emotions but my own."

- "I know what plants need."

- "My sensitivity makes me stronger."

- "My abilities are a blessing."

- "My energetic boundaries are pure and strong."

- "I willingly free myself from emotions that are not mine to carry."

- "I am happy being me, and I appreciate my gift."

- "It is OK for me to release emotions that are not mine."

- "I express my needs and desires to supportive people."

- "I am the one responsible for saving myself, and I know that I can do it."

- "I choose to release what is not mine to carry."

- "I really don't need to fix everything for everyone."

- "I am in control of how I feel in every situation."

- "I am strong and positive."

- "It is OK to say no at the right times."

- "I will use my abilities to improve my own life and the people I meet."

- "It is OK to listen to my dreams."

- "I can clear all the negative energy from my body."

- "I can control my gift."

- "I will listen to my intuition."

- "I can feel the emotions of animals."

- "I will support, not fix others."

- "I deserve to be in a loving relationship that makes me feel comfortable."

- "I will set healthy boundaries."

- "I treat myself with love and embrace my gift."

- "I will learn to accept others for who they are."

- "I don't have to fix everything for everyone."

- "I can and will set healthy boundaries."

- "I will protect my energy from draining people."

- "I can feel the energies of others, but I don't absorb the energies of others."

Empath

- "I am willing to feel only my energy."

- "I am willing to let go of all energy that is not mine."

- "I can attract gentle relationships into my life."

- "I feel safe and protected in my life."

- "I can't save the entire world and everyone in it."

- "It is safe for me to express my authentic self with the people around me."

- "It is OK to choose how I want to feel in every situation."

- "I am willing to feel only my energy."

- "I am willing to let go of all energy that is not mine."

- "I can attract gentle relationships into my life."

- "I feel safe and protected in my life."

- "I can't save the entire world and everyone in it."

- "It is safe for me to express my authentic self with the people around me."

- "I give myself permission to release negative emotions that no longer serve me."

- "I listen to my dreams."

- "I will support, not fix others."

- "I will find balance in my life."

- "I can say 'no' at the right times."

- "I can ask and receive all the help I need."

- "I appreciate my abilities every day."

- "I fully embrace my wellness, both physical, spiritual, and emotional."

- "I am strong and positive."

- "It is OK to say no at the right times."

- "I will use my abilities to improve my own life and the people I meet."

- "It is OK to listen to my dreams."

- "I am way stronger than I know."

- "I will treasure myself."

- "I will not try to hide my gift."

- "I choose to release what is not mine to feel."

- "I respect other people's feelings, but they are not my business."

- "I am healthy and full of positive energy."

- "I only welcome uplifting and positive vibrations in my life."

Empath

- "I can feel safe sharing my authentic self with the people around me."

- "I am the one responsible for saving myself, and I know that I can do it."

- "I choose to release what is not mine to carry."

- "I really don't need to fix everything for everyone."

- "I am strong and positive."

- "It is OK to say no at the right times."

- "I will use my abilities to improve my own life and the people I meet."

- "It is OK to listen to my dreams."

- "My energetic boundaries are pure and strong."

- "I willingly free myself from emotions that are not mine to carry."

- "I am happy being me and appreciate my gift."

- "It is OK for me to release emotions that are not mine."

- "I express my needs and desires to supportive people."

- "I can clear all the negative energy from my body."

Guided Meditation 2

- "I am the one responsible for saving myself, and I know that I can do it."

- "I am way stronger than I know."

- "I really don't need to fix everything for everyone."

- "It is OK to listen to my dreams."

- "It is OK to choose how I want to feel in every situation."

- "I know that some boundaries are healthy and it is OK to have them."

- "I am strong and positive."

- "I will listen to my dreams and follow them."

- "My abilities are a blessing."

- "I can ask and receive all the help I need."

- "I treat myself with love, and I embrace my gift."

- "I am willing to feel only my energy."

- "I can feel the emotions of animals and plants around me."

- "I am in control of how I feel in every situation."

- "I set healthy boundaries and this makes me feel better."

- "I will use my abilities to improve my own life and the people I meet."

Empath

- "I am healthy and full of positive energy."

- "My sensitivity makes me stronger."

- "I don't have to fix everything."

- "I release all the negative emotions that no longer serve me."

- "I it is completely OK to set healthy boundaries."

- "I will use my abilities to improve my own life and that of the people I meet."

- "I really don't need to fix everything for everyone."

- "It is OK to say no at the right times."

- "It is OK to listen to my dreams."

- "I feel safe, I feel protected and happy."

- "I can't save the entire world and everyone in it."

- "I truly deserve to feel the love I give."

- "I willingly free myself from emotions that are not mine to carry."

- "I will protect my energy from draining people."

- "I will find balance in my life."

- "I respect other people's feelings, but they are not my business."

- "I don't have to fix everything for everyone."

- "I will support, not fix others."

- "I will learn to accept others for who they are."

- "I only welcome uplifting and positive vibrations in my life."

- "I can control my gift and channel my energy to spread love and positive feelings."

- "I choose to release what is not mine to feel."

- "I will support, not fix others."

- "I choose to listen to my dreams."

- "It is OK to say no at the right times."

- "I am willing to let go all energy that is not mine."

- "I choose to embrace my wellness, both physical, spiritual, and emotional.

- "I am strong and positive."

- "I can attract gentle relationships into my life."

- "It is OK to say no at the right times."

- "I willingly free myself from emotions that are not mine to carry."

- "I am happy being me, and I appreciate my gift."

Empath

- "I will treasure myself."

- "It is OK for me to release emotions that are not mine."

- "I will use my abilities to improve my own life and the people I meet."

- "I release all emotions but my own."

- I am happy being me, and I appreciate my gift.

- "I appreciate my abilities every day."

- "I am strong and positive."

- "I feel positive and uplifting vibrations in my life."

- "I express my needs and desires to supportive people."

- "I am willing to feel only my energy."

- "I feel safe and protected in my life."

- "I can't save the entire world and everyone in it."

- "I am willing to let go of all the energy that is not mine."

- "My energetic boundaries are strong and pure."

- "I express my needs and desires to supportive people."

- "I can clear all the negative energy from my body."

- "I can attract gentle relationships into my life."

- "It is OK for me to release emotions that are not mine."

- "I will listen to my intuition."

- "I can say 'no' at the right times."

- "I can feel safe sharing my authentic self with the people around me."

- "I can clear all the negative energy from my body."

- "I will not try to hide my gift."

- "I can feel the energies of others, but I don't absorb the energies of others."

- "My energetic boundaries are pure and strong."

- "I choose to release what is not mine to carry."

Empath

Embracing Being an Empath

Living as an empowered empath is the main goal as you want to be able to use your gifts to their fullest for the betterment of yourself and those around you. You will have to develop a daily routine to maintain your level of empowerment. The first key to this success is to stop any negative self-talk. You want to get to a point where you are content with who you are and what your unique gifts bring to the table.

There are many ways to live as an empowered empath; however, here are the top 10 steps on getting to that point:

1.   You Have to Love Yourself: It is important that you have to find a way to love yourself. No more negative self-talk. Do not take on other people's emotions, and surround yourself with those that support and love you for who you are. If you are feeling down, make a point to turn a negative into a positive. If you do not love

yourself, it will be difficult to live an empowered life. If you ever doubt yourself or doubt what you are doing with your life, take note of what you have already accomplished.

2.   Take Notice of Your Accomplishments: If you have had any accomplishments in your life, write it down. Take note of even the smallest accomplishments. For instance, when you were in a bout of depression two months ago, you were able to get out of bed and clean your house. This may seem small, but if you find yourself getting back in that place, you will see that you have already climbed out of that space before, and you can do it again. Other accomplishments could include graduating from college, purchasing a new home, getting the new job you have been searching for, and rescuing four dogs. When you can recognize what you have accomplished in your life, you are more likely to feel empowered from it and for your future.

3.   Make Time to Be Alone: We have talked about the alone time a few times so far. This is because we need it, and we actually enjoy it thoroughly. If it makes you happy and refreshed, then spend as much time alone as you need. While we tend to focus on everyone else around us, we need to shut that off at times and focus on ourselves.

4.   Maintain a Healthy Diet: Food translates into energy itself; therefore, if you do not want a bunch of negative energy festering inside of you, cut down on junk foods.

5.   Use Crystals: Crystals can be a source of clarity and calm when you need to rejuvenate your energy field. One of the most popular stones for grounding and blocking negative energy is tourmaline.

6.   Learn How to Set and Enforce Boundaries: Boundaries can be difficult to set, especially with a loved one. But we are typically bad at setting boundaries no matter who it is. If you do not learn how to set boundaries, you will end up in pain, drained, and burned out.

7.   Focus on Practicing Self-Awareness: The more you become aware of your own energy, the more you will be able to figure out and decipher between someone else's. If you are ever in a situation where you suddenly feel terrible internally, take a moment to figure out whether that is coming from you or someone else.

8.   Stay Away from Toxic People: This can be difficult because empaths are typically sought out by master manipulators. It is as if they can sense it. If you are in tune with your body, you will feel when someone just is not right. If you do feel that way, run for the hills.

9.   Create Clear Goals: Make known to yourself what your purpose in life is. If you enjoy helping others, make it a point to try to make a living out of it. Be honest with yourself and know your limits when you are setting goals for yourself; make them attainable and grow from there.

10.   Establish a Routine: Routine will help you maintain a level of stability—even if it is just in the morning—so you can clear yourself for the rest of the day. A few ideas would be to wake up early to meditate, make a list of items that need to be completed that day, have breakfast, shower, and get to work. Your routine may be different, but just do what works best for you to function throughout the day.

Empath

The more in tune you are to making sure the above items are maintained, the more empowered and peaceful your life will be. Make sure to focus on yourself and your awareness to protect yourself from toxic people. Maintain your energy and love yourself, and then the rest will fall into place.

How to Become an Assertive Empath

We, as empaths, were raised in such a way that we subconsciously have the urge to help and please everyone around us. As children, we were most likely given the idea of being a good person if we followed orders from a parent or teacher. If we did not follow those orders, we associate it with a form of punishment, and that is how the people-pleasing behaviors came about to avoid punishment or letting others down. There is a way to balance being an empath while also being assertive. When you are assertive, you are claiming your views and putting forth the right to do so in a confident manner. Basically, being assertive means that you are speaking up for yourself, you are making your thoughts known, and you effectively speak out about your concerns, wishes, and ideas. When you do this, you want to make sure that you are being considerate of others and respectful of other people's emotions and personal boundaries. There are plenty of kind ways to say, "I appreciate you asking me. However, I am unavailable to help at this time."

The most important way to become more assertive as an empath include the following:

1.   Set Boundaries: Setting boundaries is particularly difficult for empaths. We tend to want to make sure everyone is happy. Thus, if they ask for help, we will fit it into our schedule. When you recognize that you are getting into an unhealthy relationship

or notice that you are always trying to save, help, or change people, you have to stop before you are the one that gets hurt. If those around you understand who you are or respect you, they will not mind when you need time to recharge. They should understand that it means nothing against them. If they are not able to understand, then they are not the type of people that you need to be around in the first place.

2.   Try Not to Take Things Personally: If someone happens to ignore you one time, you will be wondering why they are mad at you until either it is addressed or you forget about it. It may have been a misunderstanding. In fact, most instances are not intentional; however, you worry about whether or not someone is mad at you.

3.   Express Your Feelings by Writing in an Assertive Tone: Writing can be good in many ways, especially if you have been hurt or are holding on to past trauma. If you are assertive in any way, start with it in writing. Write what you want to express and express how you need to to feel better.

4.   Maintain and Control Your Own Happiness: It is important not to depend on other people when it comes to what makes you happy. If you do depend on others to make you happy, then you will most likely be disappointed every time.

5.   Focus on How You Are Presenting Yourself: Make sure you focus on how you are portraying yourself. You do not want to be so humble that people recognize that and perceive you as a weak person. For instance, if you use too many emojis, you may be seen as insecure and that you want to be liked.

Being an empath can be a struggle; however, there are ways to reduce the possibilities of being taken advantage of and keep those boundaries in place for your own well-being. One of the most difficult things for an empath to say is the word "no." The fear of confrontation and upsetting anyone else is where this stems from. People do not want to say "no," as they do not want to upset or hurt the other person. Even when an empath does say "no," they tend to worry about the fact that they did it, and it does become stressful and overwhelming.

Being assertive is not a bad trait. It can be used as a tool to manage your obligations to the point where you are not setting yourself up to be drained. Being assertive is somewhat an art. You have to make sure you maintain a level of consideration and respect for other people's feelings. I may be mistaken with passive-aggressive behavior, but it is distinct because you are focusing on other people's needs as well as your own. Once you master the art of being assertive, you will be able to control your life in a stress-free manner that works for you.

Learning How to Set Boundaries

All empaths cringe when they are told to set boundaries. Most likely, people have told you that a few times, especially if you are seeing a counselor. But you most likely will not enforce or put any boundaries in place until you get hurt when you least expect it. Usually, after a traumatic event, you will then think a bit clearer, and it is at that time that you will actively seek to put boundaries in place to avoid further trauma. The best ways to set boundaries are as follows:

1.   Focus on how you feel around certain people.

2. Utilize the word "no."

3. Become comfortable with saying "no."

4. If you become overwhelmed, leave the scene.

5. Take time for yourself.

6. Create an imaginary bubble.

Empath

Crystals

Crystals are one particularly powerful way that empaths can begin to protect themselves and their energy from the pain of other people in their lives. Crystals can help you ground yourself, protect you from negative energy, support you with having clearer and more intentional relationships with people, heal your heart, and help you with many other energy practices in your life. Most empaths who have become aware of their sensitivities choose to wear crystals in the form of jewelry regularly so that they can be intentional with their energy.

The benefit of using crystals to help in healing your energy as an empath is that crystals work on their own without you always having to consciously be "at work" with your energy. This way, if you find that you are going about your day-to-day life and you become exposed to unwanted energies, rather than having to consciously put in the work to protect or ground yourself, you can let your crystal help you. As a result, you will only really need to do the work of keeping yourself grounded or protected in any instance that may be particularly overwhelming.

How Crystal Healing Works

Crystals emit their energy at a certain frequency that also can subtly shift the frequency of the energy fields that surround the crystal. Wearing or carrying crystals with you regularly ensures that your own subtle energy field is "monitored" and balanced by that crystal's energy throughout the day. This energetic exchange happens without you having to intentionally facilitate it over and over again, as the crystal automatically facilitates the balance simply by being present.

Crystal healing can be done by wearing crystal jewelry, although it can also be done by keeping crystal specimens in your home or using them intentionally in healing sessions. Crystals shaped like wands, spheres, and palm stones are all used in intentional crystal healing sessions where the individual receiving the healing will often meditate with them, place them on their body, or sweep their body with them to cleanse their energy field. Doing this regularly helps you keep your energy protected and cleansed, whereas wearing crystals on a day-to-day basis will help you with in-between maintenance.

If you are not certified as a crystal healer, you can always find a local crystal healer who can perform a session for you. Most cities have healers who are trained to do proper healings, which means that if you feel you need a more intense energy healing, you can book a session and have it done for you. With that being said, this is optional, not strictly necessary for the healing process.

Crystals for Healing Your Energy

There are five types of crystals that empaths should have on hand to help them with healing. These include "rose quartz," "malachite," "lapis lazuli," "fluorite," and "lepidolite."

Rose Quartz

"Rose quartz" is an incredibly gentle healing stone that works wonders on the heart chakra and the emotional body of sensitive beings. This particular stone has a very gentle energy, which is why it works so wonderfully for empaths. It is a great and gentle healer and a stone that can add unconditional love and support to your energy field if you are feeling particularly drained.

Malachite

"Malachite" is a rich green-colored stone that is known for releasing stagnant energy in your field so that you have the power to be yourself. If you are healing from negative thoughts or a painful inner dialogue, malachite will help.

Lapis Lazuli

"Lapis lazuli" will help you dig into your intuitive gifts and awaken them with greater confidence and ease. If you are an intuitive empath and you want to learn how to use your gifts more healthily without being taken advantage of, lapis lazuli is a great stone to use.

Fluorite

"Fluorite" is known for helping to balance your chakras and support your psychic and intuitive abilities. This stone also has a subtle neutralizing ability that enables it to neutralize harmful energies as it balances your energy field.

Lepidolite

"Lepidolite" is an incredibly gentle healing stone that helps empaths relieve themselves of the anxiety that they can often feel when they are struggling with inner energetic troubles. Working with lepidolite is a wonderful way to calm your energies when you are feeling overwhelmed so that you can begin to feel better within yourself and your own energy field. Carry this particular stone if you are going to be around people whose energy makes you feel overwhelmed.

How Crystal Protection Works

Crystal protection works in the same way that crystal healing works. Protective crystals emit protective energies into your subtle energy body that make it so that unwanted harmful energies cannot penetrate into your space and create discomfort for you in your life. If you are looking to heal yourself from harmful energies, you will want to wear, carry, or decorate your space with protective crystals.

Crystals for Protecting Your Energy

The three best protective crystals that an empath can have are "black obsidian," "smoky quartz," and "amethyst." All three of these are powerful in protecting your energy field and keeping your subtle energy body safe.

Black Obsidian

"Black obsidian" is a dark jet-black stone that is known for absorbing negative energies from your field before they can reach your body. You can carry, wear, or keep this stone nearby when you are dealing with negativity as a way to absorb it out of your energy field and into the stone itself. This stone should regularly be cleaned using sage or by burying it in a pot of dirt to release the negative energies out of it when you are done.

Smoky Quartz

"Smoky quartz" is known for being particularly helpful for people who find themselves frequently absorbing lower energies as it transmutes the energy for you. This stone does not need to be cleansed or grounded as it quite literally turns negative energy into neutral energy, which means that the stone itself does not carry any negative energy within it at all.

Amethyst

"Amethyst" is a bright purple stone that is known for protecting the psyche and psychic energies of an individual. As an empath, you are likely a highly intuitive person and deeply connected to your psychic gifts, whether you realize it or not. Having amethyst on hand will ensure that you are keeping your intuitive energy protected at all times.

Empath

Are You an Empath?

What Type of Empath Are You?

Many people describe themselves as having traits similar to an empath: Nice, nature-loving, introverted, kind, and generous. If you are reading this, you likely already suspect that you are an empath, and you may have many of the qualities of an empath. But how do you know if you are really an empath? Here's a little text to help you find out more. Please read this list of phrases and count the number of statements you identify with:

•   "I know how people are feeling. I can tell when someone is struggling, even when they are covering up their feelings with their words and body language."

•   "I can tell when someone is lying to me."

Empath

•   "People gravitate to me. Not only the people in my daily life, but random people strike up conversations with me. I frequently find myself in deep conversations with people in line at stores as they tell me their life stories."

•   "I love alone time. I do not enjoy being social. It makes me feel tired, dirty, and confused."

•   "I find multitasking to be overwhelming."

•   "I prefer the suburbs and rural settings to cities."

•   "I experience sensory overload. I avoid places like food courts, perfume stores, malls, and movie theaters. They make me dizzy, anxious, and exhausted."

•   "I often feel that I don't fit in and that people don't relate to me. But this doesn't stop them from telling me all their problems!"

•   "I feel emotionally and physically exhausted after talking to my friend, who always needs my help and always has problems but never seems to reciprocate the support I give them."

•   "I feel unclean after I have to touch a lot of people, no matter how clean these people are!"

•   "I feel like I absorb the emotions of others. After spending time with a sad person, it takes me a long time to cheer up. When I spend time with someone joyful, I feel joyful as well, even if my own life isn't going so well."

If you did not score as high as you would like, you could still work to develop your skills as an empath. You may not have the same natural abilities as some, but you can hone and strengthen the abilities that you have. For example, you may never be able to tell how an animal is feeling, but it would certainly be worthwhile to enhance your tendency to intuit when someone is lying to you.

Understand If You Are an Empathic Person

Your journey towards identifying your empathic nature starts with self-awareness and being able to identify the unique characteristics that make you who you are. While we can all display different features based on the situation, it's easy to identify the patterns of behavior that we routinely engage in.

It's important to remember that most people, empaths or otherwise, have a natural level of empathy and consideration for others. Empaths are set apart by their higher sensitivity and ability to not just understand but also feel people's emotions. The following test should help you determine whether or not you are an empath and to what extent:

You Are a Great Listener

Empaths are known to be incredible listeners. In fact, many tend to be the "counselor" in their friend group. You may notice that your friends, family, loved ones, and maybe even complete strangers come to you with their problems and want to talk. At times, it may also feel like you are an emotional dumping ground for people's thoughts and emotions.

As an empath, you have a strong ability to listen to others and truly feel what they are sharing with you. They especially like talking to you because people feel like you hear what they aren't saying and know the problem better than they do, which can be a great relief for many. Modern society is not overly accepting of many thoughts, feelings, or emotions. As a result, many people are uncomfortable or seemingly incapable of sharing these things. Because you seem to "just know," people may be drawn to you because it feels like a breath of fresh air being understood in ways that no one has likely ever understood them before.

You May Struggle to Connect to Standard Religion

Many empaths find it extremely challenging to connect to the teachings of the majority of modern religions. Although most empaths will see and appreciate the underlying messages of connection and unconditional love, they tend to pick up on the reality that most religious organizations do not actually live or operate in alignment with these teachings. This can lead to a deep inner sense of struggle for any empaths who have been raised in or around a religious community.

You Are Drawn to Spirituality

Despite not being attracted to religious teachings, many empaths will be attracted to spirituality. Spirituality tends to be more accepting of and understanding toward empaths, allowing them to feel understood and recognized by others. This also allows them to facilitate deep connections toward the teachings and the others who follow similar paths. This type of connection can be heavily empowering for empaths, allowing them to feel supported in their journey as they also support others. Since the spiritual path is filled with empaths, many empaths trust that the individuals in these journeys will think similarly to them and, therefore, will be more accepting, understanding, empathetic, compassionate, and caring towards them. This allows them to feel reciprocated, making it far more inviting than many standard religious teachings.

You Are Likely Highly Creative

Empathic individuals are almost always highly creative. They perceive the world in an entirely different way and tend to see art where others see virtually nothing. For example, an empath may look at a blank page and see an entire image come to life, thus drawing them into wanting to create that image and bring it into reality. Empaths have visual gifts unlike any other, allowing them to quite literally think things into existence. An individual who is not empathic would likely see just a blank page. Empaths are known to become artists on varying levels. They may create art through words, objects, perception, photography, or virtually anything else. The entire world is a canvas to empaths, and they just want to create. Creating allows them to express themselves in ways that words and emotions do not always allow for. Additionally, it allows them to feel incredible self-worth, empowered and inspired by the world around them.

You May Have Suffered from Narcissistic Abuse

Narcissists are drawn to empaths because they have the one thing that the narcissist completely lacks: empathy. Empaths, as you know, have a heightened level of empathy that is above average. This makes them more desirable than the average person because they have enough to substitute for the lack of empathy that the narcissist has. Furthermore, empaths are more likely to forgive and desire to see the good in other people. This means that it is easy for a narcissist to draw empaths into their abuse cycles and quickly turn their empathic gift into a burden that they long to destroy so that they can step away.

You May Feel Extremely Close to Plants and Animals

Empaths, especially plant empaths and animal empaths, have a tendency to feel extremely close to plants and animals. Even if you are not a plant or animal empath, you may still find yourself feeling extremely drawn to them. This is because they tend to have much purer energy, filled with unconditional love. For many empaths, plants and animals are a breath of fresh air from the corrupted society that many of us live in.

If you find that you are heavily drawn to plants and animals, and especially if you feel like you can communicate with them in a paranormal way, this may be an indication that you are experiencing your empathic gifts. The unconditional love you feel between each other is simply amazing and blissful. You may even think that your plants and pets are the only things that can make you feel better when things are not going well. If you feel that you receive wisdom and advice from plants and animals, this is your claircognizant gift arising from your empathic abilities.

You Might Have Experienced Mental or Physical Symptoms

Empaths often experience mental and physical symptoms relating to their gift, in addition to the more commonly talked about emotional symptoms. These are not always directly borrowed from someone else but may actually be the symptom of feeling so many other people's energies so deeply. Many empaths may experience psychotic attacks or episodes because they feel overwhelmed by the amount of energy around them that they are always picking up. Often, empaths feel like they are a "sponge" to the world around them, which can result in them picking up and holding on to a lot of different sensations.

You May Experience Psychic Attacks

Psychic attacks are a common experience for empathic individuals. Psychic attacks are an attack on empaths with negative energy. This energy is sent either consciously or unconsciously by another individual or entity to create or inflict harm upon said person. These attacks can be felt by anyone in your life, including family and friends, an acquaintance, or in some cases, entities that we cannot see. This harm can be intended to create turmoil in the emotional, spiritual, physical, or mental state of the individual receiving the attack.

Psychic attacks feel a lot like psychotic attacks, causing you to feel like you are no longer lucid and in full control of your own body. Many reports that they feel like they are standing next to themselves, watching themselves go through the motions. While this may be medically rooted, if you are an empath, there is also a big chance that you are experiencing a psychic attack.

You Are Sensitive to Food

Empaths are known to feel their food in a way that no one else can. Many will become vegetarian or vegan because they feel too much negative energy in meats and animal byproducts. However, this is not always the case. Other people find that they can eat meat just fine as long as it has been ethically sourced. Some also like to bless their meat before eating. How you choose your diet will be highly personal, but you may find that it is chosen based on the feeling and energy of the food more than anything else.

Empath

When you are empathic, you may find that you can feel what you need. For example, say your energies are feeling off; you may feel that you need the energy that is within carrots, sweet potatoes, or other foods.

Raising Your Vibration

At each time, you're either acting or responding to lifetime, and the outcome is an increase or decline in your vibration. Every interaction or action throughout the duration of your life will impact your energy. If you make good decisions, you raise your vibration, and if you make bad decisions, you decrease your vibration. You have to be active to undergo a superior frequency. If your time is drained, then you will undergo low vibrations; also, consequently, your emotional, spiritual, and physical bodies are affected.

How to Become an Extroverted Empath

If you want to be an extroverted empath, all you need is love. That's right, all of the introverts out there can have it too! You may think that extroverted empathy is reserved for the outgoing social butterfly types with an ice-cold personality, but it's not (and they're not always that happy either!).

Introduction to Extroverted Empathy

Let's take a look at the definition of empathy: "An awareness of and responsiveness to the feelings of others." And now the purpose for extroversion: "Outgoing or positive attitude toward life." Aha! There is your root word: "Attitude." Extroverted empaths are those people who make the conscious decision to be outgoing and positive (empathic) toward others to change the world. These people are naturally inclined to put themselves in other people's shoes without an ounce of self-conceit.

Empath

This urge to be an extroverted empath is so strong in them that if left unchecked, they'll think of themselves as everybody's friend, which may not be a good thing. They must learn to balance their empathy with rational thinking and have the ability to put their foot down, especially when necessary. The key is to use their emotional intelligence and not let it use them.

Entering the World of an Extroverted Empath

For people who are wired this way, everything comes naturally: Listening attentively, reading social cues effortlessly, understanding how things work, and getting along with people from all walks of life. These individuals can have the ability to feel and understand the emotions of others as if they were their own. They notice how things make them feel and are in tune with their emotional needs, so they've learned to connect well with others. They're on an intuitive level and can get involved in a conversation without realizing that it's taking place.

Extroverted empaths aren't as social as the introverts out there, but all communication takes place through their thoughts, not words. The only way you'll find these people is when you stumble across them, that is, if their mind is not already filled with other people's (often negative) thoughts.

In a nutshell, these people have a natural ability and love for understanding others and their societies. This sense of giving back and involvement with people is how they find happiness. There's not much difference between being happy and feeling empathy for others.

They're in tune with other people's emotions without understanding what they're feeling or why they are feeling it. But you have to remember that it's not their fault! People don't like to be criticized or judged for having negative thoughts, so would you be comfortable doing it? This is why extroverted empaths need to observe everything that goes on in the world from an unbiased perspective. There's no need to engage unless it's necessary.

A Quick Emotional Intelligence Index to Get You Started

Read the Future: Extroverted empaths can't ignore their intuition and the visible signs that they see, even if they don't understand them. They feel people out like a jungle native instinctually. An extroverted empath can read someone by looking at how they walk, checking their facial expressions and body language, or getting a vibe from them that tells the empath what the other people are inside. They can figure out what will happen next just by observing someone or a group of people.

Make a Difference: People with this ability are highly intuitive and very empathic. They notice how people feel and understand how others think, but they do it without forcing their thoughts. They can put themselves in your shoes without judging you or taking your thoughts personally, which lets them work things out more quickly than most people. Other people feel safe sharing their deepest concerns with these individuals, from their biggest fears to the situations that make them angry or depressed.

Understand Emotions: These people understand and can express the feelings of others. They usually pick up on things that other people can't because they've gained this ability through empathy training. They have to understand and explain why other people are acting in a certain way. This skill has helped them become great communicators and interpreters, which has resulted in promotions, better educations, a better understanding of how the world works, and personal growth. Someone with this skill can calm you down during an argument or sympathize with you when you have your bad days. They can listen without being judgmental, which is why they're highly valued.

The Hidden, Sulking Side of an Extroverted Empath

Being an extroverted empath is a double-edged sword. For starters, it's difficult for people to understand how these people can be so wise and empathic when they don't show any emotion of their own. They're like the proverbial iceberg. You can only see the tip above the waterline, but what about the rest? Extroverted empaths keep their deepest thoughts to themselves because they have been hurt so often that no one ever wants to get close enough to them again. They can feel what you're going through, but they won't tell you about it. When people get hurt too often, they instinctively shut off their feelings and stop communicating with other people. Instead of telling you that they understand how you're feeling, an extroverted empath will go numb inside and experience life to the fullest without ever trying to make sense of it all.

There's a tendency for these people to isolate themselves from others because they've shut off their emotions. Some of them even stop eating and become anorexic or bulimic. They may spout off witty one-liners all day long, but they don't have anything else to say. They won't tell you that they understand how you're feeling, so their silence speaks volumes. If you ask them how they think about something, they'll give you a sarcastic response. This is common for very intuitive and empathic people who are dealing with traumatic experiences from the past.

Extroverted empaths turn to addiction when their emotions get the better of them, as opposed to fully expressing themselves to find out why they're hurt in the first place. These people tend to bury their feelings under surface-level, surface-thrilling behavior. It's like they throw up all of their feelings in a big fountain of superficiality, but they never learn how to express themselves openly and truly.

The Internalized Sulking Side of an Extroverted Empath

If the extroverted side of an empath is tough for people to understand, the internalized side is even more so. Being an introverted empath can be comical and downright confusing because it's difficult for them to verbalize their feelings. When you're an introvert, you process your thoughts internally before expressing them outwardly. This is why you'll see inner emotions on their faces, but they're hard to hear.

Internalized Side (Introverted Empath)

An introverted empath typically appears to be very happy until you push the wrong button, and then they shut down. They may be highly emotional one minute and appear to be fine the next, but only if you don't push them over the edge. People who don't understand this type of being may think that introverted empaths are cold, uncaring, or even rude because they seem cruel at times. This goes back to the example of having feelings and trying to stuff them down until they come out at unexpected moments.

Internalized Side (Extroverted Empath)

An introverted empath who has learned to be extroverted will still feel the energy of others but will try to ignore it. They may appear to be cold or uncaring because they don't show emotions like warmth or sympathy. They may seem callous or unsympathetic when in truth, they just don't know what else to do with the feelings of others except to push them away and ignore them until they can figure out how to react appropriately.

Older children and adults who have experienced sexual abuse or who have been sexually abused themselves may also respond with several personality changes, including increased emotional control and fearfulness, especially when interacting with others.

An individual who has been sexually abused may feel responsible for having "caused" their abuser to use them by either seducing the abuser or making advances unacceptable to the abuser. The same person may also feel responsible for "breaking up" an abusive relationship, even though they didn't ask for it or do anything wrong. Depending on where the abuse occurred, it may be too painful to discern whether the abuser could be abusive or whether the abusive relationship was a response to unresolved childhood experiences.

The Solutions: How to Talk to Extroverted Empaths

It's not always easy for an extroverted empath to deal with others, but there are ways to ease into the conversation and connect with them anyway.

Here are some tips that can help people talk about their feelings in an empathetic manner:

Know When (and When Not) to Talk About Feelings: If you're not sure how they're going to react, don't say anything at all. It's tempting to speak to them about certain feelings because they are your friends, but you don't want to push the issue. Are you feeling blue? That's okay. You can always tell people later that you had a case of the blues (or something similar). If they ask about it, tell them how you're feeling, but don't expect them to be able to understand right off the bat. If they ask again, try to make a more detailed explanation to begin to understand.

Don't Be Afraid of Stating Your Opinion: In general, most extroverts are not bashful when it comes to voicing their ideas and thoughts out loud. Be brave and be honest. If there's a topic you feel strongly about, don't be afraid to speak your mind appropriately. It would help if you never used hurtful or judgmental language with other people. That's the quickest way to shut off all communication and feelings toward the situation.

Give Positive Feedback: Even when you're not sure how someone will react, it doesn't hurt to give them some positive feedback and encouragement along the way. This can be as simple as telling them that you understand how hard they're trying even if it isn't always good enough for others or just telling them that they look nice today even when they're having a bad hair day (unexpectedly). Positive feedback can go a long way, even if it's as simple as a compliment. If they're having a bad day, you can just smile and tell them that you believe in them. That's all it takes to give them the boost of energy they need to continue with their day without hesitation.

Empath

Healing Yourself and Harnessing Your Gift

Your Gift of Healing

You Are Born to Heal: You have a great capacity to cure others and your own emotional problems. Learning to use it to empower yourself, you can achieve all your life goals faster. You can intentionally use it to transform disharmony into positive energy. Practice doing it and using it to heal others without their knowledge.

Start with Your Family and Friends: When you sense something is wrong with someone, allow their energy to get close to you, but instead of receiving it, you can turn it into a ball of energy, and then, with your mind, transform the negative emotion into positive feelings and send it back to them. Observe how they react. You are using your power to heal and help your loved one.

Some signs indicate that you are born a healer:

Empath

- You are extremely empathic or attuned to other peoples' emotions and behavior.

- You always think of effective solutions for people's problems.

- People around you are healthy and not sickly.

- People say that being with you soothes their troubled minds or heart.

- You have a strong desire to help other people.

- You often feel a sudden feeling of heightened awareness when in public places characterized by nervousness or difficulty of breathing.

- When you walk inside a room, you suddenly feel the discord and negative emotions that come from an argument or disagreement.

An empath who wants to develop the fullest potential of healing should avoid the following:

- Being a people pleaser

- Being a scapegoat for others negative acts

- Allowing people's destructive behaviors

- Giving time to careless people

- Forcing time to be with people because of guilt or sense of responsibility

- Having a feeling of codependence

- Playing victim

The above-mentioned acts and behaviors can hinder your objectivity. If you want to harness your healing gift, you should be emotionally mature and independent from the influence of others.

How to Use Your Healing Ability

- Use your voice to soothe wounded souls and your hands to transfer positive energy—or even play an instrument to send out healing colors to a crowd. The more you practice your gift, the more powerful you become. Healing others with energy makes you more aware of your capacity to heal yourself.

- Use your strong intuition or gut feeling to save people from harm. Empaths have a strong sixth sense and can sense future dangers. Use it to help others and to prevent you from dangers as well.

- Use your heightened sense of smell to avoid potential dangers or life-threatening experiences. You can also use it during food, drinks, or products selection to make excellent choices.

- Use it to inspire others to live life with more love and compassion. Empaths are natural giver and comforter. They live life with great enthusiasm. Show others how to fully enjoy life by being kinder, more generous, more loving, and more caring.

- Use your ability to read and understand emotional cues to help other people cope up with their struggles. As an empath, you know what is happening inside people's minds and hearts. You somehow know what to say or do to ease their troubled emotions.

• Use your innate power to know if the person is lying or hiding something. Some people will say that they are fine, but deep inside they are not. You can feel and sense beyond their superficial façade.

• Use your skills to see nonverbal signs of physical or emotional needs. You can heal infants, plants, animals, and people who are afraid to talk.

The empath's healing gift should be developed further to learn how to channel energy from one person to another. Using energy healing is the fastest, easiest, and most effective way to cure the emotional maladies of other people.

An empath is a good preceptor, connector, and conductor of energy. When you know how to use energy to heal yourself and others, you can be unstoppable. Use it positively.

On your way to the healing journey, always remember these 3 things:

1. Set Limits

Stop taking responsibility of other people. Some people expect you to take care of them. Remind yourself that it is okay to be compassionate, but know your limits. This is the only way that an empath can maintain a sense of balance and power.

Remember also that taking care of other people does not necessarily mean protecting them from their own feelings. Allow them to feel because they are vital for their growing up and not yours. You can care for them at a certain level, but it is important to keep yourself centered and guarded against their negative energies.

2.   Shield to Protect Yourself

It is important to create a protective shield to safeguard yourself against negative energies that can affect your personal energy. The natural human shield (aura) of empaths is said to be "thin" because of their natural caring nature.

Visualize positive energy around your body. See it pink, gold, or white. Imagine it surrounding your body. Keep it moving and flowing actively.

3.   Exercise Grounding Technique

An empath needs this exercise to keep their energy balanced. Grounding helps you remove excessive and negative emotions from your being. It allows you to feel light, free and centered. It is about letting go of energies that you do not need and keep your personal energy intact. Your own energy is what you need to heal others and pursue your personal goals in life.

To do it, close your eyes while creating a red ball image in your mind. Imagine it beneath your feet. Feel the tingling sensation it brings. Visualize it going up your legs and settling in your stomach. Unplug the excess energies by imagining the red ball absorbing all the stored energies. See it spinning and gathering the energies. After some time, visualize it dropping down to your legs and then to the soles. Release the ball and feel lightness in your physical body.

Ways to harness and maximize your gifts:

Empath

•   Seek spiritual guidance. An empath needs someone to keep them spiritually healthy. A healthy spiritual life makes them more accepting and trusting in their own ability.

•   Modify your lifestyle. Changing your lifestyle is another way of empowering yourself. Here are some practical ways to do lifestyle modification:

o   Avoid toxic people and those who are fond of playing victims or creating crises in their lives.

o   Avoid mainstream and social media, as well as books and movies with heart-wrenching themes that can affect your positive mood.

o   Avoid crowds, which can suck out your personal energy. When you cannot avoid crowds, make sure that you are protected or shielded to ward off negative energies to affect your emotions.

•   Spend more time alone. You need to restore personal balance and harmony. Make people understand your need for space and time alone.

•   Spend time communing with nature.

•   Find ways to manage your stress. Seek the help of a friend, counselor, or support group. Read motivational books or learn new things to balance your energy.

•   Keep a personal space in your home. Make it orderly, clean, and free from clutter. When you feel emotionally drained, spend time in this place to recharge your energy. You can use it to do meditation, yoga, visualization, journaling, or exercise.

- Practice energy healing regularly. As mentioned earlier, learning to use the power of your intent with energized thoughts can help you heal yourself and others.

As soon as you receive strong energy, look around and sense who is sending the intense emotion. Reverse it at once to help the person and prevent it from affecting the whole environment or your own mood. Imagine a ball absorbing the energy.

Next, visualize a white light settling down your heart and hands. Wrap it around the ball to transform the negative energy into a positive emotion. Then, send it out of your mind and intentionally throw it in the needy person. Visualize the ball, comforting and healing them.

Empath

Protect Your Energy

Most empaths are driven to give of themselves to help restore the happiness and well-being of those around them. Unfortunately, this can lead to an empath becoming emotionally, physically, and spiritually drained as a result. Even worse, empaths don't always have someone in their close inner circle that they can turn to for help in restoring their emotional energies. Subsequently, it falls on the empath to take the time and effort to protect and maintain their personal energy levels. This will address some of the negative practices that you should give up, as well as some positive practices that you should start to take better care of your overall health and well-being. Additionally, it will provide some methods that will help you stay emotionally grounded at all times. By following these recommendations, you will not only be able to avoid becoming run down and emotionally drained, but you will also be able to start thriving as an empath.

Empath

Bad Practices to Give Up

As empath, chances are you have developed several habits that serve to undermine your happiness and well-being. These habits aren't necessarily bad behaviors; rather they are good behaviors that have no boundaries. This is because empaths cannot usually say "no," meaning that good, noble traits, such as being giving and selfless, can become all-consuming. Subsequently, it is important to recognize and eliminate these practices to maintain your emotional balance, health, and overall well-being. Bad practices to give up include:

• Always Trying to Please Others: Needless to say, trying to please others isn't a bad thing in itself; however, when left unchecked, it can create a situation where an empath over-commit themselves. By always saying "yes" to others, you allow yourself to be used continuously, never giving yourself the time and space to restore your energy levels. The result is that you become drained and spent, much like a cell phone that isn't charged regularly.

• Being an Enabler: Another bad practice that needs to be eliminated from your behavior is that of being an enabler. Unlike trying to please others, however, this behavior is truly bad in nature. The reason why it's easy to enable others to behave badly is that, as an empath, you can relate to why they need to behave badly. Unfortunately, not only does this not help the other person, but it also serves to harm you as well. After all, most of the bad behaviors you enable involve how the other person treats you, meaning that by enabling them, you only allow more harm to come your way. Therefore, you must recognize bad behavior when you see it, and rather than enabling it, you take a stand and protect yourself from it. You can forgive and accept someone without actually encouraging their negative side.

• Carrying other People's Burdens: This is a behavior that affects almost every empath at some point in time. Whenever you see someone else suffering, as an empath, you feel the need to alleviate that suffering. First, it results in you taking on more burdens than you can handle. In the end, each person should only ever have to carry their personal burdens and no more. The second reason this is bad behavior is that it enables the other person to continue going in the wrong direction as they don't have to carry the burden of their consequences. Ultimately, you have to let others experience the pains and burdens in their life to learn their lessons accordingly.

• Always Taking the Blame: One of the strongest traits of an empath is the unwillingness to cause harm to others. Unfortunately, this trait can result in an empath always taking the blame for when things go wrong, even when they aren't at fault. This can create several problems, both for the empath and for the other person involved. By always taking the blame, you allow the other person to avoid accountability for their actions, thus enabling them to behave badly over and over again. Doing so robs them of learning valuable life lessons. Additionally, by always taking the blame, you carry the burden of responsibility for other people's actions and well-being. The weight of such responsibility will eventually prove too heavy, leaving you crushed under its weight.

• Feeling Obligated to Spend Time with Others: Another behavior that appears positive but is harmful is feeling obligated to spend time with others. This can significantly rob you of valuable alone time in which you recharge your emotional batteries, thereby leaving you vulnerable to emotional fatigue and even depression.

Empath

Furthermore, you may wind up spending time with people who are highly negative, resulting in your energies being drained and damaged by their negative energy.

•	Being Addicted to Victimization: Sometimes, when an empath allows themselves to be victimized repeatedly, they begin to become defined by the process. After a while, they identify with always being drained, depressed, and taken advantage of. This can become so ingrained that when an empath begins to feel strong and happy, they feel guilty—almost as though they aren't fulfilling their purpose. It is important to remember that your purpose is never to be victimized. Therefore, such things as happiness and well-being should be normal for you, not the exception to the rule.

•	Giving Energy to Those Who Take It for Granted: This is one of the main ways in which an empath allows themselves to be victimized in the first place. By giving your time, effort, and emotional energy to those who take it for granted, you will only ever drain your resources with nothing to show for it at the other end. It's a bit like trying to fill a bucket with a huge hole in it. No matter how much water you put in, the bucket will always demand more. Eventually, you need to learn to let go of those who take you for granted so that you can give your energy to those who will appreciate it and thus be more effective as a result.

•	Being Codependent: When you remain in a relationship where the other person takes and never gives, you will spend all your energy and never get anything in return. Needless to say, this will leave you in a constant state of feeling drained and even depressed. It is critical for an empath to only maintain mutually beneficial relationships. Only then will the time you spend with others restore your energies. Any relationship that is one-sided needs to be ended for your happiness and peace of mind.

Good Practices to Start

Discovering and ending bad practices is only half the formula when it comes to creating a life in which you can thrive as an empath. The other half of the formula is to discover and practice those behaviors that benefit you. Again, as an empath, you have an increased responsibility to protect and maintain your energies; therefore, you must perform the practices that will enable you to do so. The following list includes some of the more effective practices that will help you stay strong and happy under any circumstances:

• Accept Your Empathic Ability: As already mentioned in this book, being an empath is not as simple as it is often portrayed. One of the most difficult challenges any empath faces is accepting their empathic abilities. Not only can these abilities be confusing, but they can also be distressing if you don't know what they are. However, once you realize the nature of your abilities, you must accept them so that you can align your mindset with them. Learn to hear your inner voice and trust what it tells you.

• Own Your Gift: Accepting your empathic ability is only the first step toward creating a rich and fulfilling life. The second step is to own your gift. This is where you take the time to nurture your abilities so that they serve to improve your life. One thing many empaths fail to recognize is that their empathic abilities are for their benefit as well. You shouldn't feel as though you are only meant to improve the lives of those around you. Instead, you should constantly use your abilities for your benefit as well. Learn to discern those you can trust from those you can't, and protect yourself accordingly. Furthermore, use your intuition to know which paths will lead to failure and which paths will lead to the success you deserve.

•   Develop Emotional Detachment: Due to the sensitive nature of being an empath, you must learn to develop emotional detachment. This is the mindset where you can recognize the emotions of those around you without being affected by them. Buddhism and other similar traditions promote emotional detachment as a method of avoiding suffering. By engaging in such practices as meditation and mindfulness techniques, you can develop the ability to detach yourself from even the most negative emotional environment, thus protecting you from the harm such negativity would cause.

•   Meditate on a Regular Basis: Meditation is probably the most proven technique concerning developing emotional detachment. Therefore, you should take the time to find a form of meditation that best suits you. Not all forms are the same; therefore, if you don't take to one, simply let it go and try another. The important thing is that you find one that works for you. Not only will the right meditation help you become detached, but it will also help you balance your energies, thereby releasing any stress that has built up due to exposure to negative people or circumstances.

•   Practice Shouting, Running, and Other Forms of Catharsis: Another way to release stress and anxiety due to being exposed to negative energies is to expend it physically. Any high-energy activity will help to burn off excess energy, including stress and anxiety. Running or engaging in any intense exercise is a great way to achieve this goal. A less physical alternative is to release energy through methods such as shouting or screaming. These practices allow you to express your emotional intensity, thereby restoring balance and inner harmony. In the end, any form of catharsis that allows you to expel excess or chaotic energy will help keep you centered and balanced.

•	Develop Somatic Mindfulness: Sometimes, an empath can lose touch with their personal emotions due to the constant flow of emotions from the outside world. This results in them not attending to their own needs. One way to overcome this is to develop somatic mindfulness. This is a technique where you focus on different parts of your body to determine your emotional state. A tense jaw, for example, is indicative of stress and anxiety. An elevated heart rate can point to anxiety or even anger. Shallow breathing, stiff shoulders, and clenched fists can also point to anger, stress, and other negative emotions. By taking the time to assess your body, you can determine your true emotional state and thus take steps to correct any imbalances you are experiencing.

Empath

Parenting an Empathic Child

While empathy and manners can be taught with words, actions make a much more lasting impression. Teaching children the importance of kindness while also using anger and corporal punishment to discipline them sends a mixed message. While there is a place for strong disciplines, such as when a child engages in unsafe practices like running into the street, spanking generally does not serve as a tool for developing empathy.

Parents can demonstrate empathy in the way they raise their children and in the way they treat other adults. Helping children learn to process their emotions in constructive ways rather than acting them out can create a good foundation for self-control. Children can follow the example and guidance of empathetic parents as they learn to show empathy for siblings and other children.

Empath

Being too empathetic can lead to caretaking and promote unhealthy levels of codependency. This can happen when parents do too much for their children. An overzealous desire to protect a child from every possibility of being hurt or damaged can result in parental emotional fatigue and limit the child's ability to develop fully. Obviously, parents must make an effort to protect their children from harmful influences, but there needs to be a clear boundary between the parent's responsibility and the child's responsibility. Exactly where the line should be drawn depends on the age of the child and individual circumstances.

Being empathetic is not the same as being a pushover. There are more dimensions to human emotion than "hurt or be hurt." Real empathy never allows others to take advantage. Permitting mistreatment is not an act of kindness to the perpetrator or the victim.

In a parenting context, it's important to ensure that proper respect and boundaries are in place. A parent is more than a friend. Building a child's self-esteem does not require self-denigration. Rather, parents can be examples of healthy self-esteem by speaking up when disrespect occurs.

In families, familiarity and proximity can lead to disrespect if efforts are not made to prevent it. This respect need not be militaristic, but it does need to be present. The lines between teasing and verbal attacks must be clearly drawn.

Here is an example of a dialog between a mother and her teenage son:

"Jimmy, your dirty socks belong in the hamper, not on the living room floor," said the mom.

"Whatever, mom," said the son.

"Please don't use that tone with me. You know the rules," said the mom.

"If you don't like my socks on the floor, just pick them up. Why do you have to get after me all the time?" said the son.

"Because I'm not a maid. I'm your mother, and if I pick up the socks for you, I'll miss a chance to teach you how to be a good husband," said the mom.

"What do my socks have to do with being a good husband?" said the son.

"Everything. When you grow up and marry, you'll treat your wife just like you treat me," said the mom.

"No way! I'll treat my smoking, hot wife like a queen," said the son.

"Yes, you will, at first, but eventually, she'll be comfortable and familiar like me. You'll see," said the son.

In this dialog, the son's disrespectful behavior is clearly identified by his mother, who not only explains her request for him to pick up his dirty socks but also explains why. Opinions about the best way to handle various parenting situations vary widely. Children don't come with instruction manuals, and each parent must find his or her own way, but an approach based on empathy and respect has worked well for me.

Empath

While parenting styles differ among families and cultures, I found as I was raising my own children that they were more obedient and willing to listen when I took the time to create a relationship with each of them. In fact, for me, building trust with my children essentially took the place of discipline, especially as they grew old enough to understand the choices they were making.

Being a child can be difficult. Many adults find even well-behaved children annoying, and little respect is offered to the young. They are told what to do, and they are expected to immediately obey—often without even knowing the reasons why. Militaristic child-rearing may result in obedient children but not independent and creative thinkers.

In these days of multi-job households and technology, children are often ignored. Teaching is done by computers instead of parents, and one of the first lessons children learn is how to operate a digital device. Developing genuine empathy, however, requires human interaction.

Parenting in blended family situations can be quite complicated. Learning to work with shared custody and step-parenting, especially if toxic exes are in the mix, isn't easy. A few ground rules can help.

In most cases, the biological parent should handle scheduling, arrangements, and pickups. When step-parents get too involved, it can add extra tension.

It's important to keep adult issues among adults. Even if the other parent is sharing information children shouldn't have or actively working to poison them, speaking positively about the former spouse is still advisable. Telling a child it is wrong to love a parent can result in long-term psychological consequences.

Make sure the boundaries are clear when it comes to a parent vs. a step-parent's authority. Each blended family situation is unique. By offering love to natural children and stepchildren alike, parents can create a safe environment and set a positive example.

When my oldest daughter was three, she visited me at work. I am certain she threw many tantrums in her younger years, but the only one I remember was the one she threw in the hallway in front of all my coworkers. I felt very ashamed at that moment like I had somehow failed as a parent. I saw my child's behavior as a reflection on me and found myself disciplining her more harshly than I might have done otherwise.

Learning to allow children to make their own mistakes can be difficult. Even when they are grown, we may feel that every poor decision they make still reflects on us. As a result, embarrassment or shame may drive a wedge between our children and us.

The opposite can happen too, of course. Many teenagers find their parents embarrassing. It's important to understand how these dynamics impact family relationships. Shame and empathy are incompatible. Anger can get in the way of empathy as well. Showing empathy to our children sometimes requires setting aside our own fear and embarrassment.

Unmet expectations can also drive a wedge between parents and children. Often these expectations are unspoken, and parents may not even be aware that they have them. For example, it may simply be assumed that children will have the same political or religious views as their parents. Education and career expectations may be present as well, along with expectations about what type of person qualifies as marriage material. These expectations often lie dormant until something happens to trigger them, such as a child not choosing the expected path. Then they can result in extremely difficult confrontations and disappointments that may lead to damaged relationships.

On a smaller scale, expectations can also impact the quality of day-to-day interactions. I once planned a cross-country skiing trip with my family. As I was getting the equipment ready, the kids were playing on a nearby snow-covered hill. I let them play for a while, and then I told them it was time for skiing. They responded that they were too tired, and I got upset because the family ski day I'd seen in my mind didn't happen. Yet the point was for the kids to be entertained, and they were. It could have been a perfect day had I not allowed expectations to get in the way.

Flexibility limits the influence expectations can have on our interactions. As we open our minds to new possibilities, we may discover that each moment is exactly what it needs to be, even if it isn't perfectly in line with our expectations. Accepting reality as it is rather than as we wish it to allow us to set aside expectations and respond to every moment with empathy and understanding.

Teaching Empathy to Children

While it's easy to be cynical and believe that human beings are inherently selfish and self-centered, science is telling us otherwise. Even chimps and other animals demonstrate empathy at a young age. They get upset when they see another being unfairly treated or hurt—and stories of animals helping people in distress are plentiful. Evolutionary scientists now believe that there is tremendous survival value in empathy.

Have you noticed that human babies often cry at the sound of another baby crying? Or that your young child may try to help you with something they notice you struggling with, even if it's something beyond their abilities? Based on these and other similar observations of both human infants and animals, researchers from many disciplines have concluded that empathy is not something we learn. It is simply innate.

Yet science also tells us that the environment also plays an important role, especially in reducing a child's ability to be empathetic, if not careful. For example, children who grow up in orphanages or foster care are often found to have difficulty developing emotional bonds and being slower to pick up on facial cues. Because of unintended neglect or being moved from place to place or family to family, children can actually suffer in their emotional development due to the lack of personalized attention and love. Remember, the large majority of brain development actually occurs during the first five years of a child's life.

At the risk of sounding corny, loving your children and letting them know you love them is very important. So how do you discipline them without coming across as being harsh? As you may already know, shouting at and hitting children is counterproductive in most cases. In fact, it usually tends to increase their aggression levels.

The best way is to help children learn to verbalize and express themselves better. A crying baby or toddler is not a bad one. It's a human being with a problem they can't express properly. The empathic parent understands that there's a problem and can wait it out till the child is big enough to verbalize. Until the child reaches that age, it's the parent's job to serve as a living example of how to be empathic with others.

Once that child can speak, encouraging them to put themselves in another's shoes is also important. Instead of yelling at the child for hitting another, ask them how they'd feel if the other person hit them. Then sit back, assess, and react accordingly.

This is not to say that a child shouldn't be punished; negative behavior should never be encouraged. But unless a child understands why certain behaviors are wrong from another person's perspective, then punishment is seen as merely arbitrary cruelty.

Blocking Out Negative Emotions and Energy

Escaping and healing from a narcissistic relationship is one of the most challenging things that we can do. There are many things emotionally, and psychologically that could keep us trapped in an abusive relationship. Some victims may fear being physically abused by the narcissist as well. Having the ability to break the trauma bond, safely escape, regain your independence, and heal the trauma, is essential but challenging.

Breaking the Trauma Bond

One of the biggest reasons why it is such a challenge to escape from a relationship with a narcissist is because the victim forms a trauma bond with the narcissist. Trauma bonding is a form of strong emotional attachment that an abused person forms between their abuser. It is perpetuated by the cycle of abuse and reinforced each time the abuse cycle is successfully completed. While bonding in and of itself is natural and healthy under the right circumstances, bonds developed in the process of abuse are unhealthy and traumatic to the victim. People who have grown up in abusive households are more likely to develop these bonds with multiple people because, to them, this is a "normal" bond to have.

In addition to the trauma bond itself, there is also damage that occurs within the brain when we are exposed to abuse for a long time. When you have been abused, you will likely suffer from some degree of "complex post-traumatic stress disorder" (CPTSD). CPTSD is a psychological condition that is stored in various places throughout the brain, making it challenging to release and eliminate. This disorder will actually rewire your brain, causing you to chronically live in a state of "fight or flight." While you can still resume a relatively normal life following the breaking of the relationship and abuse cycles, if CPTSD is not properly healed, you will carry it with you for life. Because it will rewire your brain, you will essentially train yourself to live around the symptoms of CPTSD, which can result in you losing your quality of life and feeling like you are trapped even long after the break.

Breaking the trauma bond is an essential part of leaving your abusive relationship. It can be a challenge, but it is possible. It starts with confronting all of the denials and illusions that you have lived in, including the ones the abuser made for you and the ones you made for yourself. You must realize that this person is abusive and will never change. Of course, it is okay to grieve this as it truly does feel like a real loss. You are losing a person whom you thought you had, but you never truly did.

In addition to choosing to consciously live in reality, you need to create boundaries. There should be a no-contact boundary between you and your abuser. You do not contact them, ever. If, for some reason, you must keep them around, such as if you share custody of children, minimize the contact and keep it very focused on necessary topics and nothing else. Breaking your habits and changing these patterns can be a challenge, but they are necessary. It can be extremely helpful to seek external support to assist you in relieving yourself from the trauma bond and other aspects of trauma that linger in your brain. Healing does take time, and having professional support is extremely beneficial for your long-term health. Be sure always to choose a trauma-informed therapist, so they genuinely understand what you are going through and what you need.

You should also understand that breaking trauma bonds takes time. Be gentle and patient with yourself. Remember, the creation of the bond itself was not overnight. It took time to build, so it will take time to unravel and eliminate as well. Stay intentional and focused, but be patient with yourself and all of the challenges that you may face in the process.

Escaping Safely

The very first thing you absolutely must know before leaving a relationship with a narcissist is that they will continue to try and manipulate you. They will pressure you into believing that you are overreacting, blame you for everything that happened, and attempt to con you into believing that they genuinely miss you and that they want you back. An abuser will always make false promises of a better future to draw their victims back in. It is essential to understand that you cannot trust anything they say, ever. Anything they attempt to do is to manipulate you back into the relationship. You must try to look at the bigger picture and understand the narcissist's end goal. It may take you a few rounds of the entire abuse cycle before you finally realize this fact.

It is also essential that you quit cold turkey and allow yourself to endure the pain that comes with it. You may feel as though you are unable to do it, but trust that you can. Again, seeking support from understanding loved ones and trained therapists can be incredibly helpful at this point. Instead of contacting the narcissist in a moment of weakness, contact a loved one or a professional instead.

The Extreme Importance of No Contact

To successfully escape and stay away from the narcissist, you must enforce 'no-contact.' If you feel that you are in serious danger from this person, having a legally enforced law surrounding the no-contact order may be required to ensure that you have the support of law enforcement in this clause.

If you have any contact with the narcissist whatsoever, you are giving them easy access to manipulate you and keep you in the relationship for longer. No matter what you think, this will be true. Any time you communicate with the narcissist, every single piece of communication will be designed to manipulate you and lure you back in. If you communicate with the narcissist, you are allowing your own mind to justify and rationalize why it may be a good idea to go back to the narcissist. You have to realize that you are in a very vulnerable and weak position at this moment in time. You must vanish from the narcissist and focus on your recovery. You have to refrain from contacting them for any reason whatsoever unless it is absolutely mandatory (such as if you share children with them.) And even if you do share children, you must work towards creating an understood schedule between both parties, where no communication (or very minimal) is needed.

Whenever the narcissist begins the "hoover phase" and starts trying to lure you back in, you must also understand that they are doing so only because they are lonely and they want to exploit you for their own needs. There is nothing genuine here. They do not miss you, love you, or need you in their life, no matter what they say. This can be extremely challenging to understand and to embrace on an emotional level, especially because of how you have been abused and led on by the narcissist. Because of the number of emotions that may arise any time you feel the need to contact them, or anytime they contact you, having a trauma-informed therapist and empathetic friends or family members that you can turn to during these times will be extremely supportive in helping you stay away from the narcissist.

Realize that no matter how good your intentions are in leaving the relationship, you will have to fight temptation. It is very easy for your mind to replay the good times from the relationship and to convince yourself that things may be different the next time you go back. Many victims will leave the relationship with no intention to go back, only to be lured back in dozens of times before hopefully realizing that things will never change. This is because you have a trauma bond, which keeps you seeing the "good" in this person and justifying your return. What you are actually seeing are lies and manipulation, but as a victim, it can be extremely challenging to decipher the difference. This is because it would require you to admit and endure the reality that every aspect of the relationship was a self-serving lie fed to you by the narcissist. Which, understandably, is extremely challenging for anyone to admit—let alone endure the aftermath of the admission. This aspect can lead to complex PTSD, which makes it mentally devastating for any victim to attempt to endure or leave.

Another reason why your no-contact order is absolutely necessary is that the "hoover and idealization phases" are so well-refined with a narcissist, and you are already so mentally destroyed from the CPTSD and trauma bond that there is virtually no other way to overcome this aspect than to seek professional support and break contact. As a victim, you have become addicted to the idealization phase. What leads you back and causes you to justify the rekindling of the relationship is generally the fact that you desperately want to have that deep, passionate, tailor-made love once again. It is something that is rare to find in organic relationships, thus meaning that you have likely never experienced anything like it. It gives your mind a "high" with the hormones of dopamine and serotonin that actually physically leave you addicted to this phase. You become so addicted to it that, like anyone addicted to anything else, you easily overlook the dangerous and damaging parts of the addiction in favor of your "fix." This only further supports the narcissist's hoover phase, which ultimately leads to a relapse every single time.

When leaving the relationship with a narcissist, ensure your physical safety and maintain absolutely no contact. I cannot stress this enough. During this time, you will be extremely vulnerable to "relapse" into the addictions of the relationship, and the only way that you can completely avoid this is by quitting the relationship cold turkey and never looking back.

Healing from Your Narcissistic Relationship

The healing process is not fixed within any particular time frame. How long it takes varies from one person to the next. The following practices will help you hugely with healing yourself and healing the trauma within your brain. It is important to understand that healing trauma in your brain is a lengthy and challenging process and that it is best not to do it alone. Seeking support is always the answer, and it is also essential to make sure that the support is empathetic, caring, and genuinely invested in your healing. You are vulnerable at this time, so be cautious not to jump into another abusive situation when seeking support.

Having boundaries is essential. You should begin practicing boundaries with yourself and with other people around you. When you have been abused by a narcissist, boundaries are something you have been conditioned to eliminate so that you can be fully available to the abuser. It is time to start practicing saying "no" and being very choosy about who you let into your life. Be picky with the energy that you let into your life.

Empath

Empath's Problems and Struggles

The Misunderstood Behaviors

We have covered quite a significant amount of empath myths and misconceptions, so let's target a few specific behaviors and get to the root of both the true empath nature and how others perceive you.

Holding Space—Detaching and Becoming Seemingly "Aloof"

To hold space is to muster up all of your power and become strong, centered, and aligned for someone else's journey and path. Many empaths do this and frequently, and you may not even know you are doing it. It is in your nature to tune in to the pain, despair, suffering, or problems of others and seek to help heal them. Well, you do this through becoming a sort of conduit, or channel, for healing and light to shine through. Through your empathy, capacity for great compassion, and the love and healing thoughts you send them, you can essentially hold space—and it is from space where everything arises. Creation is space; it comes from space and permeates in and around it; creation doesn't just disappear or cease to exist. We, humans, are natural channels and energy conduits for thoughts, feelings, emotions, beliefs, epic epiphanies, and spiritual awareness to shine through. But we don't all consciously or mindfully open ourselves up to this reality. As an empath, your thoughts and inner motivations alone create a unique vibration within which essentially tells the world, "I am here for you. I am love, I am compassion, and I am nonjudgmental awareness. I am happy to listen to you, and I devote my time and energy to being of assistance." It's a powerful and extraordinary gift to possess.

Unfortunately, not everyone understands this, and those few people who are actively against healing and self-development can misconstrue your intentions and personal energy altogether. The keyword here is projection; they 'project' their own insecurities and ignorance onto you. Some people may consciously do this, such as energy vampires, narcissists, or other toxic characters, but for others, it's less conscious and apparent. The best analogy to use here is concerning sound wave frequencies and natural phenomena. Dogs and many other animals can hear parts of the sound spectrum we humans can't, but it doesn't mean that these specific frequencies and high- or low-pitched sounds don't exist! Henceforth, you appear aloof, detached, or disconnected from your physical environment, when in reality you are more connected than most.

Needing Your Alone Time and Solitude—Not Wanting to Connect or Be Sociable

The appearance of being unfriendly, cold, distant, or extremely unsociable can all be assumed and seen when, in fact, you just need your alone time. Unlike non-empaths, you need to recharge your batteries. If you don't spend sufficient time in introspection, rest, rejuvenation, or self-healing, you can become very disoriented and drained. Other people's feelings, emotions, and welfare continuously take up your time, and despite how others may misperceive you, you are incredibly selfless and generous with your time and energy. It is because of this fact alone that you require so much time in solitude and rest.

Furthermore, you thrive on connection, as it forms the basis and foundation of your whole existence. One of the main empath fears is disconnection or separation. The way you think, feel, and perceive is very different from how others experience their reality, so your truth may not be understood or even seen. Sometimes it is only when you take on a highly verbal or extroverted role and persona that people become aware of your true motivations and feelings, so before this, they may have been completely none the wiser regarding your innate empathic nature and daily reality. Just because you know what you go through does not mean others do!

Therefore, needing your solitude to recharge so you can be brilliant and beautiful, as well as being caring, compassionate, and self-infused with wisdom and strength solely for others, will often be seen as you are being disconnected and antisocial. This can, fortunately, be overcome through learning to speak up and be more expressive, and also through not feeling ashamed or selfish when speaking your truth and defending yourself. Many times in life, you will need to call the moon the moon, even when you think everyone else is already aware of it.

Empath

Embodying the Empath Blueprint—Appearing Moody

Human life is prone to illusion. In fact, we can all be seen to be existing under the veil of illusion, as life itself is both a multidimensional and mystical experience. The empath blueprint is your ultimate energetic blueprint—you at your best and highest frequency self. When you are in this space and connected to your true self, you can appear deeply moody or down. This may not be a problem if it wasn't for the fact that people treat you in a certain way because of it. Being seen as moody when you are, in fact, in high spirits and in a beautiful and empowered, shiny, and insightful space can cause some trouble and concern.

Firstly, because you are so prone to picking up on subtle energy, it can cause you to act in ways that are not representative of your true self. To you, everything is fine and dandy, yet lots of people are projecting negative and distorted vibes and energy towards you, which you pick up on. These subtle influences affect you powerfully!

Secondly, some people may actively persecute you or openly judge you for it, which doesn't do great things for your morale and mood. Thus, it is their negativity, delusions, or judgments that cause and create the moodiness they believed you to have in the first place. This in itself is a form of "energy vampire" engagement, and there are some who will consciously do this to you, judge you, and persecute you for being empathic. For others, it will simply be an unconscious thing but something which affects you all the same.

Like with the preceding point, you need to learn how to speak up and voice your truth. Singing can be highly effective in letting others know that you are happy, healthy, and upbeat. This can save you from the judgment and resentment of directly telling others how you feel, such as by having to point out that they're suffering from ignorance or disillusionment! For example, why not hum "Bear Necessities" or "Hakuna Matata" when around those who are misperceiving you? Or, let out a loud but natural and authentic laugh! Anything you do to express yourself and show yourself in your divine and inspired light will help you massively, further saving you from misunderstandings and subsequent potential ill-treatment. Don't forget, there are a lot of negative, toxic, and narcissistic characters, and many people do project their own "stuff" onto you.

The Daily Struggles

Expanding on from "misunderstood behaviors," why is it that other people are the ones who judge, act cold or hurtful, and are the unmindful and uncompassionate ones, yet you are the one to be misperceived? Well, this question alone is the foundation of your daily struggles. But your daily struggles extend a bit further than this. We will look at three highly significant struggles to the empath personality. Take note, dear empath, because you will most likely suffer from them at some point in your life.

The Inability to Say "No" (and Being Taken Advantage of)

One of your main issues in life is the inability to say "no." Connected to this is the sad but very real truth that you are often taken advantage of, at least until you have grown up and learned to have boundaries. Being taken advantage of is something that occurs when you attract abusers, narcissists, and other toxic characters into your energy field. Your selflessness and compassion are seen as a light, which it is, but unfortunately, some people don't want to shine with you; they instead wish to take. You may literally give too much through

Empath

generous and kind means, or you may be manipulated and fooled by less than pure characters. Honesty, sincerity, and purity are values that define and shape you; however, they are not qualities that define everyone. It can be very difficult for you to understand and fully accept the coldness and harshness of this world. You truly do have a very pure and gentle heart.

Learning when to say "no" and when to give is one of your key lessons. Being an empath is one of the most advanced and evolved personality types one could display and embody in one's lifetime. There are many people who both believe and recognize that we all have a soul—a timeless and eternal aspect of ourselves. It is the spirit that flows through all living things and connects us, further opening us up to qualities such as empathy, compassion, and higher awareness or understanding. Yet, our souls are our gateways to higher consciousness and directly to the empath's blueprint.

We have spoken at various points thus far about frequency and vibration, about how empaths operate and exist on a higher frequency. Well, there is great truth in this. Linked to the soul is the concept of "karma," and being an empath has a deeply karmic element to it. Karma is the exchange of energy. It is how our intentions and actions ripple out to affect external environments and our relationships. In essence, karma influences everything. The choices we make and the ways we behave have a direct influence on our future. But karma is not just limited to linear time or a 3-dimensional reality; we are also profoundly affected by karma from the past or from past lives. Now, whether you believe in past lives or the timelessness of the soul, it is irrelevant. The main thing you need to be aware of as an empath is that your core essence is unique. Your soul has already gone through many trials and tests to get to the stage it is now in this life. To reach the evolved emotional frequency and psychic or spiritual gifts that accompany it, but you would have to have evolved. The evolution of the soul is a fundamental part of being. Therefore, being an empath has a strong karmic element because you have reached a level of supreme kindness, selflessness, compassion, and understanding. The qualities that make you an empath haven't been brought out of magic; you have been on a long journey to get to where you are now and to embody the qualities you do. In this respect, empaths can be seen as the next stage in the evolutionary journey.

This means that a core struggle to your unique frequency and persona is to do with your kindness and generosity. It is natural for you to want to give, give, and give some more because this is who you are. You have transcended selfish and lower vibrational ways of being and thinking. Unlike narcissists, for example, you are primarily concerned with authentic connection and helping others, shining sincerity, and other beautiful and genuine qualities. Your proneness to always saying "yes" when you should sometimes, in fact, be saying "no," therefore, comes with karma. Your "karmic lesson," henceforth, is to respect and honor yourself, your time, your gifts, and your resources so that you can live your best life without being depleted.

Empath

Protecting Yourself from Energy Vampire

Energy vampires—quite a harsh phrase here—is used to refer to people who always want things their way while disregarding everybody else's feelings. These are toxic people who do not care about the emotions of others, provided their interests get served. Energy vampires are bad for everyone, but particularly for empaths.

Empaths are ready givers, while the energy vampires are ruthless takers. If you are not careful, they will drain you dry, and you'll have no energy left to take care of anyone else, including yourself. Common symptoms of energy vampires include:

• The insecurity that makes them feel disadvantaged. They complain all the time, outlining their perceived challenges in great detail. You're forced to walk on eggshells around them, to avoid making their situation any worse. Having such a person around you is like having a fussy baby, just without the sweet face.

Empath

- They demand attention by claiming to always have a crisis. Even when good things are happening, they find a way to turn the situation around and see a problem there. Besides, you don't dare claim to be having a problem as well. Yours will promptly be declared trivial. Theirs is always the most serious issue in the room. They thrive in the 'poor you' attention every single day, whether the problem is real or imaginary. Playing victim demands that other people lift them with their energy, which can be tiring.

- They never take the blame for anything that happens to them. It's always other people's fault. If they're flagged for nonperformance at work, it's not anything that they did wrong. It's their coworkers who don't like them. Or the boss that is picking on them. If their relationship goes wrong, they won't point out what they could have done better. It's always the other person. Or other people who are jealous of the relationship. If there's no one to blame, even the good old universe is not safe. 'No one likes me.' 'Nothing good ever happens to me.' Here they're trying to say that the universe has conspired against them. How convenient?

- The spotlight always belongs to them. Should anyone else try to occupy it, especially with a happy story, then it is instantly grabbed back. They will pour cold water on your happy news. You could have just gotten engaged, but instead of celebrating with you, they will talk about divorce statistics. They will remind you that 60% of all marriages end up in divorce. They will tell you of their peers who got engaged in glamorous weddings and didn't even last long enough to celebrate their first anniversary. These statistics may not even be true. They're simply intended to bring you down. Alternatively, they will turn the story around to be about them; how they were once engaged but so-and-so left them heartbroken.

Now the attention turns to the sorry story. They never embrace joy and thrive in deflating the joy of others.

• They guilt-trip you into doing what they want. They will make you feel like it's your fault that they're miserable. They will say things like, "It seems I'll just have to go through this on my own. Everyone treats me like crap. You don't have to invite me; nobody invites me anyway." You will feel sorry for them, which is exactly what they want. You will then go out of your way to accommodate them, even when that means jeopardizing your own welfare.

• Their opinions are made to sound like facts, and in their usual character, will be negative. They will say something mean about your hair or clothes, with zero regards to how it makes you feel. "You're going out wearing that?" The question will be asked in a sneer. You will be left feeling judged, mocked, and ridiculed. They will expect you to go right back and change—that's how highly they think of their opinion. Be ready for the second round of scrutiny even when you change—the alternative might not be good enough for their taste either. Or something will be wrong with your shoes this time. They even criticize things that you cannot change. They leave you feeling miserable, as they are too self-absorbed to even care.

• They speak of worst-case scenarios to spread fear. They can't stand positivity, so they'll always bring up those things that make people anxious. What if we lose our jobs? What if the economy crashes? Do you know how much toxins are in these packaged foods? Have you checked the statistics on cancer cases? If there is nothing bad happening, they will bring up that possibility. And that sight of your frightened faces will further cater to their twisted egos.

Empath

Dealing with Energy Vampires

Energy vampires are well amongst us; friends, family, colleagues, and peers. You can't avoid them completely. Your paths will cross at one point or the other. As an empath, keen to share goodness with all and sundry, you may be tempted to play the bigger person. To tolerate them even when they're offensive, you may even look for a way to help them change their ways. But remember that these people are thieves of energy and joy. They will leave you so deflated that you'll not have the strength to serve others, much less yourself. They will waste your gift. You have to engage them with caution.

Are energy vampires intentional or do they do so by chance? Both. There are those whose character is flawed by experiences. They grew up among energy vampires. They don't know how to be happy. They're accustomed to misery. They simply treat people how they were treated. These people have a chance of changing if somebody points out the negative effects of this habit on others.

Then some are vampires by choice. Life has dealt them a few rough cards. They're not happy, and they don't want to see anyone else happy. Instead of focusing on working through their situation, they choose to make others miserable so they can ride in the same boat. They know what they're doing, and they know they're hurting others. But they do not care.

Here is how to deal with energy vampires:

1.   Set a Time Limit

If you're obligated to deal with them, set time limits. These are people who can engage you for hours if you let them. And the conversation will be dominated by their sorry stories the entire time. It's normal for people to have challenges, but you can't have this one individual claiming to be in crisis all the time. For instance, you can say that you only have one hour to listen, after, which you will have to attend to something else. Be firm with your time limit; they will try to manipulate that too.

2.   Avoid Arguing

Contradicting an energy vampire yields nothing. They will come to you whining about a failed relationship, claiming to always be innocent. You will try to make them see the part they played in the failed relationship. As usual, they will not accept any responsibility. They will only insist that they're innocent. Do not argue; otherwise, the conversation will carry on until the kingdom comes. They are happy just to have your attention anyway.

3.   Be Brief

If you have to speak, stick to brief questions. Why? How? When? Such monosyllable questions will suffice. Here, keep your opinions to yourself. Voicing your ideas just keeps them going on and on, so they can discredit them and have theirs emerge as superior.

4.   Minimal Reaction

An energy vampire seeks to evoke an emotional reaction from you. They tell you their sorry stories, and they expect you to be sad for them. When they say degrading things, they want to see you angry and in despair. Do not give them these reactions that they're looking for. Remain passive. Listen with a straight face. Let them know that you're not moved by every whim. If your emotions fluctuate up and down as they engage you; they win. Don't let them 'win' at your expense. Nobody deserves that.

5.   Avoid Eye contact

Empaths are good listeners and love to listen with all their senses. Empathic listening includes eye contact. If you're dealing with an energy vampire, however, this rule does not apply. Eye contact makes you more vulnerable to what is being said; just what we're avoiding here. Keep the eye contact to a minimum. Avoid sitting facing the speaker. Just glance at them occasionally. This does not sound very considerate, but remember that you are dealing with a peculiar character here, who is up to no good, and you have to protect yourself.

6.   Stick to Light Topics

We stated earlier that those empaths thrive in deep conversations. Again, we have to make an exception here. You do not want to start speaking about the meaning of life with an energy vampire. They will do what they do best; water down your opinions, bring out their sad stories and create worst-case scenarios for everything. Make the conversation as light as possible. When they bring up issues of their own, just glaze them on the surface without going deeper. These are people intent on dragging you through the mud, and the closer you are to the surface, the better.

7.   Reduce Contact

Reduce the instances where you have to encounter such people. If they make a habit of popping into your home or office, let them know that they can only come with prior notice. What if they actually belong to your house or office? They could be your family members or workmates you know. A bit tricky here; right? You still need to reduce contact. The last thing you need is an energy vampire siphoning your energy in the place where you spend most of your time. If you have such a workmate, you're not obliged to hang out with them. If you go for lunch as a group, you can choose a different café, or carry a packed lunch. Do not entertain idle talk at your desk. If you have such a person at home, spend more time in your room. Distancing yourself from energy vampires is not selfish; it is a matter of self-preservation.

8.   Be in a Group

An energy vampire inflicts maximum damage when you are alone. Invite others into the conversation. If you have a workmate who singles you out to listen to sorry stories, you can request to involve the others, so they can also give their input on the issue. If they hover around your desk in the office, request them to bring up the conversation during lunch. You know the rest will be present, and you'll not have to suffer as much. In addition, someone in the group could have the courage to stand up to the energy vampire and call them out. Expect an argument, but the toxic character might just think about it afterward and make some changes.

Empath

Importance of Empathy

The living human community allows us to develop different emotions and moods, as well as behaviors that involve us all and make us act differently in certain situations. One of those attitudes is empathy, perhaps instinctive but that the world we live in today with its busy pace more covers us.

Empathetic people are better able to attract, build, and achieve rich, and healthy relationships. That is, empathy can be our great ally in building relationships, whether professional or personal.

Empathy is one of the most important qualities for a successful life. It is related to the ability to have healthy and balanced feelings and to respond well to daily crises and conflicts, establishing a sincere connection with our subordinates, peers, and managers. In a professional environment, empathy helps managers better communicate with their team.

Empath

Empathy is very important for professional development and growth, but care must be taken not to be overindulged when we put ourselves too much in the place of others and have difficulty separating personal and professional lives from those of others, our subordinates, and peers.

As with all our skills, empathy is partly born with us, and in another, we learn it, and it can be developed in this way. In general, more task-oriented and highly aggressive executives have little empathic capacity at some level, which hinders their relationships and compromises their results. It is an attitude that has to do with an instinct.

As the human being is a social being, that is, who is accustomed by nature to live with other peers, life as a whole is part of the essence that defines us and, therefore, it is very difficult, or almost impossible, to live absolutely isolated and remote of all civilization.

In this coexistence, different behaviors arise that are also inherent to human quality, and that can be from the most sensible and supportive or selfish and evil. Among them, we find empathy, which is that quality that makes one person feel or get excited at the suffering of the other. It is understood as a perhaps abstract form of solidarity, as empathy is what allows us to feel that another person is not well and, therefore, to feel that suffering in our body and soul, act to help that person to move forward, or at least comfort them.

To better understand why there is empathy in a person, it is interesting to note that it has to do with the ability to develop certain levels of emotional intelligence, which makes us sensitive and permeable to both our own suffering and others'.

While there are people who are educated and raised without the slightest interest in developing emotional intelligence but perhaps cognitive intelligence, there are also people who due to how they have been raised or even lived experiences, have high sensitivity towards what happens to others and, therefore, they show greater empathy in situations of pain or suffering.

Why Is It Necessary to Be Empathic with Our Peers?

We all know that the societies in which we live lead us to be quite individualistic beings, more concerned with our own good than with the community good.

However, empathy must become a common and normal attitude among us because that will depend on the well-being of a community. This is because being supportive, listening to the other, accompanying their suffering, or helping them is what makes us human and enriches us as human beings.

The following are the importance of being empathic that is applied directly to everyday life:

•   Solidarity: It is wrong to think that this word is directly linked only to volunteer work. Looking at others understanding your difficulties and offering help when you need it, and when you can, is a valuable way to show solidarity. So do not close your eyes to your friends, family, and coworkers who need your help for some reason.

•   Respect: Understanding that each one chooses the path they want for life and respecting this decision is fundamental for any human being. Unfortunately, this is not what constantly happens in the world, but it is not because of this that you will not act politely and kindly to anyone. Respect the lifestyle choices, religion, sexual orientation, political opinion, and all the many other topics that can cause problems in conversation. If older people didn't question what is different about them, the world would be living more harmoniously today.

- **Listen to the Essence:** Empathy teaches how important it is to listen to people in essence. This means that you listen to what the other has to say, assimilate, accept, and give your opinion respectfully. This kind of behavior demonstrates that you are concerned about getting everyone's opinion expressed in due space. This behavior is essential for a healthy debate, isn't it?

- **Learning:** You must be constantly evolving throughout your life. For this, you mustn't stop studying. Sharing knowledge with other professionals, deliberating healthily, reading, studying, and pursuing complementary courses and coaching are all ways to keep you updated and evolve regularly. So never forget to invest in continuing your education through different ways of learning.

- **Collectivity:** Collective awareness is very important in business environments as well as outside, as this is essential for a good coexistence in society. Much more than just knowing how to work in groups, the community teaches to respect each other's opinions and to include everyone, even those who have had fewer opportunities.

Did you already know all the importance of being an empathic person? If you didn't know about it yet, you are now full of valuable knowledge to apply in your daily life. Be sure to demonstrate your positive characteristics linked to the points we talk about up here.

In addition to being important to your mental well-being, these points are essential for good social coexistence inside and outside the corporate environment.

Besides, people are social beings and, therefore, sooner or later every person will be in contact with other people. And just in these moments, empathy is very important for a variety of reasons:

Empathy Facilitates Communication

Empathic people can empathize with their counterparts and thus more easily understand what others want to communicate. Of course, it still matters how exactly the other person expresses and how exactly they communicate what they want to convey. In principle, however, it is important to accurately perceive and try to understand the other person to guarantee smooth communication. As a result, misunderstandings can be avoided, which helps in both the private and the professional environment.

Empathy Creates Harmonious Relationships

Empathy is particularly important in friendships, partnerships or family relationships because, in the long run, good relationships can only be difficult without mutual understanding. Especially in conflicted situations, empathy can prevent a major conflict from breaking out.

Empathic people can understand their counterparts, and that is the first step already done. In the next step, it is important to accept the attitudes and views of the other person—but this goes beyond empathy. A conflict could be solved very easily if all persons involved not only in their own position but also in the other. Conflict situations can often escalate if too many emotions are involved, so it is advisable to limit oneself to cognitive empathy in such situations.

Empathy can affect relationships not only in conflicted situations but in general. For who use their empathy ability to get to know their fellow human beings better and better, can see how their fellow human beings' tick. "What quirks does my counterpart have?" "How can I please my counterpart?" "What should I avoid in order not to upset my counterpart?" All of these questions can be answered by empathic people bit by bit, thereby enabling a harmonious gathering together.

Self-Reflection Empathy

If you are empathetic and honest with yourself, then you already have two important qualities to reflect on yourself. Because empathy can be useful not only in contact with others but also in contact with oneself. Become aware of what thoughts or feelings you have yourself and ask why this is the case. Have an understanding of your own mistakes and quirks. Do not just think negatively but also allow compliments.

Observe yourself even in conflicted situations. Try to go through life with a high level of mindfulness so that you can perceive more. Through empathy and mindfulness, you can change and develop yourself.

Thus, empathy helps you to interact with other people and with yourself to understand and improve your attitudes and feelings and is, therefore, very important to everyone. To complete the idea, demonstrating these virtues complements your personal marketing in the short, medium, and long term. This is because all other professionals will see how much you are dedicated to improving your career and others.

Also, it is important to have quality relationships with third parties, as well as developing more respectful and healthy relationships with friends, colleagues, and coworkers. It is especially important to apply empathy with the closest relatives, such as parents, siblings, and partners. From empathy, we see that in any area of daily life, we can generate healthier relationships with third parties.

Somehow, empathy also offers us the opportunity to get to know ourselves more. This is because it requires basic emotional knowledge and emotional vocabulary, generated through that knowledge of our reactions on an emotional level in various situations. This leads us to better recognize emotions in others and use this knowledge to be able to talk with others, putting ourselves in the place of the other.

Knowing this, and everything that is known about empathy, I encourage you to start using empathy in your conversations, and you will see how you improve your relationship with others.

What Are the Strengths of Empathic Leadership?

Combined with technical skills, ability to influence by example, creativity, and good communication, empathy completes a bundle of essentials that good leadership must-have. Of course, not all managers can reach this level, but they must strive to bring these characteristics to life in an assertive way.

Imagine a leader who cannot look at his followers and understand their professional and personal difficulties and help them. Another bad situation is when a manager who cannot make the team is constantly evolving because they are very concerned about their position.

The above examples come close to selfishness, don't they? For that is what lack of empathy can create. An empathetic leader is concerned with seeing each team individually, respecting their professional and personal differences, and taking this into account when delegating demands. In addition, it is easier to bring effective and creative advice to people in adverse situations.

Have you had empathic leadership? Unfortunately, we are not always lucky. However, you can strive to be the empathic leader of the future. Through effective tools, the method teaches more about yourself, emotional intelligence, self-confidence, humanized management, behavioral trend identification, and many other points of interest to achieve positive and personal and professional performance.

Setting Boundaries

Borders have two sides: They create emotional health, and they are created by emotionally healthy people. They are something that you can start working on today with people close to you.

What Are the Personal Boundaries?

I will start from the practical and gradually get to the theoretical. Instead of defining what the boundaries really are (just because I don't want to take a nap right now), let's first talk about how they look. Some examples of weak boundaries:

• "Sorry, boys, I can't go out with you tonight, because my girlfriend is mad when I go out without her."

• "My colleagues are full of idiots, and I get late for meetings every time, so I have to explain to them how to do their job."

Empath

- "I would gladly accept the job in Sofia, but my mother will never forgive me for moving so far from her."

- "I can go out with you, but don't you tell my girlfriend Katya? She is super jealous of me if I have a friend, and she doesn't."

In each of these scenarios, the person either assumes responsibility for actions or emotions that are not theirs or requires someone else to take responsibility for their own actions or emotions.

Individuals who have read it will notice that taking responsibility for their own actions, without blaming others, are two of the pillars in Nathaniel Brandon's Six Pillars of Self-Esteem.

In other words, when the areas of responsibility for your own emotions and actions are unclear, when you do not know who is responsible, who is at fault, and why you are doing what you are doing, then you cannot achieve solid personal stability.

Let's say you are very passionate about judo, but you always blame your coach for not making progress, and you feel guilty about going to workouts because your spouse feels lonely when you're not close to them—then you have no control over this aspect of your personality. So, judo is something you do, not something you are. It becomes untrue, another tool in the game of getting public approval, not something you do to satisfy your desire to express yourself. It's called "being in need." Your dependence on external approval will lower your self-esteem and make your behavior less attractive.

Bad Boundaries in Intimate Relationships

In fact, I think the boundaries issue is the hardest one to solve at the family level. You can always lose that ass boyfriend, but you can't lose your parents.

Most likely, at some point, you had a relationship where you felt like a speed train: When things were good, they were AWESOME, but when they were bad, they were a complete disaster; and there was a pretty predictable movement from one state to another—two weeks of bliss, followed by a week of hell, followed by a month of bliss, followed by a terrifying separation, and then by a dramatic gathering. This is the hallmark of a relationship of interdependence, and it usually testifies to two people who are incapable of having strong personal boundaries.

My first serious relationship was just that. At one time, it seemed to me to be filled with passion—as if we were both facing the world. But now it is clear to me that things were extremely unhealthy and that I am much happier without that connection.

People have no boundaries because they have a high level of need for others (or in the language of psychiatrists—interdependence). People who are insecure or interdependent have a desperate need for love and affection on the part of others.

People who blame the rest for their own emotions and actions do so because they believe that if they blame others, then they will receive the love they have always wanted and need. If they continually present themselves as victims, someone will always come and save them.

Not surprisingly, these two types of people are very attracted to each other. Their pathologies fit perfectly. And they often grew up in a family where both parents shared the same traits. Therefore, their model of "happy" connection is based on the need of others and on the weak boundaries.

Ironically, neither manages to meet the other's needs. In fact, they both only manage to perpetuate this need for others and the low self-esteem that prevents them from satisfying their own emotional needs. The victim generates more and more difficulties to solve, in addition, the savior saves and saves, but the love and appreciation they always needed never reach the other.

This is exactly what happens in interdependent relationships. The victim produces glitches, not for the reason that there are real ones, but because they believe that this will make them feel loved. The savior does not save the victim because they care for the problem, but because they believe that if they solve the problem, they will feel loved. In both cases, their intentions are driven by the need of others and are, therefore, unattractive and self-destructive.

If the savior really wanted to save the victim, they would say, "Look, you blame others for your own problems; deal with them alone." That would be a manifestation of true love for the victim. And the victim, if they really loved the savior, would say, "Look, it's my problem; you don't need to solve it." That would be a manifestation of true love for the savior, but things don't usually happen that way.

Victims and savers are emotionally addicted to each other. It looks like an addiction in which everyone satisfies the other, and when met with emotionally healthy people, they are usually bored or say that there is no chemistry. And so strong, confident personalities are passed because the solid boundaries of a confident partner do not excite the loose emotional boundaries of the insecure person.

In terms of "attachment theory," victims tend to be impatient to attach, and savers tend to avoid attachment. Or as I like to call them—bumps and asses. Both types often repel those who want a confident attachment.

For the victim, the hardest thing in the world is to hold themselves accountable for their own feelings and their own life, not that of others. They spend their entire existence believing that they SHOULD blame others so they can feel intimacy or love, and is therefore horrified by the idea of stopping to live that way.

For the savior, the hardest thing in the world is to stop fixing others' problems and stop trying to make them happy and content. They spend their entire life feeling valued and loved only if they have fixed someone's problem or been helpful to anyone, so getting rid of that need also terrifies them.

The behavior of needing others makes you unattractive to most people, limiting you to people with a similar level of need for others—hence the thought that you become one—with who you have a relationship. If you only start attracting low self-esteem drones, then you too will become a low self-esteem drone and say, "High demands. Oh, my queen!"

This is a topic that many people ask, "Ah, nice, but what does it look like?" I will answer it with a few examples. Personal boundaries, while particularly important in intimate relationships, also greatly affect our friendships, our family relationships, and even our professional relationships. Therefore, below I will give examples from different areas.

- "Theodor, we have been working with you for five years. I

can't believe you embarrassed me like that in front of the boss."

• "But you had messed up the report. It was extremely important to indicate accurate values."

• "Yes, but you had to support me. It made me look like an idiot. You didn't have to show your disagreement in this way to everyone."

• "Look, I like you. You are my friend. But I have no intention of doing your job. Let's be clear. End of conversation."

• "But I am doing my job!"

• "Okay, so what I say shouldn't matter."

Some friends may be too close. This situation occurs in various forms in the lives of each of us: A longtime friend stumbles, but instead of taking personal responsibility, they expect you to take some of the responsibility because "that's what friends do."

Accepting this leads to interdependent and unhealthy friendships. Yes, even friendships can see the need of the other and be unattractive. Have you seen two friends who are constantly complaining about each other or talking behind their backs, but when they are together everything looks great? They are very likely to have serious problems with boundaries, just as in the example above. Friendships of this kind are like factories that constantly produce drama. Stay away.

• "I'm so sad when you and your sister don't come to see me. I feel very, very lonely."

- "Why don't you go out anymore, Mom? Find your friends."

- "I tried. But no one likes old women like me. You are both my children. You have to take care of me."

- "And we do it."

- "No, you don't. I spend so much time alone. You have no idea how difficult it can be sometimes."

- "Mom, I love you and will always be there when you need me. But you are responsible for your own loneliness. My sister and I are not the only solutions to all your problems."

Familiar situation with familial guilt. I used to like to say, "Guilt is a worthless emotion." In fact, I no longer believe so. Guilt is important when it is justified and when you have felt it yourself.

Guilt is worthless and harmful when used as a tool to manipulate loved ones. Guilt can be terribly painful when used in this way, not only because it requires you to be responsible for emotions that are not yours, but also because it implies that you are in error or you are a bad person, so you are not doing it.

Lately, nothing else has annoyed me as much as someone who tries to make me feel guilty. I resist immediately, and if I do not know them well, sometimes I end that relationship at the moment.

Self-Sacrifice

The strongest counterargument—or rational explanation, depending on your point of view—is that sometimes you have to sacrifice yourself for the people you love.

Empath

This is true. If your partner has an overwhelming need to call you every day, even if you talk for three minutes, then it may be wise to make small sacrifices to please them.

The catch is that, if you sacrifice yourself for someone you care about, then it must be because you want it, not because you feel obligated or because you fear the consequences if you don't. We return again to the point that acts of affection and interest-only make sense when they are carried out without expectations. Therefore, if you call your partner every day, but hate to do it and feel that it threatens your independence, and you resent and are terrified of their anger if you do not call, then you have a problem with boundaries. If you do it because you love it and you don't mind, then you do it.

Love and Sex

As you already know, empaths feel the world more intensely than others, and when it comes to love (which in itself is a very intense feeling), everything gets even more magnified. Empaths literally wear their hearts at their sleeves, and they feel very deeply. But this habit of feeling everything intensely can also be a bane in intimate relationships because then they have to learn how to set healthy boundaries, which are something they clearly don't know. But on the other hand, it is necessary because otherwise, the empath would become overloaded with more emotions than they can handle.

But also, when an empath is in the right kind of relationship where their emotions are values and where their partner understands them completely, then they feel empowered, and it also makes them feel more grounded. But when you are together for a long time, intimacy also has the power of suffocating empaths, so you have to make sure that doesn't happen to you. Since empaths are very sensitive beings, they have this habit of absorbing all the emotions of their partner and making it their own, which sometimes can make them feel unsafe, although, on the other hand, even empaths seek companionship.

Therefore, do you see how conflicting it can get? Empaths want to be loved and needed just like they do with others, but they do not want to get burdened by the needs and emotions of other people. But running away from such situations and seeking shelter by completely isolating yourself from the world is not the solution. The solution lies in protecting your sensitivities by learning how to navigate the world of love and sex as an empath.

Tips to Find the Right Soulmate for Empaths

Empaths become stronger when they feel that they are valued. But to make togetherness a bit easier, I am going to talk about different types of emotional people who can be better for an empath as a partner. Basically, it depends on the needs and temperament of the person, but this list is going to make things a bit easier for you:

• Intellectuals: These people are bright individuals and are also incisive analysts. They have highly rational thinking, and they use it to filter the world around them. No matter how heated the situation is, intellectuals always know how to keep their cool. Whenever it comes to something playful or light-hearted, they might even hesitate a bit before engaging with it. Empaths tend to be more sensual, whereas intellectuals will most likely be prone to staying inside their heads. They are very big fans of solving problems and fixing situations. You as an empath should tell your intellectual partner about your needs of having some "me time," and then you both can together figure out solutions and creative ways in which you can strike a balance in your relationship.

•   Empaths: Yes, empaths can definitely be with empaths. They both are highly sensitive but loving at the same time. All you have to do is learn how to be supportive and honor the sensitivities you both face. But look on the bright side; you both are easily able to understand things, and so you can easily understand what the other person is feeling. However, the challenge will be in determining your needs and keeping them separate from that of your partner's. You need to learn to set boundaries. If both of you become overwhelmed with each other, there can be a lot of anxiety in your home. So, figure out how you both can have some alone time. In the long term, it is often seen that two empaths can really make a relationship work like no other.

•   Rocks: These are those people who are stable and have a strong personality. You will not face any hesitation while expressing your emotions in front of these people. They will never judge you or upset you. But the problem with these personalities is that they are not able to express their feelings easily. But rocks and empaths together can make a wonderful couple. They can help each other grow by balancing each other. The empath can teach the rock how they can practice compassion and also express emotions more clearly. Rocks need just a little nudge, and then they will be able to express whatever it is that is going on in their mind. But remember, you, as an empath, will have to initiate things and don't rush anything. Express one feeling every day.

•   Gushers: These people are the ones who love to express their feelings, and they can also get over negative feelings very quickly. But you must be wondering what their downside is. Well, they tend to share more than necessary, and this can lead to burnout in those who are listening. That is why when they are with an empath, they can make the empath feel overloaded. That is why both of you will have to learn emotional sharing.

Tips to Make Relationships Work for You

When you are an empath, then you keep absorbing other people's emotions, and that alone can be so exhausting that you might not want to be in a relationship with someone else. This is even truer in the case of live-in relationships where the empath has to share the other person's companionship at all times. This can lead to the development of unstable emotions, and a balance between relationships and life, in general, can become quite difficult.

Always Find Time to Meditate and Decompress

An empath needs to engage in self-preservation regularly, and that can be done by finding some time out of your daily schedule and keep it reserved only for yourself. You can also practice keeping certain short breaks throughout the day. You should also talk about this with your partner and tell them how important it is for you to have some time alone with yourself. During this break, you will be able to think deeply about the issues that are bothering you or maybe some relationship problems that you are facing. This will also assist you in understanding your partner in a better way. If you think that your partner will not understand your idea of alone time, then you are wrong. You simply have to make them understand lovingly, and this will prevent them from feeling rejected. Any relationship would indeed require several compromises to be made, but that doesn't mean you will compromise your soul and your feelings in that process.

Make Changes in Your Physical Space

The physical state around an empath can impact them in great ways and alter their energy levels. That is why you should be having certain ground rules with your partner about what makes you comfortable and what doesn't. You need to figure out the system that is the best for both of you. It can be something as simple as having a separate nook in the house where you can sit alone and read books or do whatever you want, or it can also be something like using different bathrooms. The adjustment can be anything, and they usually vary from one empath to the other. You can also make similar adjustments for those times when you are traveling together because you don't want emotional overloads in vacations, right? If you are an empath who is sensitive to smell, then you need to have a look at your chemical sensitivities too and arrange your surroundings accordingly. But whatever it is, if you do not come out with your preferences and tell your partner what you need, they will never be able to understand you. For example, if you are sensitive to any particular perfume or essential oil, you need to insist on not using them (at least not in front of you).

Figure out How Much You Want to Socialize

Empaths love to stay alone, or they are sort of introverts. That is why they feel overwhelmed in social gatherings. So, if you are in a relationship, you also need to sort out how much time you actually want to spend socializing. For example, not every empath likes crowded cruises; some simply love a casual day by the pool.

You Can Consider Sleeping in Different Rooms or Beds

Most of us sleep alone while we are growing up, and then suddenly, when you are in a relationship, you are expected to share a bed. Some people might love it while others might not, and there is nothing wrong with that. So, if you, as an empath, want to sleep in a separate bed, your partner should be able to honor your decision. Or, you can also sleep together three days a week, and on the remaining four, you can choose to sleep alone. Empaths also get easily disturbed by snores or any other noises during sleeping, and it is also one of the reasons why they prefer sleeping alone.

Stop Taking Things Personally

Maintain harmony in your relationships by not taking things personally because not every time the comments are personal. You need to learn how to be less reactive.

Don't Try to Always Fix Your Partner

You need to understand that your partner is completely fine and does not need any type of fixing. Your partner might not always love to take instructions from you on any matter. They also have their personal opinion, and you should be able to respect that. You need to let them face their difficulties in their own way.

Focus on One Issue at a Time

Your relationship might be facing several issues at the moment, but you need to promise yourself and focus on only one at a time; otherwise, you will get stimulated. Don't repeat issues. Try to communicate your problems as clearly as possible, and then when you are done, stop overdoing it by reiterating the same thing.

Decide on Your Bath Time

This can seem funny and irrelevant now, but this is so important for empaths. They usually love long and uninterrupted warm showers. So, if your bath time coincides with that of your partner, then you need to settle it with them. Or, suppose you love to take a long bath before going to sleep, but your partner wants you in bed by them at that time, then that is also something you need to resolve.

Are You a Sexual Empath?

Since empaths can feel everything so intensely, even during lovemaking, they can easily feel and absorb the other person's energies. Sexual empaths have stronger abilities to sense other's emotions than a normal empath, and that is why it is also advised that sexual empaths should choose their partners wisely, and only then will they get the same amount of respect and love reciprocated.

But when a sexual empath is without a partner for a long time, they jump at the first chance they get and enter into a relationship with literally anyone who sparks their sexuality. They become eager about developing sexual connections that they forget about all other intuitive signs that show the person is not actually the right fit for them from the emotional point of view. They start thinking that they finally got to engage in a sexual relationship with someone who interests them, and so, the red flags should not matter. But that is also how they make themselves prone to get hurt. They start building an attachment with those who cannot love them back with the same intensity or cannot handle their complex personality.

Empath

Empath in Workplace

Depending on what type of job you have, the office environment can be an interesting dynamic between coworkers. There may be cliques, there may be those who keep to themselves, and there may be those who do not do what they are supposed to do. The workplace can be an odd collection of different types of personalities and work ethics.

Empaths may work in a wide array of jobs, some more depleting than others. In order for an empath to feel fulfilled with both their individual and communal senses, they could potentially have a difficult time finding the right job for them. Here are some positions that would work best for an empath to use their gift:

•   Nurse: Since empaths are caregivers, being a nurse would be a great fit for an empath. Empaths want to help, and using your gift to help comfort sick patients would fulfill your needs as well as the patients.

• Writer: Empaths can also have a way with words, and it can be quite therapeutic for them to get their feelings out and on paper. When an empath can get creative, they release the powerful emotions that they may have held inside. People would most likely relate to them as they have plenty of feelings and emotions to relay.

• Psychologist: A psychologist is also there to help those who have an illness of sorts, just on a mental scale. Since empaths can feel so deeply and understand what others are thinking, they are able to help those who have a mental illness on a better level.

• Artist: Many artists see things differently than the rest of us and have a unique collection of perspectives. Since an empath is more connected to their surroundings, they tend to be more creative than others when it comes to art and the emotion that goes into it. With that, their creativity will be second to none when it comes to being an artist.

• Veterinarian: Empaths care not only for people but also for all living things, including animals. This could be a very rewarding job for an empath, as they will be able to assist with the care of animals as well as their owners.

• Musician: As an empath, your feelings can pour out on paper, which, in turn, could make an amazing song. Many musicians pour their hearts and souls into their music, making their songs more relatable to others.

• Life Coach: Empaths have lived through a lot of nonsense when they hit a certain point in their life, and with that, they want to help others either avoid trauma or help them heal trauma. You want the best for people, and you want to help them become better people. As an empath, you prefer that all people around you gain a level of success. You do not get jealous; you feel happy for them. This is an uplifting and rewarding position for an empath as you will be using your gift to the fullest and helping people be the best they can be.

• Teacher: As a teacher, your goal is to help kids get to where they dream to be. You will help them along the way and make a big impact in their life, and that, in return, will make your life more fulfilling. When a teacher is able to pick up on the quirks and emotions of their students, they can change their students' lives forever. They will understand the student, but they will also know how to offer the right amount of motivation and support to assist them. There are many times that teachers make more of a difference for children than anyone else, and empaths are definitely up for that support system challenge.

• Guidance Counselor: Being a guidance counselor is similar to being a mentor; you will be guiding a child or adult toward a better life. You will be able to figure out what people have in terms of character traits and personality, which will help find them with a list of positions that may fit them as a person so that they can lead a successful life. Since empaths tend to understand how others think and feel, it will be an easy task to figure out how to guide someone in the right direction.

• Social Worker: Social workers have a difficult job, but they are around to help their clients through terrible situations. This type of position is great for an empath, as they love to make a difference in other people's lives. When this position works out well, and there are times it will not, the empath will be involved in the achievement of happiness for those around them as well as themselves. The only downfall would be that an empath may deplete all energy and emotions due to an unhappy ending when something does not end very well. Empaths who are very secure and have thick skin would be best for this type of position.

• Nonprofit Organization Volunteer: This could be many things, but all of which are set to help someone or another. For example, if someone has a child in an ice hockey organization that they have also played back in the day, they may love to sign up to help coach a team. There may also be board-level positions that could provide a lot of fulfillment by helping educate the parents about the organization's programs. These types of organizations need workers that are empaths as they strive to make a difference. They need people who want to make a difference to fulfill their level of happiness as opposed to those who are money-driven. Volunteering is more fulfilling as it will let you help without expecting anything in return, and that is typically where empaths thrive.

• Self-Employed: Since an empath may battle ups and downs, with bouts of isolation, being self-employed would help them as they could make their own schedule. Being self-employed, they are on their own to make decisions; empaths would thrive in this type of environment. There is no need to risk having toxic people around them as they would be in control of their environment. This is the perfect work for empaths who have waves of needing isolation or do not have enough energy to deal with coworkers.

• Lawyer: This job is not typically where an empath would excel at. It seems that there are more snakes as lawyers than those who want to look for others' best interests. Because empaths do love to help, can be assertive, and can look out for their clients' best interest, a position like this is great for them.

While this list is not all-inclusive, and some of the positions may not seem like they would be a good fit for an empath, many do utilize their strengths.

Empath

Empath's Friends and Family

Family relationships and friend dynamics are a huge part of everyone's life. Our families are our parents that we are born to and our relatives on both sides of the line. We have siblings, cousins, aunts and uncles, grandparents, and beyond. They influence our lives and make us who we are with their own characteristics, beliefs, personalities, and energies.

Our friends are the family we make outside of our genetic family line. We choose our friends, and they choose us. We learn from them, and explore and adventure with them and turn to them for comfort in a way our immediate family can't always provide for us. Friends are who we turn to in times of need and who help us know ourselves better as we walk our own unique paths in life.

The empath will have a lot of ups and downs with both family and friends. The gift you have can actually influence who you are as a child and how your family reacts and relates to you in either positive or negative ways. Certain types of people may be drawn to you because of what a good listener you are and how easy you are to talk to without always giving the same balance in return.

Our path, as empaths, is to find the people in our lives that allow us to be true to ourselves, and in many cases our family and friends allow us to do this. In other cases, we struggle to deal with the emotional energy and personalities of our dearest loved ones because they are a part of our lives and we want to make them feel supported and loved.

This will talk more in-depth about the friendships and familial relationships that can cause difficulty for the Empath. There are certainly plenty of healthy and balanced bonds that exist for many empaths, but for those looking for solutions to the relationship challenges of this kind, then this is for you.

That's What Friends Are for

Friends are so valuable to our lives. They witness our growth and empower us to become more of ourselves, or they don't. When you are an empath, you are often in a position to offer someone a lot of compassion, empathy, trust, and a lot of time and patience to listen to their stories and what they are all about. It can happen quite often that the empath will provide their friends with the good company they deserve and then go home feeling like they are drained and tired from hearing about their friend's ongoing work saga and romance troubles.

Then you wonder, "Did they actually ask me any questions about what is going on in my life?" You may come up with a few situations with friends when you realize that you barely spoke more than a few sentences and some nods of agreement, asking a few questions to get more information about their story, but really you hardly spoke at all.

Empaths are often a shoulder to cry on, and hey, that's what friends are for, right? Friends are our shoulder to cry on, and that is one of the greatest gifts of friendship: Having someone close to you that you trust and can pour your heart out to. Not all friendships are balanced in this way, though.

If you are always someone's shoulder to cry on, whose shoulder do you cry on when you are having a hard day? Do your friends give you that support in return as often as you need it? Empaths need a shoulder to cry on as much as anyone else does, regardless of how skilled they may seem at holding their own and taking in all the emotions of other people.

There may be a long-term friend in your life who has always been a drama queen, taking up all the conversations and hang-out time with their great emotional down-pours of how terrible their life is or how they can't believe so and so said this and that. When you are in a long-term friendship with someone like this, and you have never shown them any boundaries or any idea that you don't enjoy listening to them talk that way all the time, you run the risk of creating even more drama if you say something now.

A drama queen is often in the friend company of an empath, and here is why: The drama queen is drawn to the empath because of their good listening skills and because the empath is dazzled by the drama queen due to their capacity to feel free and live life excitingly, opening up the potential for the empath to be more outgoing as well.

This is also how some romantic partnerships can get started for the empath. The relationship imbalance for the empath and the drama queen is only obvious after you begin to realize and ask some of these questions:

- "Is my friend always upset about something?"

- "Is my friend usually wanting me to help them figure out a problem by listening to their latest drama?"

- "Does my friend ever take the time to ask me any deeper questions about my life?"

- "Does my friend usually criticize or judge my choices?"

- "Is my friend also a good listener?"

- "Do I want to spend time with them when they call me or do, I sometimes feel like I have to make an excuse to avoid the drama?"

- "Do I feel exhausted or drained after talking to or hanging out with my friend?"

- "Are there people in my life who make me feel differently after I spend time with them?"

- "How does my friend react when I create a boundary with them and their drama?"

- "Do I give too much and get too little with this friend?"

These questions can really help you understand the dynamic of your relationships with friends. You can ask them for any friendship and determine the quality of the relationship. It might be more out of balance than you recognize, and you can find new ways to incorporate your sense of self and your power as a person with your ability to sense these imbalances and differences.

If you have a mostly good relationship with your close friends, then you may not need to worry too much about this, but it can help you when making new acquaintances avoid becoming someone's shoulder to cry on without receiving the same courtesy in return.

Family Are Always Family

Parents can be so infuriating for all people. Brothers and sisters too. Parents and siblings can also be loving and kind, and they can teach us about closeness, connection, and bonding. Our families are where we come from and how we learn to see and understand the world when we first get started here. There are many family experiences that mold and model who we become as people, whether or not we become a more empathic person.

The relationship you have with your family is always colorful and complex. Families stick together, or they don't. Families argue at some point down the road. Families challenge your identity and your concept of what you believe and value as you grow older. Empaths are highly sensitive to their family energies and dynamics, especially as children since the way that you experience your family as an empathic child can change the course of your entire life.

As you grow into adulthood and are separated more from your parents, you begin to notice that you are not at all like you were shown to be by your parental figures and that you were really just responding to their emotional needs and energies. This can be a very eye-opening and challenging life experience because it can afford you a great growth experience so that you can live more fully as yourself away from mom and dad, but it can also challenge the relationship that you have with them when you stop protecting their emotions and feeding their emotional wants and needs.

The challenges of adulthood are exciting and intense, and when you are a grown-up, your relationship with your family alters, whether you are an empath or not. You can begin to live as yourself more fully, and as you get more like you and embrace your gifts more and more, your parents or caregivers may not understand why you are different and why you are challenging to be around all of a sudden.

This is a common tale told by many adult children and their parents. As we adapt and settle more into our own identities, realities, and personalities, we change our early life relationships and have to grow from them in a new way.

Your mother and father held you when you were born and kept you alive. They saw you at a certain age and continue to carry that idea of you close to them. When you are a young empathic child, all you care about is making your mother and father happy, especially when they have intense emotional states and hardships.

When you are an empathic child, you become the caregiver for your parents on an emotional scale. This is rarely taught to parents, or shown to children as a possible reality. We just fit into the roles we have to in order to survive. When you grow up, you maintain that relationship, even when it is unhealthy, because it is what you were shown or taught to do unconsciously.

The empath will grow up having learned how to be an emotional caregiver and will foster other relationships in the same way, with their friends and romantic partners, and even their children. The empath will have a very loving bond with their offspring because of how easily they can sense the feeling and emotions of their own child. This can be very challenging as well since, when we are younger, we have to go through a lot of growth and change very rapidly, which can cause outbursts, temper tantrums, and behavioral problems.

Raising children as an empath is just as challenging as it would be for any parent, but the empath can have an advantage and will be able to use a well-balanced and well-nurtured skill to help their child feel loved, nurtured, and secure by how well they can sense and feel their child's emotions.

Empath

Emotional Health

An undeveloped empath has a little safeguard against the energies of individuals around them. Specifically, they are delicate to misery, discouragement, struggle, and outrage. They disguise these imbalanced feelings and energies, and they stress the torment of seeing someone. Subsequently, they lose control and are disturbed without any problem. However, they additionally attempt to control these feelings. If these feelings and energies endure, they go to substance, liquor, and food maltreatment to adapt.

For example, an undeveloped empath can feel more terrible in the wake of conversing with an individual about this current person's passionate agonies. This individual will feel better after the conversation. However, the undeveloped empath has encountered serious feelings without acknowledging what they are accustomed to. Then, at that point, they learn later that a friend or family member is encountering a similar inclination as well. In a room

Empath

loaded with individuals, an undeveloped empath may encounter a limit change starting with one feeling then onto the next. However, they quiet down when they are without help from anyone else.

An undeveloped empath may think that it's hard to focus when they are around others as a result of the different feelings they are feeling. They can't relinquish others, since they feel answerable for them. In many cases, their treatment matters appropriately, even though they want not to. They carry on their character when they are around specific people. However, they can undoubtedly return to themselves without them. Besides, an undeveloped empath acts and feels plastered if they are around tanked individuals, even though they didn't drink liquor.

Practical Choices

As a result of expanded torment insight, an undeveloped empath gets unfortunate and watchful, and careful in deciding. Since they are a profound scholar, their dread of results turns out to be too incredible that they get hesitant. Accordingly, they get isolated, bashful, and shy.

Besides, an undeveloped empath may not understand what they need and want. As a general rule, they possess the ability to take some energy for them to choose. However, they may in any case even think that it's simpler to stand in opposition to what others need from them, rather than them deliberating their requirements and needs themselves.

Relationships

An undeveloped empath is amazingly delicate. On the off chance that they are uninformed, they become harmed effectively because they don't see how to manage their feelings and energies. They can't shield against outer confusion. Subsequently, they muddle their connections, particularly when others don't get them.

Moreover, the undeveloped empath can't define limits, because the anguish, outrage, and frustration of their friends and family influence them profoundly. They believe they are continually losing eventually, regardless of whether they go to bat for themselves or do what their friends and family need.

An undeveloped empath needs an adoration association—like the remainder of the world. Nonetheless, the dodge heartfelt closeness and associations since they are anxious about the possibility that their accomplice's feelings will overwhelm them. They need to cuddle, yet they roll because they need the space for their own energy. Indeed, the staggering affection for one another can make them extremely upset since they can't deal with the extraordinary feelings.

Besides, an undeveloped empath thinks that it's hard to blossom with harmony. He may stow away or bolt for some space to breathe because they are engrossing the feelings of their accomplice. Their depletion or tension can make them look for decompression in their own energy space. An undeveloped empath in a relationship can feel a feeling that is multiple times more than what their accomplice feels.

Reactions to Outside Stimulus

When all is said and done, an undeveloped empath can't keep up concentration in perusing printed news or watching the news. He

Empath

can't do it, because the worldwide outrages influence them. They will in general cut off from the web news sites, papers, and TV news communications. They avoid pictures or recordings to disassociate themselves from the circumstance.

Moreover, the undeveloped empath is delicate to the major feelings described with the news. Injury, enduring, torment, loathsomeness, dread, and fear are only some uplifted feelings of the empath. Consequently, they will in general stay away from even computer games, books, and bloody motion pictures.

Reactions of Other People to an Empath

People may think that it's awkward to be around an empath because they accept that this individual sees their mysteries. In this way, the undeveloped empath may see that different people are keeping them away from them. They have no idea why they get outsiders. A couple of outsiders may think that it's simpler to uncover their biographies, regardless of whether they meet the empath.

The Cloud of Fear

An undeveloped empath has some impediments. Truth be told, exploring empaths online can cause them to understand that pages upon pages talk about safeguarding oneself from the cynicism of others. As an empath, they should understand that they draw in the difficult energies of others. They feel them on their psyche level, yet they have no idea about the incredible force that they have.

An undeveloped empath can exploit various systems to shield themselves from their extraordinary detecting capacity. However, they may not understand how to dispose of capacities that have lost their usefulness. Therefore, obsolete mental and enthusiastic internal ideal models, even though might be forgotten totally, can in any case run the empath's life. Subsequently, zeroing in on procedures only isn't useful, because the undeveloped empath is really battling them. They are assuming liability and drawing in the energies of others. Then again, they are additionally attempting to dispose of them; however, safeguarding is just an impermanent fix to empathic torment and wiping.

All the more, regularly, an undeveloped empath has low confidence since they have a lot of duties without seeing how to deal with them. They are confused about the best way to insert the energies of others into their own. In basic terms, they need to feel sublime about being an empath. However, since they have collected the energies of others, it is hard for them to feel superb about themselves. Truth be told, they feel agony and distress from every one of these undesirable energies.

It is practically difficult to feel glorious when the empath's body doesn't feel incredible. They can't handle their feelings. All the more critically, they are confused about some solution for them, and they can arrive at a specific point where they will be twisting down to self-deterioration. The will in any case help others since they feel commendable doing it. However, they are just intensifying their fundamental issues.

The Effects of Emotional Vampires

A passionate vampire assimilates the energies of an undeveloped empath. Truth be told, he can even assimilate the empath's joy and excitement. Albeit a few connections can be disposition lifting and positive, associations with passionate vampires can ingest the serenity and hopefulness out of an undeveloped empath.

Undeveloped empaths may not know it; however, a passionate vampire can exploit anyone. In this manner, it is huge for an undeveloped empath to see how to distinguish a passionate vampire. Some signs can help an empath perceive if an individual close to them is a passionate vampire or not.

In the first place, the empath feels languid, their eyelids become weighty, and their temperament weakens every one of them unexpectedly. In addition, they wind up needing to gorge on solace food varieties or sugars. The likewise feel negative, discouraged, or restless, and in conclusion, they feel put down.

Do You Need Healing?

Being an empath implies having the ability to retain what others are feeling. It is having this unusual, yet special endowment of interfacing with individuals through their feelings and actual circumstances. This can be depleting and tiring over the long haul. You are THE audience. Individuals are drawn to you since you discharge the sort of energy that tells the world "YOU CARE." You tune in. You identify. You mentor. Your support. You recuperate. Indeed, you give it a second thought.

However, imagine a scenario in which you, the empath, are the person who additionally needs mending. Imagine a scenario in which you are the person who needs care. How might you know it, if you do or you don't? Is it true that you are mindful of what amount of being an empath is transforming you? It is safe to say that you are beginning to think often more about others than about yourself? Would you even have the option to distinguish or perceive the side effects that could be revealing to you that there is a requirement for you to mend?

Why Empaths Get Sick

Outrageous empaths are individuals who don't have power over their capacities. They get so associated with what's going on to individuals around them that they truly are told to get genuinely and intellectually wiped out.

A limited empath can be consistently wiped out. It tends to resemble having a year-round influenza, or on the other hand, a sensitivity that can't be pinpointed. You could be wheezing and hacking each day, throughout the entire year—winter, spring, summer, and fall—and no measure of a prescription can cause you to feel much improved. No kind of clinical trial can figure out what infection you truly have.

Sooner or later, you will basically be another clinical secret. No treatment for your agonies. No decision except for you to remain debilitated. No determination for what you have. In any event, no finding is satisfactory in the clinical field.

You are experiencing being a limited empath. An excess of sympathy is making you genuinely sick. It occurs, you know. You may not know about it; however, being too empathic can obliterate your personal satisfaction without you understanding it. What you know about is that you get the sentiments and energy of those around you. You have acknowledged that. You've likely even accepted that. You realize that you are helping others. You have the blessing; you are exceptional. However, do you realize that you can likewise experience the ill effects of uncommon diseases? That can be a sort of ailment that you will most likely be unable to move away from or the sort that could, in the long run, cripple you forever.

Clairsentience is the mystic capacity presented to empaths. The capacity permits you to feel the enthusiastic energy around you; energy that others don't generally feel. On the off chance that you are an undeveloped empath, one with unmanaged capacities, you don't simply feel the energy, but you likewise retain it.

You transform into a wipe for passionate energy. You kiss up and clutch every one of the types of enthusiastic energy that you approach. You feel and retain, and afterward, your issues start. The enthusiastic misery, psychological maladjustment, and actual torments begin to kick in.

The energy you feel gets moved to you, assimilated into your own vigorous field. Presently, what the exchange will truly mean for you relies upon a few variables, including your energy type, vivacious state, and current lively immersion degree.

In less difficult terms, that energy can be shown as passionate change, similar to the burdensome occasion or mental episode. It can likewise be an actual disease, which turns out to be the most well-known outcome. If there is a major development of moved passionate energy on your framework, you become truly ill or consistently wiped out.

CONCLUSION

Thanks for making it to the end of this book. After reading this, you should have all the information you need to get started in developing your gift. You should be able to understand who you are as an empath. You should be able to determine whether you are a physical, emotional, intuitive, earth, animal, plant, or psychometric empath.

I can't highlight how significant it is that you are fully aware of why you believe your empath gift is a curse and not the blessing it was designed to be. I had accepted that I was cursed for a long time until I became fully aware of why I thought this way. To free yourself from this bondage, ask yourself the following questions. Does people-pleasing leave you exhausted? Do you suffer from depressive episodes? Do you attract toxic people? These are common problems among empaths who are struggling with their gift.

Empath

Your next step is to understand that change requires work. All the negative experiences you are having as an empath are because you have developed a series of bad habits that cause you to react in a way that is counterproductive to your gift. To get to the next level, you will need to develop good habits to replace the bad ones with since they are keeping you in bondage.

Protecting your energy as an empath is essential. You can't give everyone access to your soul. You must take the necessary steps to keep yourself free from negative energy. That means you've got to put the appropriate boundaries in place.

Once you've got into the habit of protecting and strengthening your energy, it's time to really dig deep and start practicing the techniques required to take your empath gift to the next level. This includes summoning supernatural help, sharpening your intuition, transmuting negative energy, getting clear on your purpose, and refusing to give away your power.

I would like to stress that awakening your superpower is not going to be an easy ride. If you really want to walk in the totality of your power, you will need to put in more effort than the average person. Meditation, visualization, shielding, and everything else that comes with awakening and maintaining your gift takes time and practice. If you are going to get any of these things done before you start your day, you will need to wake up early. When I got back from work, I completed my routine before I engaged in any other activities.

Without self-discipline, you will never master your gift. "Knowledge is power" is a common phrase, but I would like to change that to "knowledge in action is power." Without applying what you have learned to your life, transformation is impossible. You will remain at first base if you don't put the knowledge you've learned in this book into practice. I can tell you with confidence that it works because I went from zero to hero within six months.

Listen, the world desperately needs you! I once had a bad habit of complaining about how jacked up the world was. I would watch the news, read the papers, listen to the radio, and listen to people and just think there's no hope. I was depressed for a lot of reasons, but one of them was that I felt so sad for the planet. Our creator has given us this amazing universe, and mankind is destroying it. I felt hopeless. It wasn't until I started regaining some strength and understanding my purpose that I realized not only that it is my responsibility to change the world but that I have the power to do so.

A part of awakening your superpower is starting with what you've got. Another reason why I was so depressed about the state of the world was that I wanted to be the savior of the world, and I knew that wasn't possible. The reality is that some people don't want help. They are content to remain in their negative energy field, and they don't want to get out. In other words, you couldn't save everyone even if you had the power to do so because some people you would try and help would reject it. As much as I would love to save the world, it just isn't possible. So, I focus on doing the best I can with the people (like yourself) who are ready to become all who they were created to be for the betterment of humanity.

With that being said, it's time to go. Remember, don't overwhelm yourself with trying to do too much. Start small and work your way up.

Empath

Psychic Abilities Guide

The survival path for highly sensitive people: Practice meditation to discover the power of your mind with intuition, telepathy, aura reading and clairvoyance. Open your third eye and find a connection with your spirit guide.

Tara Brakh

Introduction

A psychic ability guide is a support designed to offer you a comprehensive, unbiased introduction to the subject of psychic abilities. It provides information about what psychic ability is, how to test for them, and the different types of clairvoyance that exist.

While psychic ability is still a taboo topic in many places around the world; know that it can be an enriching experience for those who can receive messages from loved ones who have passed on or simply want some guidance in their lives. While we don't guarantee with any certainty that anyone will be gifted enough to receive messages from another person's mind, we firmly believe that being open-minded and kind are worthwhile virtues themselves.

We intend to help people understand psychic ability and apply some of the principles quite easily in their lives. If you are interested in using such an ability for your own personal benefit, or just want to have a better understanding of this phenomenon, then you've come to the right place.

This guide will start by examining the theories and then move on to showcase some techniques that anyone can use regardless of age, gender or race. You'll learn about clairvoyant abilities such as clairaudience and clairsentience and also how you can test yourself for them.

It's a fascinating subject that can be quite useful in the right hands, so why not have a look at all of our courses.

This guide may help novice mediums as well as anyone who wants to learn more about a psychic phenomenon. We've also included a list of our other training courses that may be of interest to you. Take your time and get comfortable with the topic!

Psychic ability is the ability to perceive or feel the energy, through clairvoyance and/or mediumship. Clairvoyance involves seeing something without having visual contact with it. Many people are unaware of this form of psychic ability, as it is often categorized as a form of extrasensory perception (ESP) instead. However, his/her ability may not reflect the person's outstanding psychic aptitude in the same way that those with psychokinesis (PK) demonstrate a great deal of talent in their unique field of expertise.

Psychic ability can come in a wide range of forms, though. The most common are clairaudience (the ability to hear), clairsentience (the feeling of emotion or vibration), and clairvoyance (the ability to see). Generally, an individual with mediumship will have all of these types of psychic abilities, in some combination. Each type of psychic ability is unique and therefore requires a unique method of testing to determine whether one indeed has it.

There are four basic ways that psychics tell us they accomplish their tasks: physical mediumship, astral projection, remote viewing via PK, or telepathy. Physical mediumship involves channeling entities such as spirits or angels. Though not as easily defined, astral projection is the ability to perceive and travel through the astral dimension. Telepathic abilities are a form of PK that allows a person to manipulate information unconsciously, thus bypassing normal processes.

Many people with any number of psychic gifts choose to see themselves as spiritual healers, which is definitely true in many cases. However, most individuals do not see themselves as religious leaders and typically do not undertake those types of direct actions for religious reasons. The ability may be used for either personal or spiritual purposes, at the individual's discretion. Nonetheless, both are possible and have happened in the past.

What Is Psychic Ability?

This layer involves an expanded awareness of our place in the cosmos. This is not an "intellectual" awareness, but a somatic, "felt" experience. As a result, you'll have an expanded grasp of information available to you through non-sequential, intuitive channels extended beyond our normal sensory awareness.

When you read that earlier, it probably seems like the kind of gobbled-gook you could read from many pseudo-gurus of mindfulness. (By the way, "The Pseudo-gurus of Mindfulness" would make a good name for a rock band).

But now, after we argue coincidences, the above description might make a little more sense. But let's break this definition down and make it crystal clear.

As I said earlier, my best guess about all this is that the Programmed self has access to events and information from "reality" that we aren't normally conscious of.

Instead, more often than not, our Programmed Self filters out a lot of these events and information—"signals" if you will—from our normal sensory awareness. But as we saw during our exploration of synchronicity, with the cooperation of the Programmed Self, we can sometimes receive these signals in a more direct, unfiltered fashion—a way that seems more "intuitive" in nature.

In addition, these signals often appear to be non-sequential in that they don't follow the orderly sequence of cause and effect that we expect.

Our Programmed Self seems to be able to pick and receive signals not just from the present, but from the past and from the future. It may also pick up information that is distant in space, from an event that is not where we are physically located at the time.

For example, the coincidence of thinking of your friend and then having them call you to contain at least one event (their decision to call you) that you don't have direct access to. However, the Programmed Self does seem to have this access, in a way that defies logic. You might see what this is leading up to.

Acquiring knowledge of events that are distant from us, or having premonitions of future events before they happen are experiences we usually identify with "psychic abilities."

That's when I think psychic training can be helpful for mindfulness, if it's the right training and if it's training done with the right mindset.

And that is our focus in the work we'll do with the "intuitive extension" level of the ECS.

From Psychic to Magic to Intuitive

When I first started teaching these practices, I referred to this "intuitive extension" level as the psychic level. But I think that term has too many associations with the paranormal and the supernatural for our use.

I've also at times referred to this next level as the magic level, a term that has been associated with these mystical practices since at least the 1600s.

But I stopped using that term because some people associate it with a belief in things like Wicca or Satanism. As I mentioned before though, our work isn't about belief. It's about experience and insight.

So not too long ago, I recently began calling this the "intuitive extension" level. I think that name fits with our goal here—to discover how to extend our intuition.

We're not doing these exercises to become psychics or mystics. We're doing these to gain "intuitive insight" into our True Selves.

From working with my in-person students and the online members of our Mindful Masters group, I know that a number of you have had psychic experiences in the past.

I hope that as we go through this work, you'll learn to see those past experiences in a new light. Especially if your experience was intense—positive or negative—you may feel some resistance to letting go of your past interpretations of the experiences.

Just realize that these past interpretations may have been heavily influenced by your Programmed Self. Now that you have understood some of your programming, our Level 9 "intuitive extension" work may cause you to re-examine these past experiences. You may see them differently, feel differently about them, and understand them in a new way.

Especially if your psychic experiences have been negative; I know that you will find great comfort in this new approach. But if you aren't a "believer" in psychic abilities, don't worry. You don't have to be.

If a grumpy, old info-phobe like me can open him up enough to experience "intuitive expansion," then anyone can!

Aping up My Psychic Abilities

As I stated in the overview of this book, my own mindset on psychic training changed over time. I told you how I came to embrace much of the earlier psychic training that I had formerly rejected.

I told you the story, but I didn't tell you what caused it to change. Well, it changed as a direct result of—yes, you've guessed it—Archetype Met programming.

Before I tell you how AMP brought me full circle back to psychic training, let me just make something clear. I'll be telling you how I experienced one of the archetypes in my AMP practice. This is my personal experience. If you are doing AMP right now, I don't want you to take my story as an example of how you should work with this archetype. Working with archetypes should always be made personal, relevant to you and your situation. Your experience with this same archetype during AMP will be totally different.

With that in mind, you'll see my interpretation of this archetype actually was personal and extremely relevant to my situation. You'll see how working with this archetype led me to open myself up to the "mindful" importance of developing psychic abilities. In other words, AMP did its job!

It found a "stuck" area in my life and freed me from it. That happened a lot to me with AMP. I know it will happen for you as well during your own AMP practice.

Just What Is Behind That Curtain?

About two months into my AMP practice, after having worked through about four or five archetypes, I drew the High Priestess archetype.

With this archetype, I started by following the standard AMP process. During the first week after choosing the archetype, I developed my personal symbols for the card. I also researched the universal symbols. Keep in mind; this was still the early days of the internet (2001 and 2002). So while some research material for universal symbols was online, a good portion was still only available offline. I did most of my research using mostly hard-to-find and out-of-print books.

Thankfully, where I live (Portland, Oregon) has Powell's Books, the world's largest independent bookstore for new and used books. I don't see how I would have done this research without them.

Of course today, much of that hard-to-find information is online. Most of it is even in Wikipedia!

Side note: I sometimes think that AMP was more challenging—and even more fun—when this information wasn't so readily available online, and you had to hunt for it. But then, maybe that's just me being a grumpy, old info-phobe.

Getting back to the universal symbols. If you look at the illustration of the High Priestess, you'll notice several unusual objects in and around her on the card.

She's holding a scroll that says TORAH that is partially obscured by her robes. There are two columns with the letters "B" and "J" on them. The priestess sits between the two columns, blocking our access to what might be beyond the columns. There's also a curtain or veil behind her. So not only is our access blocked, we can't even see what's beyond the columns. The veil contains pomegranates (possibly the "forbidden fruit").

I'm not going to go into details of all this symbolism, since you can get most of it from the web. But I will say that my exploration of all of these symbols pointed towards the idea of "hidden knowledge."

The High Priestess appears to be protecting and blocking access to whatever this knowledge might be. The more I investigated those symbols, the more I wanted to know just what was behind that veil. What secret knowledge was held in the temple that the High Priestess was guarding? What instructions ("torch") were being hidden?

As part of playing the role of the High Priestess, I decided to include an exploration of "occult teachings." As I mentioned a few times, the word "occult" in contemporary times has come to mean "paranormal" or "supernatural." Organized religions often use it to refer to evil or forbidden practices. But the original meaning of the word was "secret teachings," "hidden knowledge," or "hidden abilities."

These secret teachings and abilities often became "forbidden fruit" by the restrictive religious and social orders. So as part of my High Priestess role, I actively sought out this forbidden fruit.

At first, I began by simply reading about occult teachings from a variety of Western mystical traditions. But as I continued to play the High Priestess archetype, I began to realize that not only would she protect these secrets, she would be intimately familiar with them.

So playing the High Priestess role, I would have to not only read about these teachings, I would have to experience them.

I decided to learn some of the actual practices and rituals associated with these mystical, esoteric systems of knowledge. Normally in AMP, you only play an archetype for one week. With the High Priestess, I played the archetype for one month to give me time to explore these Western mystical practices. Even after that month, as I moved on to other archetypes, I continued my explorations. Interestingly, these explorations were supported by a number of the AMP archetypes I played over the coming months.

(Once again, I want to remind you that this was my personal experience with these archetypes. I am not suggesting that you do the same thing when you work with the High Priestess or with any of the other archetypes. Follow your own path here).

But the result has been a growing understanding and use of "intuitive extension" in my life.

Through the High Priestess and other archetypes, I've opened myself to the important role that psychic practices play in living a mindful life.

But then again, maybe I haven't totally opened myself up, based on what happened to me while I was writing this part.

Reveal Abilities

Psychic abilities are said to be supernatural powers. These are abilities that others would consider impossible. However, it should be noted that psychic abilities are possible and that there are people who possess such abilities. In fact, every human being possesses some psychic abilities to a certain degree. The problem is that most people do not develop their abilities. Consequently, they are not able to use and take advantage of their abilities. If only people could take more time to meditate, then you will see that psychic abilities are supposed to be very common. Regular practice of even the basic breathing meditation can help you awaken your latent psychic abilities.

From now on, you should not see psychic abilities as something extraordinary. Realize that you possess these abilities. It is just a matter of developing and making use of your abilities. Yes, you need to learn to use them effectively.

Psychic Abilities Guide

Psychic abilities have become controversial. In fact, some completely do not believe in the existence of such abilities. This is due to the sad fact that those who surface and claim to possess psychic abilities are mere hacks and scams who do not even know how to meditate. Do not allow these people to dispirit you from pursuing a noble and magical path. After all, the best way for you to ensure that such abilities truly exist is by seeing them for yourself.

The Different Psychic Abilities

There are numerous psychic abilities in the world. Although it would be great to master all of them, it would be practical to just find which ability you prefer the most and use your time and efforts to master that ability. If you can dedicate more time, then you can branch out and learn another ability. Keep in mind that when it comes to learning, you need to focus on the quality of your learning. So, feel free to learn as many psychic abilities as you want, but are sure not to sacrifice the quality of your learning.

So, what are the different psychic abilities? Well, there are many. One of the most heard of is clairvoyance. Clairvoyance or clear-seeing is the ability to see beyond what the physical eyes can see. It can allow you to look beyond and divine the future, see and read auras, as well as see subtle energies and entities, among others. The ability of clairvoyance is closely related to your Ajna chakra, which is the seat of intuition and higher consciousness. If you want to develop this psychic ability, then you need to develop your Ajna chakra.

Another psychic ability that you should know is clairsentience, which means clear feeling. It refers to the ability to receive intuitive messages through emotions and feelings, which may also include physical sensations. People who have this ability are often referred to as empaths. This is due to their ability known as empathy. This ability will allow you to feel people and understand them on a much deeper level. This is characterized by a heightened sensitivity to subtle energies, feelings, and emotions. The more that you engage in meditation, the more that you can develop this ability. To be more specific, this ability is more associated with the heart chakra. Of course, the Ajna chakra also has an important role to play in the development of this psychic ability.

Clairaudience refers to clear hearing. Think of it like a little voice that tells you the right thing to do. You are probably aware of the saying that there is an angel beside you that sometimes tells you the right thing to do. Well, many times, it is actually the psychic ability known as clairaudience that should be given credit. This ability is also linked to the Ajna chakra as it makes use of intuition. It is also worth noting that messages from the spiritual world are often received through this psychic ability. You cannot expect those in the spiritual plane to manifest strongly in the physical plane, as they are in a different realm or plane of existence.

Almost everyone has a good memory of some experience with this psychic ability. It is that "voice" that speaks in your head and tells you the right thing to do or idea to think about. You might think of it as the messages from your guardian angel. Although we can indeed receive messages from our guardian angel, it is also true that some of these meaningful messages may come not from an angel but from your intuition and are communicated to you psychically. The more that you do meditation, the more that you will be able to notice this "voice" in your head. It is your intuition talking to you. Listen to it.

Psychic Abilities Guide

Another interesting psychic ability is known as claircognizance, also known as clear knowing. It is the ability to just know things, even without any logic or fact. You can consider it as some kind of inner knowing. For example, having this "knowing" that you should not trust a certain person, only to find out that person really cannot be trusted or is a bad person. Take note that this is different from clairaudience. In this case, there is no voice of any kind that you have to deal with. Instead, you simply know things as they are. You do not have to do anything; you just know. Although all your chakras should be well developed to master this ability, two main chakras are primarily needed for this psychic ability: the crown chakra and the Ajna chakra.

Though, it should be renowned that many other psychic abilities exist. Unfortunately, the world only considers the above abilities to be the "main" abilities. The truth is that many other abilities are just as wonderful.

Telekinesis

Telekinesis is the psychic ability to move objects using the power of the mind. This is one of the most charming abilities that you can learn. It is also very popular. However, the question remains: Is it real? The answer to this is yes. However, learning telekinesis takes time and practice. If you want to learn telekinesis, then here are the instructions that you need:

Place a light object in front of you, preferably on a table. You can use a feather, small stone, or anything light enough. Now, just relax. Focus on the object in front of you. Now, visualize forming a tunnel between you and the object. Nothing should exist in front of you but the object of your focus. Now, visualize your astral hand reaching out and pushing the object. Another thing that you can do is to visualize a ray of prana pushing the object. Watch it move.

As you can see, the steps are unassuming. It is up to you to practice this technique until you can do it properly. Once you get good at it, you can skip the part where you have to envision a tunnel between you and the object. After all, its purpose is only to aid you in your visualization and give you better focus.

Growing Abilities

There is a difference between developing spiritually, and developing your psychic abilities, although one can lead to the other when done right. When you're psychic, you can read people and places just by energy. As for spiritual development, it involves growing on all levels where you exist, in all aspects of life, developing your thoughts, understanding the reason you are alive, and why your relationships with yourself and others matter.

In other words, you can be psychic and still spiritually underdeveloped. The trouble with this is that it can cause you to become very centered on your ego. However, developing yourself spiritually will give you richer, more meaningful connections with the world around you, so you always come from a place of empathy, from the heart. This is the best route to take, considering your psychic abilities will develop at the same time.

Psychic Abilities Guide

So, while having psychic powers is cool and all, you want to approach this with the sincere desire to develop your spirit while developing your psychic abilities. Make this simultaneous, and there will be harmony in your life as you bring together every part of you into one balanced whole.

Chakras and Psychic Abilities

To develop your abilities, consider what you're naturally good at, intuitively speaking. This means becoming more aware of your chakras. They allow your abilities to come through and be the path you take to develop spiritually.

The seven energy centers have their own unique gifts.

- Muladhara gives you information from other dimensions.

- Svadisthana improves your intuition.

- Manipura gives you those "gut feelings."

- Anahata balances energies from the spiritual and physical realms.

- Vishuddha allows you to communicate, and of all chakras, it has the most psychic senses.

- Ajna gives you psychic visions and psychic intuition.

- Sahasrara is what ties you to your higher self and all things spiritual.

With these energy centers, we often give and get information, whether we're conscious of it or not. They are especially useful for picking up on subtle, psychic messages. You'd have a hard time manifesting these abilities without having these chakras active and open first. Many people have chakras that are naturally active, which means they naturally have psychic abilities that correlate to those chakras. Though, if you weren't "born this way," you must open your chakras first. Think of them like a door or a psychic portal that allows you access to all sorts of dimensions and information energetically. As you open them, you will become more and more aware of your gifts.

Meditation

Meditation is key for opening your centers up because it's a great way to keep your awareness centered where it should be. By channeling your focus on each chakra for just five to ten minutes daily, you will notice your intuition and awareness growing to greater levels. Here's how to meditate so that you can improve energy flow and increase your psychic abilities.

•   Sit somewhere quiet and get in an upright position. You may lay flat on your back if you prefer.

•   Inhale, and as you do, see energy as white light in your mind's eye, coming up and moving through your body, flowing directly into the blocked chakra.

•   Exhale, leaving that energy locked in there. Notice the chakra glowing brighter, looking more vibrant and alive than before (in your imagination).

•   Inhale again, drawing in more energy, and then exhale, locking it in, seeing a brighter glow.

• Continue this for some minutes.

• You can now put your palm on the chakra, directing energy to and through it for 15 minutes. You might notice some cool, warm, burning, or tingling sensations in there, during or after meditation. This is simply your chakra receiving energy.

You can do this with all chakras. The key is to be consistent. A fair warning: You might notice no substantial change for weeks or even months but stay consistent and patient. In time, you may notice you are much more psychically aware and that you're developing certain abilities.

The Third Eye and Psychic Development

The third eye is important when it comes to developing psychic powers because it regulates your subtle body's energy flow. It gives the wisdom and understanding needed to comprehend life beyond the physical. It allows you to get past the idea of duality and become more aware of the truth of who you are, a spirit having an adventure as a human. You are more than your flesh.

For some people, the level of spiritual awareness they get through developing this center can be incredibly overwhelming, especially when they have done no work on the lower five centers. So, again, never try to run before you can stand. Work with your chakras, beginning from the root and then moving on up. Don't rush this process.

When you have worked through everyone and approach the third eye, it opens as it should with no terrible side effects. You will notice you have an inner knowing of sorts. You will also sense the fullness of your being, "I Am." You will find that your emotions, beliefs, fears, and judgments are simply experiences and not the definition of who you are.

Opening Ajna

When your third eye is open, you see yourself laid bare before you. There's no room for self-deceit. You can see your insecurities, false assumptions, and judgments. You can see when playing the victim. You'll also notice the many hats you have when it comes to interacting with people. You can see when you connect with others based on their thoughts and assumptions about your person, and you can step beyond all that and the illusions by which most define their everyday lives. Now, you will become aware of a spiritual reality before you do this, which means your sense of identity will change. Accept this, and you will be fine.

Exercise 1

1.   Sit somewhere quiet, where you won't be bothered. You'll need a pen and a notepad.

2.   Think about who you are right now.

3.   Write down as many sentences as you can, in a list form, beginning with the words "I am." You could write, "I am beautiful, I am a wife, I am a writer, I am lonely, and so on."

4.   Next, think about how you were ten years before now.

5.   Create another list based on who you were back then.

6.   Pick two more periods from these times, and then repeat the process.

7.   Now, look through all lists, and notice the differences. Notice how your self-perception shifted and changed over time.

Exercise 2

With this exercise, you're going to act. Don't worry; you don't need to win an Oscar. When you act, you can access so many emotions, and those emotions usually affect the way you behave and how you perceive yourself. You're going to generate emotions using your memory.

1.   Recall a funny experience. Make yourself laugh at it. Force the laughter, if you must, until it's natural.

2.   Recall a sad experience. Make you cry—and feel it.

3.   Recall an infuriating experience. Scream angrily into a pillow, saying whatever you want.

The key to this exercise is to exaggerate the feelings, but don't remain in these feelings for long. What you will learn from this is that emotions do not define you. You are not your emotions.

Exercise 3

This exercise involves keeping a dream journal. When you dream, your third eye is active. The more you journal your dreams, the easier you will recall future ones, and the more detailed they become. You will also become more connected to your unconscious, which is the home of all your blind spots. Have a dream journal app on your phone to make things easier for you.

1.   When you wake up from bed, don't move. Just lie there.

2.   Remember the last thing that happened in your dream.

3.   Work your way backward.

4.   Once you've got most of the dream, open your dream journal.

5.   Write down the key images you saw that would remind you of each part of the dream so you don't lose that memory.

6.   Now, write out the dream in detail, referring to the keywords to make sure you're not leaving anything out.

7.   As you go to bed each night, run through your day in reverse until you hit the point when you woke up in the morning because doing this will help you with dream recall.

8.   As you fall asleep, gently affirm to yourself with conviction, "My dreams are crystal clear. I remember them all."

The Underrated Vishuddha

The third eye chakra is powerful, but the throat chakra is the main psychic center, housing three of your psychic senses. Clairvoyance allows you to see without physical eyes. You get images of places, people, and events using your third eye, and you can also see past the illusion of the physical realm or Maya. When you have clairvoyance, you can enter a room and perceive energetic images and imprints of what's been going on before you got there. This ability sits in the brow chakra.

Clairsentience is clear feeling and sensing, and this ability is in the Svadisthana. When you have this ability, you can feel emotions and things like cold and heat, even though it isn't cold or hot. You are an empath. This is usually the very first of the psychic senses that most people develop and come before the third eye's abilities.

Now the throat chakra holds three psychic abilities, including clairgustance, clairscent, and clairaudience. With clairaudience, you hear things without needing your actual ears. This easily lends itself to telepathy. You can get information from the spirit or hear messages about past events or experiences that have been energetically imprinted in a place. Clairscent allows you to smell things that aren't there. If you have ever smelt a perfume of a loved one who isn't around, and they didn't just spray it recently, then you've experienced this. If they've passed on, it means they're right there with you. Clairgustance allows you to taste without needing to use your tongue. It might seem like quite an odd ability, but it's pretty useful. For instance, getting a terrible, metallic taste in your mouth if you're interacting with someone could tell you about the state of his/her health.

Since Vishuddha has more psychic senses than other chakras, you need to keep this chakra balanced to develop your psychic power. If you intend to work as a healer, pay attention to this chakra to work with it well. As a healer, you must pass on valuable information and use your skills to the best of your abilities during your sessions. You cannot give your best if your throat chakras and others aren't in alignment. Only when balanced, healthy, and aligned can your psychic abilities work as they should? When you give attention to the throat chakra, nurturing it, you must be a psychic powerhouse, functioning at an energetic rate (high and efficient), being a blessing to those around you when you share your gifts with them.

Divination

Perhaps the most fascinating psychic tradition is that of divination. Different forms of divination have been in use from prehistoric times to the modern-day, involving everything from animal sacrifice to the reading of everyday playing cards. Needless to say, some of these forms are not everyone's idea of a good time. That is assuming you aren't the type of person who would be willing to sacrifice a goat just to know whether you should ask someone out on a date! However, most forms of divination are far less extreme, requiring nothing more than a deck of cards, a canister of sticks, or a bag of tiles. These forms allow the average psychic the opportunity to tap into their subconscious and gain insights that would otherwise be beyond reach. In fact, divination can be seen as the waking form of dreaming in the respect that it allows the practitioner the opportunity to access deeper levels of knowledge, much like a psychic dream. Additionally, many of the 'languages' of different divination tools are very symbolic, reflecting the language of psychic dreams.

There are far too many types of divination to cover in such a short space, so this part will focus on four of the main forms used in the modern-day. These forms cover two basic variations of divination—single question divination and big picture divination. Single question divination covers the forms that usually produce a single reading, meaning that they are intended to convey the possible outcome of a particular course of action. These usually involve such questions as "What will be the outcome if I accept this job offer?" or "How will my date with so and so go tonight?" Big picture divination is a more complex form of divination, given to exploring the dynamics of a situation. These forms often produce detailed readings involving numerous cards, tiles, or other devices. Readers of big picture divination will often get insights into energies working for them, energies working against them, and several choices that the reader must make. These forms of divination usually require a great deal of study to master, and they require the utmost concentration and devotion to use properly.

The first type of divination to explore is that of single-question divination. While there are various forms of this practice, perhaps the two most well-known and commonly used are the I Ching and Chinese fortune sticks. Both of these forms of divination come from Ancient China, and they serve as a testament to the mindset of the Ancient Chinese. The average person in Ancient China believed that the gods were there to help guide them in making the right choices at any given time. This meant that the spirit realm was an extension of the physical realm, not something to be feared or worshipped. Subsequently, the divine forces were there for everyone, regardless of status. To do a reading in I Ching or fortune sticks was to ask virtually the gods for advice. The fact that these divination forms exist to this day suggests that this outlook on the spirit realm is very much alive and well in modern times.

In the case of the I Ching, there are 64 hexagrams or sets of six-line readings. Each hexagram represented a story or legend from Ancient China, one that conveys a lesson or a message. To determine which hexagram was relevant, the reader would cast three coins six different times. These coins would land heads up or tails up, and the reader would use this to determine each of the six lines. After the sixth cast was complete, the full hexagram would be revealed. The person who reads would then turn to the suitable hexagram in the book for the message revealed. This practice was used in other Asian cultures as well as China, and in fact, it is reported that the Imperial Japanese Navy used the I Ching before the attack on Pearl Harbor in 1941. The fact that such significant decisions were based on psychic readings demonstrates how much faith the Eastern cultures place on divination and its ability to provide direction and wisdom.

The second form of divination used for single-question situations is Chinese fortune sticks. There are numerous differences on this theme; however, the most commonly used format also provides 64 different readings. Unlike the I Ching, which requires six different castings of three coins, the fortune sticks require only one casting. In this scenario, the reader has a canister with 64 separate sticks, each numbered accordingly. The reader will shake the canister in a way that will make the sticks slowly emerge. This process will be performed until a single stick leaves the canister and lands on the table or the floor, depending on where the reading is being performed. Once the stick is identified, the reader will turn to the appropriate number in the book that contains the fortune stick readings. Like the I Ching, this book contains different stories and fables from Ancient China, each with a unique message and subsequent advice. Sometimes two or three sticks will fall out at once, and in this instance, the reader must make a choice. Many people choose to treat all the fallen sticks as significant and read all the readings that they convey. Others choose to put the sticks back in the canister and do it again until only one falls out. In the end, there is no real right or wrong answer. The trick is to do what is right for you.

Single-question divination is an excellent way to answer a pressing question at the moment. For the most part, these readings allow the reader to decide whether they should pursue a certain course of action. There are times, however, when a more in-depth understanding of a situation is required. For these events, big picture divination is a better source for answers. Just as with single-question divination, big picture divination has many forms. Again, there are far too many to cover in the limited space available here. Therefore, we will examine two of the most commonly used forms in existence today—Tarot and Runes. These forms of divination have origins that go back into history, although they aren't necessarily as old as the Chinese forms we have examined.

In the case of Tarot cards, the earliest known Tarot deck goes back to the middle of the 1400s. The purpose of the original Tarot cards was not for divination; rather they were actually playing cards much like our modern playing cards, containing different suits and numerical values. However, as time passed, the rich symbolism of these cards attracted mystics who were looking for a medium for discovering the wisdom and deep insight. Eventually, a system was devised which gave each card a specific symbolic value, meaning that the Tarot deck became a way to tap into the wisdom of the subconscious. A great many spreads became available, meaning that any number of situations could be contemplated using the cards. There are 11 such spreads commonly used today, ranging from the single card spread which allows the reader to gain insight on a single-question, much as with fortune sticks or the I Ching, to spreads of as many as eight or more cards. A spread of three cards allows the reader to gain insight into the progression of a situation by revealing the past, present, and future. Other spreads provide deeper revelations, including energies that stand in favor of the situation, those that oppose the situation, and even lessons that the reader needs to learn from the situation at hand. The standard Tarot deck consists of 78 cards, meaning that there is an endless source of wisdom and insight available to the reader.

One of the wonderful things about the Tarot deck is that it has gone through numerous changes over the years. The earliest and most original of the decks are still available today, but other decks with different imagery are also available, meaning that the reader can choose a deck that best reflects their personality. Additionally, different decks can be used to better represent the specific situation at hand. While this may seem fairly superficial at first it actually represents a very critical element of divination—the connection between the reader and the source of the wisdom. Whether you believe that divination is a way to communicate to the divine, or whether you believe it is merely a way to tap into your own subconscious (some would argue one's subconscious is divine), the important thing is that the medium represent your personal vision of that which you are accessing. Therefore, different imagery options allow a person to find the imagery that best captures their vision of the source that the information will be coming from. This personalization makes the experience all the more meaningful, as it makes the reader a more integral part of the process.

Finally, there is the divination tool known as Runes. Like Tarot cards, Runes were originally not designed for use as a divination tool. Rather, Runes were the characters of the original Germanic alphabet used by the Scandinavian and Germanic cultures in the era commonly referred to as the Dark Ages—a thousand-year timeframe beginning in the 5th century and ending in the 15th century. Different variations of Runes emerged across the different Germanic cultures, but the version that is used for divinatory purposes is the one knows as Futhark Runes. Specifically known as the Elder Futhark, this group consists of 24 different Runes, each with a phonetic and symbolic value. The name Futhark itself comes from the phonetic value of the first six Runes, Fehu, Uruz, Thurisaz, Ansuz, Raidho, and Kenaz. The first letters of each Rune combine to form the name, just as the first two letters of the Greek alphabet are used to form the word alphabet—alpha and beta. While the Runes were originally just the alphabet of the Germanic or Teutonic peoples, they became a tool of divination that is unsurpassed in symbolism and rich imagery.

Unlike Chinese divination, which uses poetry, legends, and stories to convey wisdom, Runes use more primal images in their language. Uruz, for example, represents the Auroch, a wild bison that covered Northern Europe in prehistoric times. This Rune symbolizes the raw strength and power of the Auroch; therefore, when a reader draws Uruz, they are inspired by the promise of strength that it portends. Thurisaz is the Rune for thorn, and it represents the barriers that thorns can be. In the case where a reader draws this Rune, they are cautioned that the road ahead may be full of challenges, much like the rose bush is full of thorns. Certain pains will be experienced in the course of achieving the goal. The simplicity and primal quality of Rune symbolism make it a favorite for anyone who embraces a more shamanic relationship with the divine side of life.

Empathy

Familiar personality and what they are afraid of, what they find to be overwhelming, and how their world always seems to change.

If you are an empath person and have found yourself feeling like you can't get a break or experiencing exhaustion at the end of every day or if your relationships are souring with people that you thought were friends, it may be time to take a closer look at what may be going on.

You may be an empath, and this condition seems to affect different people in different ways. Being empathetic means experiencing sadness when others are sad and being able to sense other's thoughts, which can make it difficult at times.

The energy of others will affect you on a deep level because you feel their feelings and emotions as your own. Empaths are sensitive people, and they often become overwhelmed with life, making it hard to maintain a healthy social life and relationships.

Empaths are often confused about being psychic because of their ability to sense energy or read other people. Some empaths can even feel the emotions of inanimate objects like plants, animals, nature, and others who aren't even present.

If this is something that you believe you are dealing with, here is a brief look at what empaths experience with each sign.

Aries (Mar 21–Apr 19)

Fear: Loneliness/Rejection

They will often do whatsoever they can to avoid this feeling because being rejected or abandoned triggers deep feelings of pain and sadness. They are not comfortable being in situations where they don't have control. They want to be in every case by themselves and wish that someone would understand how sensitive they are.

Taurus (Apr 20–May 20)

Fear: Unmet Needs/Being Alone

This is a challenging situation for them because they become overwhelmed when their personal needs aren't met and feel like they cannot function properly without love and appreciation from others.

Gemini (May 21–June 20)

Fear: Being Wasteful/Manipulated

People with solid empathy often go into situations where they feel like they are doing the same things repeatedly, but only to find that nothing gets done. They dream about being free to do what they want when they want to do it.

Cancer (June 21–July 22)

Fear: Being Misunderstood/Burdensome Situation

They can become overwhelmed by the emotion of others because their sensitivity makes them feel everything deeply, and in some cases, it can feel like an emotional rollercoaster for them. They are often the ones that others come to in times of distress because they know how to make everything seem better.

Leo (July 23–August 22)

Fear: Being Exposed/Overwhelmed by Joy

People with this type of empathy can become overwhelmed by joy and feel like it takes a lot out of them if they experience too much happiness. This is not something that they are comfortable with because they believe pleasure should be shared with others. In some scenarios, this can result in them judging things that other people do or have.

Virgo (August 23–September 22)

Fear: Being Judged/Rejected

Empaths are quickly judged, and for the most part, they like to avoid this. They are sensitive people who know how to project well and do not feel comfortable provoking hurtful feelings or emotions in others. They will do of any kind they can to evade situations where they feel judged by others. They want people to see through them instead of understanding them, which is more likely to happen than the other way around at times.

Libra (September 23–October 22)

Fear: Being Alone/Lacking Control

Sensitive people with this type of empathy are often afraid of being alone or feel like the world is changing too quickly for them. They are typically always looking for a relationship or someone they can share their lives with and want to be in control. They don't like to be influenced by their surroundings and often need space because they become overwhelmed.

Scorpio (October 23-November 21)

Fear: Being Overwhelmed/Rejection

They will do whatever it takes to avoid feeling overwhelmed, and for the most part, they feel like there isn't enough time. They are always looking for time out of their busy schedules to relax. They can become very angry or emotional at times and are quickly rejected by others because of their sensitivity.

Sagittarius (November 22-December 21)

Fear: Being Ignored/Overwhelmed by the Mundane

They are not comfortable being ignored or left alone. If they feel like they don't have friends or people who genuinely care about them, they can become sad and fail. They do not enjoy being around negative people and can often become overwhelmed by the thought of mundane situations.

Capricorn (December 22-January 19)

Fear: Feeling Used/Being Ignored

They step back from situations when they feel like people are trying to make them the victim. They are very cautious of their personal lives. They will try to avoid problems where they fear being used because they prefer to deal with issues right away instead of letting them slip into something that may be more difficult to fix.

Aquarius (January 20-February 18)

Fear: Being Ignored/Losing Control

They are most comfortable when they are in control of their lives. They want to make the best way for everyone around them to get what they want. This is why they can become confident and influential leaders. They surround themselves with people that give off magic and often have a hard time believing in what others say or how things should be done.

Pisces (February 19-March 20)

Fear: Being Overwhelmed/Feeling Alone

They are not comfortable being overly emotional or depressed because of how much they can connect with others. They don't like feeling alone, even in the most solitary situations, and will find a way around being alone to get things done. They love to keep busy and always have busy agendas for themselves, so they feel like they are always overwhelmed by the mundane aspects of life.

Like every other personality test that you may take on the Internet, this is based solely on what you answer to questions from the test creator. It is meant to show you which star sign or which star signs you can connect to and how. Suppose you do not feel like you are associating with your own personal Empathy Profile after taking this test. In that case, other tests can be taken on the Internet that will do the same thing and give you a more accurate reading for yourself. If this test does not seem to match up with some of your personality traits, then take another one until one seems to match up with how you feel and think.

Your Empathy Profile Test Results

Dramatic Expression Profile (Emotions)

Unlike the prior profile that simply listed your personality traits, this profile is more in-depth. It will give you a better understanding of how you are most likely to react to different emotions. There may be some emotions that will seem very similar, but some may seem opposite. Every person will have a unique view of what their emotions mean and what they mean for others. The best thing that you can do when taking this test is to see how your results relate to who you are as an individual. The test creator is trying to get you to come up with why certain emotions are occurring within you and what they mean for you. If emotion does not seem to fit into who you are, this may mean something else.

You will be shown a series of emotions related to situations that could happen in life and how you would react to them. You will be able to click on each emotion link as it pops up, and it will give you more information and follow-up questions about what the emotional reaction would be. You may notice that some of the links seem similar or similar but have different answers. This indicates that it is possible that you have more than one emotion, and you will need to work on all of those before they are resolved in your being.

This may take 10 minutes or more, but because it is self-directed and you are the one doing it, you can take as long as you like. The longer you spend on a particular step, the better. Anything under 15 minutes would be too rushed. 15-30 minutes would be considered average and of course, if you have the time, then use even more time for yourself. A more extended test could provide you with a lot of information about yourself because it is more in-depth than the other tests that have been given.

Here are the emotions that you can expect to be shown on this test:

• Overwhelmelm: Overwhelmed by normal life situations and situations where they feel they have too much going on. This could involve work, love, and other personal relationships.

• Unsatisfying relationships: They may feel that their relationships are being ignored or taken for granted, leading to them feeling frustrated. They may have different feelings about certain people than others, and they will want to express those thoughts, especially if they feel like people are taking advantage of them somehow.

• Rumination: They may feel like they cannot move on with life because of what has happened. They are often kept in the past and stuck on insecurities that have been built up over time.

- Feeling unwanted: They may feel like they are not wanted by others, which could cause them to have feelings of sadness or depression if the person they want to be close to doesn't want them back.

Medium

So far, we've talked about psychic reading. Here, we will talk about medium reading. So, what's the difference? Well, someone who does psychic readings may not have mediumship abilities, which are acting as a vessel and a bridge of communication between the spirit world and the world of the living—but all mediums have psychic abilities, as this is what they use to contact the spirits of the dead.

Mediumship or mediums may be a term you haven't heard before. As mentioned above, a medium is a person who is a bridge between the dead and the living. They can communicate with those that have passed over and convey messages to the living for them. Suppose you've ever used an Ouija board. In that case, this is one form of mediumship, as you are contacting, or attempting to contact, the spirits of the dead—although Ouija boards are usually used as a form of entertainment more than anything serious.

Psychic Abilities Guide

The forms of mediumship used by practicing mediums are when the spirit of the dead speaks through the medium and when the medium receives messages clairvoyantly (or clairsentient, claircognizant, clairaudient) and relays the message to the living. A living person often asks the medium to contact and create a communication channel with a dead loved one because they miss them. There is unfinished business or unanswered questions between them; they want a sense of closure. The spirit of the deceased loved one likely feels the same, so these sessions can be very healing.

Suppose you wish to become a medium, an intermediary between the spirit world and the living. That being so, you will need a stronghold on the four intuitive types (even if you favor one more than the others) as the messages will come through. You will perceive them via clairvoyance, clairaudience, clairsentience, or claircognizance. This is something to try once you've been practicing your psychic abilities for a while and feel confident. You can still be on a beginner's path, but make sure you've got the basics down. If you feel that you are a natural psychic medium, someone who has sensed the presence of spirits of the dead from a young age, you may already know how to communicate and use these spirit channels. It is not a necessity to becoming a medium, however.

If you know any mediums, you can get in touch with, ask them about their craft. How does it feel to communicate with spirits? When did they start, or when did they first notice they had this ability? What are some examples of mediumship experiences they've had? You can also search online to read first-hand experiences from mediums; you can contact where you live if there are none. Just be careful that the person you are learning from is not a scam artist, as the world of psychic practice is rife with frauds looking to exploit people for money.

To begin practice towards contacting spirits, you must be in a state of total relaxation. Find a calm, comfortable spot without bright lights. Feel the energy of the whole universe flowing through you, and relax your mind, letting other thoughts that poke at you fade away. Now it's time to call upon the spirits. Before you do this next step, make sure you've mastered psychic protection against negative spirits and entities, as it's possible to invite a negative spirit into your home. To help reduce the risk of an opposing spirit entering your space, think of a specific deceased loved one you would like to contact (this can also be a pet). That way, your call is not extended to any spirit who happens to be around. They are not invited; only your loved one's spirit is. Now call upon them out loud. Ask them into your space and maybe ask a question of them or ask if they have anything to communicate. Call upon them mentally too. Summon up an image of them in your mind, quite detailed, and mentally welcome them into space. If you feel their presence, ask them a question you have prepared beforehand.

You may sense them in different ways, whether you smell the cologne they used to wear, hear their laugh or a song they used to sing, see their favorite color or a piece of clothing they used to wear in your mind's eye, or a sudden shift of emotion where you feel warm and full of love. These are just examples to show you that the way you sense them may not be seeing their image speaking to you in your mind's eye. The way they answer the questions may be through images that must be interpreted or through words you see or hear in your mind. If you answer a question and get a strong emotion immediately afterward, this may also respond. Or if they answer claircognizant, then you will know the answer. Remember not to force or make up their presence or answers. Just let them flow, and if they don't show up or answer any questions, then that's okay. Just keep reaching out and practicing and stay relaxed. If you pick up nothing, don't force it. Release and try another time again.

You can also try practicing as a medium for a friend, and you can call upon the spirit of their loved one, asking the spirit any questions your friend may have of them. If you want to challenge yourself, don't ask your friend who they want to contact. Go in blind. Ask them only to picture and think about the person they wish to get. Keep your mind clear and relaxed, and be open and receptive to any energies and messages you may receive. If images or feelings start popping up, describe them to your friend. You can go online and look up videos of psychics in action to see how this is done. For example, if you're sitting there with an empty mind and suddenly, a figure of a man pops into your mind, and then the color red. Then the concept of Thanksgiving dinner, and the smell of cigarettes, you would say, "I'm seeing a man, now the color red, and something to do with Thanksgiving. I also smell cigarettes." You obviously will not know what this means, so ask your friend if it has any significance for them. After all, when acting as a medium, the message isn't for you but for the other person, the one the spirit of the dead is connected to.

If this is a legitimate message, your friend will get it right away, and if they feel like it, they can tell you what it means to them. Maybe the man was their uncle, whose favorite color or shirt or car was red, and he always hosted a big family Thanksgiving at his house—it was an annual family tradition. And he smoked, which was a familiar and comforting reminder of his presence to all who knew him. It is an example of how a medium reading can progress.

You may hear words or phrases from the deceased as well, which you should relay to the living person. Tell them everything you see and hear in your message, even if it may not make sense to you, as it may make sense and be vital to them. If not, then keep going. You probably won't get everything right, especially since you are just beginning, so keep telling them what you are sensing and make sure you aren't forcing these messages. Make sure they are coming to you naturally and clearly from the spirit you have contacted.

Psychic Abilities Guide

Clairaudient

Clairaudience is the capacity of getting a natural vocal message from the universe of spirits or a higher being. Clairaudient individuals can stretch out their hearing to rise above the ordinary physical world and the known degree of mindfulness, to arrive at the world past. Clairaudients are profoundly natural individuals who can tune in to a voice other than their own when the soul world transmits a message to them.

The message may incorporate specific words, names or expressions, incoherent sounds, or music. The voice now and then sounds incredibly unique concerning the voices we typically hear. It might seem as though it's being spoken right by you, inside your head, or resounding as though from another measurement. It likewise may seem like one of your friends and family who has passed away. The voice may make itself heard now and again of an emergency, a crisis, an intersection, or at another huge time. Clairaudient

Psychic Abilities Guide

dreams are additionally a known wonder, where an individual may hear the voice of a soul during rest.

How Does Clairaudience Sound?

Clairaudience is normally heard inside (in your mind).

Some of the time, clairaudient messages can be heard with your "customary hearing." However, recall—those in the Spirit world never again have a physical body—in this manner, needn't bother with a physical "voice."

Tip: If you need to be an expert instinctive, clairaudience can be too useful to create. Then again, if a psychic hearing isn't your most grounded instinctive blessing, no stresses! You don't have to have every "clair" wide open to be a stunning instinctive!

5 Ways You Can Receive Clairaudient Messages

You Hear Your Very Own Voice in Your Mind

Clairaudience is delicate and unobtrusive. It regularly seems like when you are contemplating internally. Consider it a clairvoyant method for imparting.

When you've built up this natural blessing, you'll have the option to separate between your own voice and the say of Inner self, as well.

Sounds

You may hear noises, words, or melody in your thoughts. They may have exacting or representative implications.

In case I'm giving a checking and Spirit needs me to realize they as of getting on had a birthdate, I may hear the Happy Birthday tune in my mind.

Physical Sounds from the Ether

At some point, my back rub specialist and I started hearing the most excellent music, yet there was nobody else in the structure and no radio set around! We could together hear this otherworldly music with our regular hearing.

The Voice of Spirit

Most mediums hear Spirit clairvoyantly in their very own voice. Remain that as it may, at this time and there, the voice of Spirit will seem as it did, although they were living.

These kinds of clairaudient encounters are sure and not unnerving.

Clairaudient Alerts

On the off unintended that a specific one is in trouble and their soul group needs to stand out enough to be noticed immediately, they MAY hear a clairaudient cautioning unmistakably.

These marvels aren't intended to be alarming; however, can be frightening (this is another motivation behind why Spirit likes to speak with delicate, clairvoyant messages).

Furthermore, trust me, if your otherworldly group ensures you by shouting "STOP," you'll be overly appreciative they did!

Where Do Clairaudient Messages Come From?

271

Psychic Abilities Guide

When you are far-off adequate along in your psychic improvement, you'll start to get a feeling about who is sending you a message and why.

- It may be from your Spirit Guides.

- It could be from somebody you adore who's passed on.

- It could be from your Higher Self.

11 Signs You Might Be Clairaudient

Numerous clairaudient individuals are strolling around this world who don't realize they have this super-cool instinctive blessing. It is safe to say that you are one of them?

Hear Somebody Saying Your Name When Nobody Is Near

Does it ever appear as though you hear individuals talking, yet nobody is near? Perhaps you hear delicate voices out of sight or could have sworn you heard somebody saying your name.

In the event that this transpires, it's a pretty darn great pointer that you might be clairaudient.

When you have psychic hearing, you can now and again hear things that other individuals can't. It might be a delicate, unpretentious sound (like music), or something increasingly emotional (like a voice).

You Appreciate and Need Calm

Instinctive individuals are generally exceptionally delicate, both genuinely and physically. Along these lines, you might be touchy to clamor in case you're clairaudient. For instance, a noisy gathering or TV may make you feel—goodness—like you are going to slither out of your skin! By and by, this is my solitary protest about being clairaudient. A lot of commotion may make you feel:

- Tired.

- Irritable.

- Ungrounded.

- Give you cerebral pain.

It tends to be truly disappointing when you have a psychic hearing; however, your loved ones don't see the amount it influences you.

You Converse with Yourself Frequently

Do you have thoughts with yourself in your mind all the time? It could imply that clairaudience is one of your overwhelming instinctive endowments. Why?

All things considered, since you are as of now great at "being in your mind," it will be simple for you to figure out how to perceive when you're taken advantage of Spirit.

In the event that you converse with yourself a great deal, you're most likely getting Divine direction without acknowledging it!

Thoughts and Inventiveness Move through You

In case you're clairaudient you may have numerous inventive, enlivened thoughts that course through you—particularly when you are feeling loose, euphoric, or thankful.

This is because when you are cheerful, your vibration is high and you are most associated with your spirit!

This is the reason clairaudient individuals look for calm. We instinctively realize that in that isolation we can interface with the Divine.

It's even regular for individuals with psychic hearing to get bunches of motivated thoughts while cleaning up! I propose bath colored pencils so you don't miss any of the directions you get.

Your Closest Companions Were Nonexistent

Contrarily! "Fanciful" companions can be heavenly attendants, Spirit directs, and even withdrew friends and family.

If you conversed with a fanciful companion as a youngster, either clairvoyantly or on the off chance that you heard a physical voice, you are presumably clairaudient.

Music Makes You Feel Associated with Your Spirit

Recently, Tom Petty was on TV conversing about how music originates from the spirit.

When you focused on it, it's generally because your spirit needs something and you're not tuning in. That is the point at which you get in your vehicle, jump on the closest nation street, and play the music that you cherish! Inside only a couple of minutes, your vibration is lifted, and you feel reconnected to your spirit. On the off chance that music moves you to this degree, you might be clairaudient. You may likewise be:

• Musically slanted or improvise.

• Write music – You may "hear" the music before you compose it, or it might feel propelled by a higher power.

On a side note, in the event that you start seeing pictures in your mind to coordinate the melody verses, it might likewise mean you are extrasensory!

You Lift Others up

• Do you appreciate managing and elevating others?

• Do individuals reveal to you that you should charge cash for offering guidance or that you have a "blessing"?

• Do individuals call you to "vent" since your words are so alleviating?

Hear Ringing or Shrill Commotions in Your Ears

You may likewise hear humming, or feel your ears "pop." If it's too noisy, it's OK to state, hello folks, cut back the volume!

You Learn Through the Sound-Related Channel

Your favored method for learning can be a piece of information concerning which psychic blessings you have. Numerous clairaudient individuals adapt best through hearing. Or on the other hand, you may appreciate tuning in to a book on Audible as opposed to perusing a book.

You Can "Hear" Creatures

Hearing creatures doesn't mean they open their mouths and start visiting like Mr. Ed or anything, it's progressively similar to "squares of the idea" that fly into your head.

For instance, I was petting my feline one day when an idea flew into my head that my little girl has been disclosing our kitty privileged insights! I referenced this to my girl, and she yelled, "He did! Did he reveal to you what my mystery is?" He didn't. Shucks for me.

You Get "Signs" in Melody and Discourse

Signs can make you feel associated with Spirit, feel approved, and are a TON of enjoyable to search for! Signs from Spirit can come to us in every single various way.

On the off chance that you request a sign from your aides or friends and family in paradise, pay heed to how they come through for you.

Does the direction you've been looking for come through in the following tune that plays on the radio? Or on the other hand, do you wind up saying, "Entertaining you should state that," when a more bizarre says precisely what you have to hear? Provided that this is true, these are attributes of clairaudience.

Clairvoyant

This is a French word meaning clear seeing. It is the intuitive sixth sense, which allows people to perceive energy. Every human being can hear, smell, see, taste, and feel; however, people have other psychic senses beyond these five senses they can use to gain more subtle information. Clairvoyants, for instance, use their spiritual eye, also called the mind's eye, to perceive the knowledge of their soul, as well as the collective knowledge of the universe, including the knowledge of past souls and souls not yet manifest.

Clairvoyants get intuitive information through symbols, dreams, images, visions, and colors. This ability is so subtle that people often think they are making things up or imagining stuff. In fact, it can happen even if one's eyes are open. This ability manifests several times during people's lives, but they do not recognize it for what it is; therefore, they discredit it as a wishful thought, daydream, imagination, or wondering of the mind.

Psychic Abilities Guide

People's intuitive powers stem from the right side of their brain, which is the same side that houses their imagination and other creative centers. People's imagination contains some seeds or aspects of the clairvoyant symbols and visions. In other words, clairvoyance often appears similar to one's free and creative thoughts with imagery. Essentially, it does not always manifest in a clear vision or extensive dream.

Therefore, many people are walking around and living their lives who do not know they possess this amazing psychic gift. Some of the most common signs to look out for determining whether one may possess powers of clairvoyance include:

Seeing Colored Dots and Flashes of Light

People who often see colored dots, floating shadows, and glittering lights in the air might mistakenly think they are losing their minds. However, nothing is farther from the truth. In reality, they might have a cool gift. According to practicing clairvoyants, colored dots and flashes of light are an indication of the presence of higher spirits, which may be seeking attention to delivering vital information. One might see the following:

a.   Flashes of light and movement in the corner of one's eye.

b.   Colored dots or floating orbs in the air.

c.   Flashing and glittering lights in the surrounding space.

d.   Shadows that look like they are suspended or floating in the air.

The thought of spirits scares most people; however, according to practicing psychics, this fear is unwarranted. They insist that higher spirits usually deliver their messages and guidance with love, and this guidance is fun, valuable, and useful.

Daydreaming a Lot

Some people tend to zone out, daydream, and wander off into their own thoughts several times a day, or have imaginations that almost seem like they are living inside their head. This may be a sign of clairvoyance because a large part of this psychic ability involves visualization and seeing.

Frequent and Vivid Dreams

Vivid dreams feel so real and are so close to reality that it is easy to pick out which is which. Even in sleep, clairvoyants possess an extremely active sight because they are visual people, which is why they often have vivid dreams. For them, a vivid dream can tell a story or be a vision that offers insight into things that are taking place in real life.

Deep Appreciation for Beautiful Things

Clairvoyants love looking at beautiful art and have a deep connection to bright flowers, sculptures, and other attractive physical objects. In addition, they tend to gravitate towards careers such as photography and graphic design, as well as creative hobbies like drawing and painting. This mainly stems from their strong visual senses.

Seeing Things Moving in the Corner of One's Eye

Often clairvoyants tend to see things from the corner of their eyes, and these things seem so real that they actually turn or double-check to determine whether they just saw someone. However, when they do this, they do not see anyone. According to practicing clairvoyants, these things are earthbound spirits inhabiting certain places. Essentially, they are the emotional or mental spirits of the dead who, for some reason, did not fully cross over. Therefore, in addition to seeing their spirit guides, clairvoyants can see these earthbound spirits of deceased people.

Ability to See a Light or Aura around People

According to many self-confessed clairvoyants, they often see differently colored auras around different people. These auras consist of electromagnetic energies, which also contain certain information about people's lives. By looking at a person's aura, a clairvoyant will identify and understand that individual's emotions.

Ability to See How Things Fit Together

Clairvoyants are good at solving complicated problems or difficult puzzles, as well as perceiving in their mind's eye how things should be for them to work in the right way. In other words, while others are struggling to solve a complicated problem at work or in any other setting, a clairvoyant will easily see how different pieces fit together to create the big picture. Essentially, they naturally understand how ideas and things connect together, which also stems from their strong visual senses.

Ability to Envision Plans in One's Mind

Certain people tend to create entire scenes about the future in their minds. These scenes tend to have new designs and details that often seem real. Some of these people might actually have the gift of clairvoyance. This is because people with this gift possess a highly developed sense of mental sight and vision, which is why they can envision things and see their results, even before they begin a project.

A Heightened Sense of Direction

People with clairvoyant abilities tend to have such a strong sense of direction. In a certain way, they act as human GPS systems. Their strong visualization skills help them see things in ways other people do not. If this ability is real, then maybe Sire should ask them for directions instead of them asking it for directions.

In psychological terms, clairvoyance is the ability to know certain information that others do not know. This information comes from extrasensory perceptions, not from any normal channel of reasoning. According to some in the paranormal community, this ability is rich in people who experienced or suffered tragic events.

Meditation

Find a comfortable place to meditate. Somewhere you can be calm, quiet, and undisturbed for the duration of this soothing guided meditation process.

The most comfortable position, and the one which is most helpful for some of the visualization exercises included in this process, is to sit in a chair with your feet planted firmly on the floor, your hands inactive casually in your lap. If this position isn't possible for you, simply get yourself into the position that's most ideal for remaining awake and alert, whilst also becoming pleasantly relaxed.

Close your eyes, relax, breathe normally, and let yourself become soft, calm, and centered.

Openhanded you while and space to focus on yourself and your spiritual development processes is one of the most pleasing things you can do for maintaining calm and balance in other areas of your life. So, try to be fully present during this process and prioritize it among all your other activities, so that you can reap those benefits and improve your psychic abilities at the same time.

So, with your eyes closed and your breathing nice and relaxed, easy and natural, begin to open up your perception, to allow divine loving light, to connect with your energy field and lovingly begin to open you up, to prepare for your psychic, intuitive or healing work. Begin by visualizing, sensing, or feeling a beautiful divine white or golden light pouring in through your crown chakra, and bringing with it a feeling of pure, peace, a feeling of complete and total, expansive, comforting, reassuring, all-embracing, soothing, heart-opening unconditional love.

That's right, just relaxing into its soft and loving embrace, as it lovingly enfolds you, and makes you want to release all the heavy burdens of life, and simply accept that you belong right here, right now, enjoying this precious divine embrace.

See, sense, feel or imagine this light streaming in through the top of your head and filling each chakra. Overflowing as it fills you up, and cleansing and clearing from each of your chakras, anything of a lower or toxic nature, as it travels down through, the entire chakra system and comes cascading down around your body, clearing your aura and each one of your energy bodies.

Feel this cleansing, clearing, healing, loving light filling up your third eye and cleansing from it anything that prevents you from seeing the true nature of all things. As this brilliant, bright divine light travels into this sacred space within you, you may see a flash of light, or feel a slight throbbing sensation between your physical eyes.

There's no need to be concerned about these things. You can simply relax and allow this divine healing light to take you deeper and deeper into relaxation, trusting and knowing that you are safe and protected and that all is well.

Feel this loving light curling and swirling around inside your head, clearing away any thoughts, impressions, or trapped energies that do not serve your highest good or your purpose at this time.

Let it drop down into your throat chakra, and, at the same time, feel it filling the surrounding spaces, cleansing and clearing your aura, your personal space, the room you're sitting in, and all your belongings, bringing everything within and around you into perfect harmony and resonance with the highest sources of love and light within the universe.

As it falls into your throat, simply allow it to clear from this area anything that is not in alignment with your peak virtuous, anything that prevents you from expressing yourself fully. Sense it curling and swirling around inside your throat, removing from it anything that is not in arrangement with celestial love, light, and truth.

As it falls into your heart, feel this beautiful, shimmering, golden and white light, this powerful divine light, building, and swelling, as you simply allow it to clear from this area anything that is not in arrangement with your highest good, anything that prevents you from loving fully, deeply and unconditionally, anything that prevents you from seeing yourself as a beloved being of light.

Sense it curling and swirling around inside your heart, removing from your heart chakra anything that is not in alignment with divine love, divine peace.

As it falls into your solar plexus, allow it to clear from this area anything that is not in association with your highest truth, anything that prevents you from knowing how powerful you are, anything that prevents you from feeling a sense of peace, personal power, freedom, and autonomy. Sense it curling and swirling around inside your solar plexus, gently removing from it anything that compromises your personal truth and sovereignty.

Breathe deeply and inhale deeply into your body, a divine breath filled with this powerful cleansing light. Feel its sparkling iridescence, lighting you up from inside, taking away all that keeps you from knowing that you are a blessed and beloved divine being.

And as it drops even lower, all the way down into your sacral chakra, allow it to clear from this area anything that is not in alignment with your highest vision for your life, anything that interferes with your sacred manifesting power and your ability to create the life that was always your true destiny.

Feel the energy building within you, as it falls into your root chakra and begins to clear from this area anything that is not in alignment with your highest good, or anything that stops you, blocks you, or prevents you from creating an empowered life of peace, stability, security, safety, and abundance.

Sense it curling and swirling around inside your root chakra, removing from it anything that prevents you from moving forward in life, knowing that you are divine love, divine light, and divine truth.

Feel this light all around you now, cleansing, healing, building, and strengthening your own personal energy field, and connecting you powerfully with All That Is. Feel it traveling all the way down through your legs now, and into your feet, as well as through the root chakra, traveling deep into the crystalline center of the new Earth, anchoring you there fully and firmly. Simply set your intention that these roots will travel down into the highest and most divine center of the template for the ascending new earth, and when they get there, you can begin to visualize, see, sense, or simply imagine, a beautiful world, full of light, filled with ancient trees, sparkling waterfalls, rivers, and lakes, teeming with flowers of exquisitely vibrant colors and shades, a secret crystalline paradise, at the heart center of mother Gaia.

Once you are able to see this place, imagine the roots of light which have traveled here from the soles of your feet and your root chakra, connecting with the roots of a beautiful, ancient, sacred tree, and feel the ancient and sacred love from this beautiful, wise forest being, returning to you through this connection.

Immerse yourself fully into this step of the preparation process. Notice how you feel and what has changed or shifted in your energy field. Do you feel less spacey, more peaceful? More connected to life and to yourself? How does it feel to have this much energy moving through your body? How does it feel to be this grounded and connected to the earth and to your body?

Give yourself time to enjoy processing. Indulge yourself with this time, space, and the opportunity to connect with more of who you are and discover more of who you can become.

And as you sit there, simply breathing easily and naturally, you might begin to visualize a beautiful, thick, deep electric blue cloak all around you. You might see it being placed around your shoulders by Archangel Michael, or you might simply sense or even just trust that this is happening. Don't worry if you don't believe your visualizing ability is very strong; you can still sense and feel changes in your energy field if you simply sit quietly with these intentions in mind while listening to this recording.

Notice whether you feel anything changing, as this beautiful, heavy, protective, velvety cloak is carefully zipped all the way up to your chin, and its hood is gently placed over your head, covering your third eye. Feel Archangel Michael lovingly zipping up your cloak, even sealing it under your feet, giving your body one hundred percent, complete and total protection from all unwanted energies.

Once again, immerse yourself fully and totally into this step of the preparation process. Notice how you feel and what has changed or shifted in your energetic field. Do you feel safer, warmer, or more peaceful? More connected to yourself or to spirit? If this process feels good to you, this may be a good time to make a mental note to give yourself time and space to practice it daily, whether you intend to do any psychic work or not.

Give yourself time to enjoy this feeling of safety and protection. Indulge yourself with the time, space, and opportunity you now have, to feel safe and to know how it feels to connect with your feelings and think your own thoughts, without feeling, sensing, or hearing telepathically, the thoughts, feelings questions, or agendas of others. Breathe, relax, and release all tensions and worries. You're safe to relax now and feel a peace you might never have experienced before.

Moving on to the next stage of the process, you may now see, sense, feel, or imagine a large golden pyramid or dome, carried from heaven by beautiful divine angels of love and light. See this magnificent structure slowly descending over the entire room you're sitting in. Observing, as each of its four corners touches the corners of the room, and it slowly lands on the ground, covering a much wider area around you.

A thick, plush carpet of gold is carefully and lovingly rolled out under your feet, sealing you into this safe and sacred space and causing you to be one hundred percent, completely and totally protected and shielded from anything within the general environment that is not for your highest good or does not support you in your higher purpose at this time.

You might like to see this structure inscribed with protective, sacred symbols. As you develop a stronger bond with your guide, you can ask him/her to provide you with the most appropriate structure and symbols.

Take your time, once again, to wait until you see sense or feel these structures taking shape all around you. Then take time to notice the energetic impact their presence has on you.

Sit quietly; drinking in the soft and sacred atmosphere within this protective sanctuary you are building. Breathe. Relax and enjoy the new feelings you're feeling within this sanctuary of safety and protection.

And as you sit there, basking in the precious divinely loving frequencies all around you, you can silently ask Archangel Michael to send his army of loving, protective angels to surround your home and keep it safe and protected as you work.

Spirit Guide Communication

Creating a Spiritual Practice

"Leave your ego at the door and the rest will be opened to you."—Carolyn.

Morning Meditation & Ritual

It is important to establish a spiritual routine, but it is also important to be spiritual throughout your day without it seeming like a chore. It should come naturally and eventually will over time. As witches and psychics, we need to be prepared, protected, and shine as bright as the sun to overflow our positive energy into the world around us. It is our job to keep ourselves in balance this way.

Now we need to put it into practice. Easier said than done, I know. But, having a daily spiritual practice can literally change how your day unfolds. It can create a shield of protection from not only the unseen world but the physical world as well. It also keeps you in tune with the God and Goddess and your higher self's wisdom, not the Ego. If you want to open up your psychic abilities, this is what is needed.

It's empowering to know that you can go out into the world each day with your higher knowledge to lead and guide you. Like a spiritual tuning fork, we do these practices to be in tune with ourselves, our world, and the higher realms.

When we are in tune with those vibrations, we are limitless and can access all the best of our higher self's qualities. We can access the knowledge of the spirit realms, whose psychic messages and wisdom guide us when we are at odds about our choices or what we should do.

I have created an outline that we will be studying for these spiritual practices; including both morning and evening meditations so that you can begin to integrate them into your everyday life. This is only an outline and you should create your own routine that best fits your spiritual needs. As time goes on, your own psychic self will guide you on what will work best.

Morning meditation:

1.   Cleansing the physical body.

2.   Center & Anchor your spirit.

3.   Opening prayer to the God and Goddess.

4.   Surrounding yourself with Angels, your Guides, and loved

ones.

5. Balance the chakras and expand the aura.

6. Prayer for self.

7. Meditate.

8. Journaling.

9. Closing prayer of thanks.

Upon waking, think of the new day as a clean slate; a fresh start. Every day is a gift and we should show gratitude for that. Wake up smiling and think only good thoughts; gratitude for the breath in your lungs, for your eyes, which can see the sunrise, for the ones you love and who love you, knowing that they are safe and happy. Think of this while you are going through your morning routine. When you take a shower, imagine yourself being bathed in white light, a light so beautiful; that nothing negative can reside there.

Once you are cleansed, dress in something breathable and comfortable. You want to be in a state of relaxation. I like to make a cup of herbal cleansing tea before meditating so that it warms me inside; this relaxes me more, but that is up to you. If you meditate outside, you can easily get a small box to hold your meditation tools, whether they are candles, gemstones, incense, or statuary.

I have a travel altar that I use, where everything I need is in a small wooden box and I use the actual box as a mini altar, placing its contents on top. You don't necessarily need those things to help you in meditation, but if it aids in the process, that is fine. If you are meditating inside, simply sit in front of the altar and get into a relaxed position.

Now, you must center and anchor your spirit. This is a feeling within, so as you close your eyes you can feel the energy click within the center of your chest. It's as if your heart opens up to receive the Universal energy and you are preparing yourself to take it in.

You have come here intending to honor the God and Goddess and your spirit. Feel that loving energy in this relaxed state. Take a few deep cleansing breaths and once you feel rooted and ready, light your candle and incense, and then say your opening prayer. This can be anything you wish. For example:

"In honor of the God and Goddess and honor of my spirit, I lovingly ask that they surround me with their loving light, energy, and love. May they guide me this day in wisdom, grace, and honor, with the ability to see the world through their eyes? I thank them for my life and for this day."

This is only an example, depending on our life situation; you can change this to serve your purpose. Just remember that the idea here is to honor them, you, and the new day before you. Invite them to connect with your spirit and acknowledge their presence. Once this is done, we now want to call on our Angels, Spirit Guides, and any loved ones who have crossed over:

"I lovingly call upon the Arch Angels, my Guardian Angels, my Spirit Guides, and my loved ones on the Other Side. Please surround me, protect me, guide me, and open my heart to your divine wisdom and love. I love you and thank you all for your unending support from Home."

In doing this, you are creating an arsenal of assistance that will help you throughout the day. Good or bad, they will be there to protect and guide you. While they are always there regardless, this is a way of acknowledging and thanking them for their loving service. We want to show appreciation for their guidance and loyalty in loving us unconditionally.

At this moment, you should be feeling at peace and in a state of grace. You should be feeling the vibration of the higher realms flowing within and without you. Take a moment to breathe in and out slowly, enjoy this, and smile, feeling relaxed, and at peace now.

Sometimes, I will imagine that when I breathe in, a white light enters through my nose or mouth and when I exhale, any negativity I may have will flow out in a black smoke until it fades to white. That is another powerful way to cleanse.

Balance the Chakras & Expand the Aura

In this state, you are ready to visualize and balance the chakras and then expand the aura. Remember what I had said about sensing energy with your dominant hand. Using your dominant hand and without touching your body, take your hand and hover it in front of the root chakra, which is located at the base of your spine and groin area.

Wait to feel the energy, and in your mind, visualize the root chakra as the color red, spinning in perfect harmony and brightly lit. When the energy between your hand and the root chakra pulsates, you can move to the sacral chakra.

Again, with your hand placed over the sacral chakra, visualize the color as being a bright orange ball, letting the energy pulsate. If you have trouble visualizing this, think of things in nature, like the color of the sun before it sets. As time goes on, with practice, you will find that this sequence will go quickly. That your chakras will instantly exchange energy between themselves and your dominant hand, or even ignite immediately on their own.

Continue to do this with every chakra; root, sacral, solar plexus, heart, throat, third eye, and finally, the crown. When you reach the crown, you will literally feel the top of your head open up to the Universal energy. Imagine this energy flowing from the source like a bright white beam of light, pouring into your crown chakra and enveloping your body, both physical and etheric. This will feel almost electrical, so much so that you may twitch a bit from receiving this energy from them.

When the crown chakra opens, you are in such an elevated state that the energy coming in can almost feel like having an intense orgasm. Truly, it is the only way I can describe the feeling. I have had several meditations where, once the chakras are aligned and I open my crown chakra to receive this Universal energy—it had brought me to tears. Everyone experiences it differently. If that doesn't motivate you to meditate, I don't know what will!

In your mind's eye, keep focused on this light that is now surrounding you, because we are going to use this to expand the aura at the same time. As this light is pouring down into and over your body, imagine it enveloping and surrounding you. You can see this light as white, gold or whatever you prefer.

I use white at first and then when I begin to expand it around myself; I envision another layer of purple light and then another layer of gold surrounding the whole. Layering myself in spiritual light and then expanding it from my physical body makes me feel protected and allows me to be able to sense psychically and touch those around me with that light.

This, in turn, affects their energy with my own, but in a good way. When you are done with this and feel elated, then you can seal it with a closing prayer or affirmation such as:

"My chakras are balanced, whole, and in unison with my higher self and that of the God and Goddess. With my aura expanded, I lovingly ask that it protects me and also touch those who come within my sacred space, blessing them with my loving energy, light, and love."

Once this is done, we can take this opportunity to pray for ourselves and others. If there is something that concerns you, if there is something you wish to have insight into, or if you want assistance with something for yourself or others, now is the time to say a prayer and request it.

Since we will be going into meditation soon, you will find that saying this request of prayer will bring the answers you seek through psychic channels. For me, and I think it could be because I am an artist, I see very strong visually.

There is no place, no location, nor any time in history or in my life— past and present, that I cannot visit and see within my mind while being there fully in spirit. I know that a lot of spiritual people use meditation to quiet the mind and the ego, but I find that I receive the most unbelievable insights into myself, my life, and the lives of those around me when I allow information to flow.

Psychic Abilities Guide

Information will come that is so amazing, that oftentimes I cannot believe how lucky I am to be able to access it. Your meditations are your own, and what you choose to get out of them is up to you. Whether it is to cleanse yourself, your mind, your spirit, or a way to access psychic information and to get the answers that you seek, it is always about connecting with the higher self and the divine.

Psychometric

The next psychic ability to explore is psychometric. This is the ability to ascertain specific information about an object just by holding it. In other words, someone with psychometric skills can hold a coin or piece of paper currency and see where that coin or banknote has been in the past. Needless to say, this ability is not restricted to money; instead, it can be performed with any item at all, including objects of clothing, pieces of furniture, and even houses or other buildings in general. The basic premise behind this ability is that an item absorbs a certain amount of energy from every person and event that it encounters, much like a thumbprint. Therefore, it has a memory of that person or event, and someone with psychometric abilities can tap into that memory, thereby catching a glimpse of the past, albeit recent or far back into ancient history. This subdivision will converse the specifics of psychometric, including its uses, whether it is the right psychic ability for you, and ways to harness and strengthen any psychometric abilities you might have.

Psychic Abilities Guide

What Is Psychometric?

The word psychometric is Ancient Greek and roughly translates as "soul measure." This definition can have two different meanings. On the one hand, the "psych" portion of the word can refer to the fact that psychometric is a psychic gift, one that is performed with your inner senses as opposed to your five physical senses. However, it can also indicate that what you are measuring is the energy of the object itself. This, in essence, suggests that you are tapping into the very soul of a particular object or place, much like telepathy is tapping into the mind of another person. Whether you believe that objects have souls or they simply accumulate residual energy is of little consequence. The bottom line is that a person with psychometric abilities can read the energy an object contains.

Again, a decent way to imagine this is to imagine that every person that touches an object leaves a small amount of their energy on that object, much like they leave behind their fingerprints when touching that object. And, just as fingerprints can be used to identify a person, so too can the residual energy left behind on an object. This is mainly true in the circumstance of an object that is used by the same person regularly. Something like a hairbrush, wallet, or pair of glasses can contain a huge amount of residual energy from a single individual, making it easy for someone with psychometric skills to get a clear image of who that person is/was. Furthermore, items associated with specific events, such as sporting equipment or military equipment, can possess the energy of an event, allowing a psychometric expert to see a touchdown being scored just by holding the game's winning ball.

Perhaps a better way to imagine it is to think of the residual energy as a snapshot, a single image reflecting where that object has been.

Someone with psychometric skills can literally read the images contained in an object, thereby seeing the history of the object. This is where most things can get a bit dangerous, though. For example, weapons such as bayonets or swords may contain the image of the brutal slaying of an enemy combatant. Likewise, buildings such as hospitals or prisons may contain residual energy of a negative nature, making for bad reading when it comes to the images presented. Therefore, it is always vital to choose the objects you will read with great care as the images they contain can be anything at all—from the most wonderful to the most horrifying. Additionally, it is commonly accepted that the more intense a situation is, the more energy that situation creates. Therefore, items may have clearer images of more negative events, as those are usually the ones that create the most intense energy. This makes it all the more chief to choose the objects you read with great care.

How You Can Tell If Psychometric Is Right for You

When it comes to determining whether you have psychometric skills, this too can be an exercise fairly negative in nature. The reason for this is that most of the telltale signs of psychometric abilities are stressful and unpleasant, often causing a person great distress. One such example is if you feel overwhelmed or oppressed whenever you are in an antique store. While many people can spend hours looking at all the wonderful and mysterious relics from the past, anyone with psychometric abilities will tend to become depressed and even anxious in such a place. This is because all the residual energy in the objects present will overwhelm their senses, much like hundreds of radios being turned on at once. Therefore, if you feel uncomfortable whenever you are around old items, especially in the case of being in an antique store or a thrift shop, then you are probably a good fit for psychometric.

Another way to know if you possess psychometric skills is if you feel heavy or sad in older buildings. Again, places such as hospitals, prisons, or any other place where the energy would be highly negative will doubtlessly have an impact on almost any psychic, even those without inherent psychometric talents or skills. However, if ordinary places such as old houses, railway stations, or even old buildings turned into restaurants cause you depression, fatigue, or even anxiety, and then you are probably someone with natural psychometric abilities. Not being comfortable in second-hand clothing, using old furniture, and other such issues with anything that has been used before is almost always a clear sign of psychometric abilities.

The feelings you get from old places, or old objects, don't always have to be negative, however, to indicate psychometric skills. This originates down to the meek fact that empathy is at the heart of psychometric. Thus, when an empath can control the flow of information coming in, they can avoid the negative impact of such places as antique stores and the like. This is because they don't become overwhelmed by the energy surrounding them. As a result, rather than becoming stressed or fatigued, they can simply feel the energy around them, much like hearing the ambient sound of numerous conversations in a restaurant. Therefore, if old places feel different to you, or old objects have a quality that sets them apart from new ones, psychometric is probably right for you.

Real-Life Applications of Psychometric

As with any other psychic ability, psychometric can have some very useful real-life applications. That said, those applications will be far fewer than the ones associated with talent, such as telepathy, where real-time information can be obtained, helping a person make the best decisions and choices every time. Nevertheless, psychometric can prove more useful than a mere talking point at parties. One way that psychometric can be put to use is in the area of antiques themselves. Forgeries and fakes are commonplace in the antique market, providing a lucrative business for those who can pass off such fakes to would-be buyers. However, a person with psychometric abilities will be able to tell the difference between a real antique and a fake just by the energy signature of the item. No matter how old an object looks, if it is relatively new, it will lack the depth of energy that a true antique possesses. Even the most novice practitioner of psychometric can tell a new item from an old item just by plotting it for a few seconds.

Another application, perhaps one more likely to occur in day-to-day life, is in the area of identifying the owner of lost objects. While a lost purse or wallet will usually contain a photo ID of the owner, things like keys, a phone, or a jacket won't. This means it can be all but impossible to know whom to look for if you spot a set of keys laying on a picnic table or chair in a restaurant. However, if you have psychometric abilities, you will hold that item for a moment and catch a sight of the person it belongs to. At the very least, you will know if it is a man or a woman, someone old or young, and hopefully, you will even be able to see the color of their hair. This can make all the difference when searching the nearby crowd to see whom the keys might belong to. Needless to say, when you see someone matching the image in your mind looking around as though they lost something, you can be sure they will appreciate you returning their keys or phone to them.

Psychic Abilities Guide

Equally as important as knowing how psychometric can be used in real life, so too, you must know its limitations. Unfortunately, television and movies often depict psychometric in a very unreal and irrational way. This is particularly true in any situation where a telepath holds a murder weapon in order to identify the murderer. There are several things wrong with this depiction, not least of which is the fact that no law enforcement agency would ever base an investigation on such a tip. Furthermore, this idea significantly underestimates the impact of the images that a telepath can see from an item. Not only would the images of a murder weapon be devastating to your heart and mind, but the energy itself, full of horror and pain, would be immeasurably traumatizing. Therefore, no sane person would ever willingly use their psychometric skills in conjunction with a murder weapon, a torture device, or any other object knowingly used to create pain and suffering in another living being.

How to Develop Your Psychometric Skills

As with any skill or talent, the best way to improve your psychometric skills is with practice, practice, and even more practice. Fortunately, the process for conducting a psychometric reading is very straightforward, requiring only five steps to accomplish. This means that you can practice virtually anytime, anywhere, and as often as you like. The following are the basic steps of a psychometric reading:

• Step one: Wash and dry your hands thoroughly before handling an object. This will remove any dirt that might interfere with the reading, as well as any residual energy left from handling a preceding object. If you can't wash your hands, simply wipe with them a few times on your pants leg, just enough to brush off any surface residue.

• Step two: Rub your hands together vigorously for about ten seconds. This will generate energy in your palms and fingertips. The more energy you have in your hands, the easier it will be to absorb energy from the object. A good way to know if you are ready is to hold your hands together after rubbing, slowly separating them to about a quarter of an inch apart. If you can feel a tingling sensation or a resistance to pulling them apart, you know you have generated the energy you need. If you don't feel anything, rub them for another ten seconds and try again.

• Step three: Pick up an object and hold it in your hands. If you are a beginner, it is recommended that you start with an object that would have been used daily, such as glasses, a hairbrush, or a set of keys. Not knowing the owner can also be useful, as it will prevent your mind from conjuring up memories of the person, such as a friend or a loved one. This will ensure that any images you see are the result of the object and not your memory or imagination.

Flower and Random Visualization

No Self-Pity

Empaths are extremely wonderful, but they lack self-awareness and have low levels of self-worth. Stop wallowing in self-pity and take steps to improve your self-confidence and self-worth. If left unchecked, an empathy's need to be loved can create a victim mentality. Your empathy is not a weakness; it is your strength. It's the key to unlocking your true purpose in life. Most empaths are often overwhelmed because of their empathy, and it creates a variety of mental, physical, and spiritual imbalances. These imbalances make it easier for the empath to develop a victim mentality. Stop victimizing yourself and, instead, concentrate on the positive aspects of your life. Think about all the different instances when your empathy helped you. Whether it is your sense of intuition or imagination, it might have helped you at some point or another. Once you concentrate on the good things that empathy brings into your life, your self-worth will increase. Once you have a higher level of self-worth, you will feel stronger and more confident in yourself. You might be stuck feeling pathetic, but stop making excuses for your behavior by victimizing yourself.

Listen to what people are saying to you. If someone is making a positive statement, then respond with some positive affirmation. If you don't say anything, it will create the opportunity for that person to make negative comments about your empathic nature. Always focus on the good things that people have said about you and your empathy skills. In a matter of seconds, you will take a positive approach to your life and increase your level of self-worth. Just listen, look, and respond accordingly.

Look After Your Mental and Physical Health

Your empathy levels can cause many physical imbalances in the body. If your energy fields are out of balance, then you will feel tired or drained often. You might find that you are not able to focus on one thing for too long without feeling exhausted. It is important to learn how to take care of yourself physically so that you can maintain your energy levels throughout the day. Take a nap or go for a walk when you need to recharge your batteries before facing more challenges in life. It is also important to learn how to eat properly, drink plenty of water, and get enough rest. You should also find a doctor who can help you with any physical imbalances that you are experiencing at home.

Learn How to Achieve Empathy Goals

By learning how to achieve empathy goals, you will have a much better chance of progressing in life. The finest method to do this is through visualization techniques and imagination exercises. Spend some time each day finding a way to visualize reaching your goals for the day. Visualize yourself achieving your desired outcome as many times as possible. Eventually, these visualization exercises will help you reach your goals by creating an energy field that allows you to accomplish the object in question. You will learn how to achieve great things by visualizing them in your mind and feeling as if you are achieving them all in real life.

Reach Out to People with Trust

Empathy is an extremely powerful tool that allows you to feel what others are feeling. If you can't trust the surrounding people, then social interactions will be limited at best and dangerous at worst. Try not to make friends with people who may betray your trust or manipulate your emotions. Instead, find quiet time every day where you can just sit down and talk with a friend or family member.

Psychic Abilities Guide

Eliminate Negative Things

Shielding means protecting you against negative, harsh, and lower energies. It is a way to make sure that your energy remains clean and high, especially when you're working in or traveling through a harsh environment. Below are some of the most effective ways to shield your energy:

Crystals and Gemstones

Crystals are powerful stones, rocks, and minerals that can protect, magnify, and transmute various energies. Holding, wearing, sleeping, or working near these protective gemstones help repel negative energy and enhance positivity. Some of the most effective shielding crystals are the following:

Amethyst

Psychic Abilities Guide

This beautiful purple gemstone is excellent for protection and purification. It enhances intuition, helps release addictions, improves spiritual awareness, and lifts the energy in you and around you. At the same time, it wards off negative energy –both ethereal and spiritual. Having this crystal around will greatly help you in coping with your empathic abilities.

Blue Topaz

This crystal will help you think clearly and ease the tension brought about by your work, social, or love life. It will also help you communicate your thoughts, desires, and pleas to the universe and see the bigger picture.

Black Tourmaline

This powerful protection gemstone is particularly helpful for empathic healers. It fends off all negative energy, including those that are being purposefully directed at an individual and general negative energy coming from the world around you.

Green Aventurine

This crystal possesses great vitality, making it an excellent healing stone for any situation related to health, friends, finances, growth, confidence, and everything else. This is an important stone to have in an empathy's arsenal.

Obsidian

Wearing this gorgeous black gemstone will help you ground yourself. It deflects anger, psychic attacks, and negativity.

Citrine

This stone represents happiness and creativity. If you're feeling down or stuck in a creative block, this lovely yellow stone can definitely help you. It gives a powerful boost for all things related to finances, abundance, and prosperity. It also manifests radiant energy, which pushes away negativity and attracts positive vibes.

Lepidolite

Lepidolite enhances the power of other nearby stones and crystals and relieves anxieties that commonly plague empaths. This stone is well-known for its peace, power, and ability to foster love, luck, and sleep.

Malachite

Malachite is perfect if you want to eliminate emotional blockages and pressures that may occur when dealing with stressful situations. This gemstone has a great tendency to absorb negative emotions you may be keeping inside.

Rose Quartz

The energy of this pale pink crystal is really gentle, calm, and compassionate. It provides a feeling of genuine, unconditional love, and protects you in romantic relationships. It also heals and soothes the heart chakra, and pushes away all the negative feelings around you.

Clear Quartz

This stone is highly versatile and can act as a powerful amplifier of any frequency, including the natural electromagnetic frequency (EMF) in the human body. This clear crystal can refract sunlight into rainbows and deflect negative energy and vibrations.

Smoky Quartz

This crystal releases negativity from your past relationships. Place it close to your bed and let it do its job while you sleep. You will wake feeling lighter and with a more positive outlook.

Lapis Lazuli

This stunning bluestone is another excellent protector, but its influence is more inclined to spiritual growth. It helps you maintain an objective attitude and take others' actions lightly and not too personal. This stone helps keep your energy unbound and your mind clear of muddled thoughts, great for use in the office or other workplaces.

Jade

This is a popular crystal amongst lovers, but is great for empaths, too. Jade helps balance the opposing energies of romantic partners and prevents them from inflicting harm on themselves and others during spats and quarrels.

Turquoise

Turquoise drives negative energy out of your space and creates a stronger, more resilient bond between your physical body and the energy field. Even a small piece of this stone can go a long way, filling an entire home with positive vibrations and soothing energy. Many people consider turquoise as the ultimate anti-negativity gemstone.

Unakite

Although not as popular as the other stones, Unakite can be a great inclusion in your arsenal. This crystal helps balance your emotions and bring your spirit close to the other side so that you can stay connected to late loved ones who may be checking on you every once in a while.

Zoisite

Zoisite is another uncommon yet valuable crystal. It is perfect for artistic empaths because it promotes creativity, individuality, and connectedness to other people. Many artistic empaths are introverted and tend to shut everybody out. This stone reminds the spirit that human contact is not only important but can also be fun.

Fossils

While not exactly a crystal or gemstone, fossils are also important to an empathy's well-being. Fossils will keep you strong and grounded, and constantly remind you that energy is fluid and everything will change inevitably.

Picking the Perfect Crystals

After deciding on what crystals you need, you will then have to pick out the right ones. Certain stones work better for some, but not as well for others. Follow these three steps to find the perfect crystals for you.

1.   Set your intention. Before you begin the process of finding the perfect gemstone or crystal, you must first set an intention. Speak inside yourself or aloud about what crystal you're hoping to find. Example: "Amethyst, thank you for becoming my new crystal. Please show yourself to me."

2.   Follow your senses. As empaths, we have strong intuitive senses and physical senses. Intuitive senses include claircognizance (clear knowing), clairgustance (clear tasting), clairalience (clear smelling), clairsentience (clear feeling), clairaudience (clear hearing), and clairvoyance (clear seeing). Turn on all of these senses when picking your perfect gemstone.

3.   Wait for a feeling. There are times when a gemstone or crystal just stands out among the others. If you come across a stone, which keeps grabbing your attention, then that might be the one for you. Also, some crystals vibrate or emit a certain kind of energy when handled by the right person. Wait for that feeling.

Angelic Shielding

You can appeal to the protector Archangel Michael to protect you with his royal purple and royal blue light. Say this either silently or aloud, "Archangel Michael, please shield me with your protective light now." This archangel is limitless, so can instantly protect anyone who calls on him.

You can also call upon God and ask Him to send additional guardian angels to look after you, your home, your loved ones, your friends, or any other important person, thing, or place. Angels are infinite, and all you need to do is ask and more will come for you.

Clearing

Clearing your energy is as important as shielding it. Whenever you get confused, feel exhausted, or become prone to accidents, take a break to clear your energy. Most of the time, these are signs that you have absorbed too much negativity.

Like shielding, there are different ways to clear you, and this also includes calling upon Archangel Michael. You can say: "Archangel Michael, I ask of you to clear away all the energies within and around me that aren't of God's light and love." The archangel instantly comes to the aid of everyone who calls on him, for he loves all of us and can help everyone at once.

Another fine way to clear your energy is to take a warm bath enhanced by Epsom salts (sea salts are fine) and essential oils. You can further improve it by adding pure flower essences to your bathwater and surrounding your tub with white candles. The candles will serve as focal points for your genuine intention of clearing yourself.

Massage and similar bodyworks also have excellent clearing abilities, especially if your massage therapist is skilled in relieving physical tension and energy.

Detoxing and tweaking your diet is another effective way to dispel energetic and physical toxins. You can work with juices, supplements, or herbs that flush out contaminants and heavy metals attached to the energy toxins in your system. Consult a naturopath or a trained staff at your local supplements store to get the best recommendations.

Psychic Abilities Guide

Grounding

Grounding means your consciousness is contained inside your body instead of floating freely above it. Many empaths leave their physical bodies when the earth plane becomes too much to handle. They "go home" inside their consciousness and you can say they are not really "here." It is okay to do this during meditation or dream time, but during your waking hours, remember the reasons you are in your physical body.

Besides wearing obsidian crystal to help you ground yourself, eat organic, non-GMO vegetables such as turnips, onions, carrots, potatoes, and radishes. You can also get a foot rub or visualize yourself as a tree, with roots growing out of your feet. Feel the earth's energy connect with the bottom of your feet.

Another way to ground you is to connect physically with nature. Take your shoes off and touch the soil, sand, grass, or water. This will help you shift your focus back to your physical reality.

Trust in Yourself

Trust Your Gut

Empaths have a strong sense of intuition because of their highly sensitive nature. You can understand what others feel or experience without needing verbal cues. You can see beyond this and know their true intentions. Any psychic images you receive, any signals you get from them, their energy vibrations, or the little voice in your head, listen to them. This is your empathy at play. If your gut says something is wrong, go with it. Chances are your gut is right. Have there been occurrences in your life when you made a decision, even when all logic defied it? Did a little voice tell you what to do? What were the outcomes in such instances? Were the outcomes positive and helpful? If you think about these examples, you will understand it was your intuition guiding the way. If your gut says you somewhat are wrong, something certainly is amiss. Work on improving your intuition and trust your gut. The more you trust your instincts, the more fine-tuned your intuition becomes. It also helps you stay away from toxic individuals and instead create healthy and positive relationships.

Establish Boundaries

This book repeatedly mentions that empaths need to establish personal boundaries. By now, you are perhaps aware that dissimilar people have different effects on you. Some individuals make you feel instantly happy while others drain you of all energy. Start considering how you feel in certain situations and around people. If something feels off, something is definitely off about the situation.

Use your intuition to set limits and personal boundaries. The establishing of boundaries is a sign of self-esteem and self-respect. It lets you know the extent to which you can push yourself and when to stop. It also teaches others what is and is not acceptable to them. Don't just implement the boundaries, but also ensure there are consequences if the boundaries are violated. If you feel rough in a situation, it is a sign that one of your boundaries is compromised. With practice and conscious effort, you will finally understand when you are supposed to walk away for good and restore your empathy. It also helps you say "no" in the right situations and reduces stress. In turn, it gives you more time to concentrate on the activities you love and enjoy.

No Negative Energy

As an empath, you are an expressive exfoliator. You do not discriminate the energy you absorb from others. It can be positive, negative, or anything in between. Whatever it is, you pick it up and carry it with you as with your energy. You need to stop doing this if you want to grow as an empath. Remember, there is only so much you can give to others without compromising yourself. It is not your accountability or duty to fix everyone's problems. Help whenever possible, but that is about it. Don't take these energies or negative emotions on as if they are yours, and stop carrying this emotional baggage with you. All this increases any anxiety you feel and will worsen your overall mood. The first responsibility you have in life is toward yourself.

There are dissimilar methods you can use to get rid of negative analogies in different situations. For instance, place plants at your workspace or home so they absorb negative energies. Similarly, you can use protective crystals such as amethyst or quartz to safeguard your personal energy field from unwanted energies. Another simple practice you can use is to change any negative thinking to positive thoughts. Always maintain a positive attitude in life, and it quickly dispels negativity. Spending time by yourself after a tiring day can also eliminate negative analogies that might be carried unknowingly. Try to look for comicality in every situation and start your day with gratitude. Be thankful for all the good you have in life, and do not wallow in self-pity. If you want to, you can use positive affirmations to improve your quality of life in different aspects.

Healing Power of Breath

Whenever things start getting a little overwhelming for you, take a break from the situation. If you cannot walk away, channel all your energies inward. Concentrate only on yourself and your breathing. By shifting all your focus to your breathing it helps reduce any stress you might be experiencing. It also gives you a well logic of control over the situation. It is easy to get overwhelmed, but it is tricky to regain control of yourself. The good news is you always have this power and choice. Don't let anyone or anything make you feel helpless. There is always a choice provided if you are willing to make it. Learn to breathe consciously and mindfully. Whenever you breathe in, visualize that you are breathing in the healing power of the universe and exhale all negative energy present within and around you. Your breath is an incredibly powerful healing force.

If possible, head outdoors and practice this simple breathing exercise. Whenever you inhale, repeat the mantra, "I am breathing in positivity." When you exhale, repeat the mantra, "I am breathing out negativity and am filled with positivity." Do this implementation for a couple of minutes, and you will soon feel better about yourself? Enchanting a few unfathomable breaths calms you down and expels any negative energy. Once your mind is free of stress and negativity, it becomes easier to think about the situation logically and rationally without getting overly negative.

Self-Love

Your life's purpose is not to take care of others; it is about taking care of yourself. Self-love is quintessential for everyone, and even more so for empaths. You deserve the same empathy you reserve for others. Be compassionate toward yourself, your thoughts, and your emotions. Develop and follow a proper self-care routine and spend time taking care of your needs and requirements. Do not ignore any unprocessed feelings and certainly do not suppress them. Be accepting of yourself to bring about a sense of positivity into your life.

Do not shy away from your emotions and embrace all your

sensitivities. Vulnerability is not a sign of weakness; it is your strength. Accept that you can be strong and vulnerable at the same time without any compromises. Don't forget to congratulate yourself whenever you listen to your intuition and something good comes out of it. Hold on to all the happy memories you have in life and try to amplify them. Don't allow negativity to bring you down. Love yourself unconditionally and always be there for yourself. After all, you are the only one who will be there for you.

Try Read People Mind

Mind reading, along with psychic abilities and powers of intuition, certainly is powerful, but it is actually not a trick. It really is about using all the tools that you must at your removal to the best of your ability and honing them with practice.

When you're trying to read the mind of another person, the first and most important bit of advice I can give is to make sure that, as with everything else in life, you are doing it with a good intention in mind. If you go into something with a nasty motive, you should be aware that others also have strong powers of intuition, and that they can sense when something is off. Don't do it for vindictive reasons or to make someone uncomfortable. Let's always keep that empathy at the front of our minds.

Reading someone's mind isn't as far removed as we might think. Sci-fi and fantasy movies will give us the impression that we can simply gaze into the eyes of another person and know the exact verbalizations of what they are thinking. As cool as that may sound, that isn't how it works, and I'm not sure anyone would really want it to work that way, anyway.

Psychic Abilities Guide

The way to read minds is by asking appropriate questions and listening. It's all about combining all the tools you have in your arsenal; your innate ability to tell if something is off, wrong, or very good, your ability to look at a person's face and body language and be able to tell, nearly instantly, what their mood is or whether they have something on their mind.

Often, the ability to read minds begins in our close relationships. We spend so much time with certain people that we begin to be able to pick up on what certain tics mean, what it means when they start a sentence in a certain way, where their hesitations are, and such things. However, it is never good to do a reading on someone that you are particularly close to. Your results can often be affected by your own emotional interference because you don't want to hear the answers that dear person is actually giving you. You also don't want to hear that you could be wrong about something you may personally have held up as a truth.

Choose someone you are acquainted with to practice on, but again, you don't want it to be someone you know too well. Ask questions and listen. It's like an interview, except in this case, you also need to listen to yourself and what your intuition may be prompting you to respond with. Never start with anything too personal. Just as you would with a date, you want that person to build up a comfort level with you. Start with the things that exist more on the perimeter of their life, and then work your way into the personal things, and therefore, likely more important. If you are stuck for things to ask or for how to begin, you could even begin the session by asking the person what it is that they would like to talk about first. Perhaps something is pressing in their life that they wish to address immediately.

When they answer the questions that you pose to them, always go with your gut feeling. Don't accuse them of being dishonest if you don't like the answer, but perhaps try to steer them to be more open. Never steer or skew their answers to your liking, however. You must remain impartial. After each answer you receive, ask the next question that seems logical to you. Here is where your natural intuition will guide you to the answers they need to know.

Practice Seeing Aura

Many people are left wondering what an aura is and what they mean. This confusion generally stems from a lack of understanding, and with so many ideas about what an aura is, this is understandable. However, like most anything else, all it takes is a little education to make things much clearer. If you know about auras, the next time it is brought up in conversation, you will have some correct information to share. You might also find that a lot of people will be very curious to hear what you have to say. There are people interested in auras and aura reading than you may think. There are still skeptics out there who make some people hesitant to ask questions or seek out information on their own.

On a fundamental level, it is the magnetic field surrounding every living thing that makes up an aura. A person's aura is unique and reflects their own specific liveliness, it is this energy that impacts their ability to attach and cooperate with others. Most people's auras extend about three feet around them, but those who have suffered a tragedy or trauma usually have a larger aura. Much of what we do in our lives leave some type of mark on our aura. That is why experienced readers can tell so much about a person during a reading. Our aura is so intimately connected to both our minds and our bodies that it is difficult to keep secrets from experienced readers. This is why it is good to choose a reader that you think you can trust and that you feel comfortable with.

The study of chakras is an ancient tradition and was often treated more like a visit to a doctor. It was known that the chakras held information about both our mental and physical health, so it would make sense to see someone about chakra alignment if there was an issue. Our auras originate from these chakras and therefore, can also reveal what ails us. Many people believe that getting regular aura readings keeps them healthy because the aura can reflect some diseases or illnesses before more classic symptoms arise, increasing the likelihood of a speedy and full recovery. Knowledgeable aura readers do not even need to meet their subject in person to give a proper reading; they can just do it from a normal photograph. That is how deeply connected we are to our auras; they show up in regular photographs, meaning they must be pretty powerful for that to happen. Auras can always change because they reflect our thoughts and emotions, so while some of the basic traits, both good and bad, remain the same, other aspects of our aura shift along with our moods and circumstances.

An aura is not one single unit laid on a sheet; instead, it is made up of many layers. The aura's layers interconnect and mingle that forms the cohesive body that is known as the aura. Each layer of the aura holds different types of information; these are known as the subtle bodies. The energy created by the chakras is what creates the auras. The size of a person's aura depends on spiritual, emotional, and physical health. These auric layers will contract or increase depending on these facets.

The 7 Layers That Make Up an Aura

The first layer, also called the etheric layer, remains close to the body, generally only extending an inch or two from the body. The etheric field reflects your physical health and is usually different shades of blue. This layer will change shade and radius along with your physical health. This layer originates from the root chakra and it is what makes up the link between your physical and higher bodies.

The second layer that is influenced by emotions generally extends only about one to three inches from the body. This layer holds your emotions and feelings, which we all know change regularly depending on your particular circumstances. Usually, this layer is bright and combines many colors, but negative feelings and emotions can act as a block that can dull or darken the color. The sacral chakra is associated with this layer, which is fitting because it is beneath the heart's location, the figurative source of emotion.

The third layer of the aura is the mental field, and it can spread out from the body anywhere from three to eight inches. The mental layer is generally a shade of yellow, varying from bright to dull. For those sorrow from despair or anxiety, this layer is greatly affected. This layer also relates to the solar plexus chakra.

The quarter layer is the astral coating, which acts as a bridge to the spiritual realm and is connected to the astral plane. This layer extends about a foot from the body and contains all the colors of the rainbow, with the brightness correlating with a person's spiritual health. The astral plane is a part of the multi-dimensional planes that surround us. This plane vibrates on a higher frequency than the physical plane that we live in. The fourth layer is connected with the heart or fourth chakra and is often referred to as the 'layer of love' for this reason. It also joins the higher three and lower three auric layers.

The fifth layer is called the etheric template; it protrudes around two feet from the body. This layer contains a guideline of the entities in the physical world, and because of this it is not usually associated with a specific color. This layer can also create negative space because it does deal with the physical world, but this is not negative, it just means that many colors can be associated with it. The throat or fifth chakra is related to this layer and represents your personality and identity.

The sixth layer is also known as the celestial aura and can protrude up to two and a half feet from the body. This layer is also linked to the spiritual realm and any communication with that realm is reflected in this layer. The celestial aura also mirrors feelings of ecstasy and unconditional love. The colors in this layer appear shimmery and are usually pearly pastels. This layer originates from the third eye or sixth chakra; intuition and perception are the focus here.

The final layer can extend up to three feet from the body and is known as the Ketheric layer. This field contains all the other layers and basically acts as a barrier to hold them together. The Ketheric layer vibrates at the highest frequencies and contains bright gold threads that weave throughout it. This layer reflects the trials and experiences that have made an impact on the soul. The Ketheric layer acts as your own personal connection to the Divine and aids in your journey of being personally connected to the universe. The crown chakra is related to this layer, and it represents our connection with all that exists.

Even though these layers all make up the aura, the first layer is not actually the aura, it is the energy that leads to the creation of the aura. This is also known as the Energosma, and the aura really starts where the Energosma ends, which is why auras can vary in size from person to person and from day to day. As our emotions and thoughts change, so do our auras, since they are a manifestation of our overall health.

One person's aura can also be affected by another person's; this is known as an auric connection and can make communication easier. This happens because the energies from the two people become stronger and take on a greater role in the communication, usually without the people knowing it is even happening. This helps to explain those inexplicable connections we have with some people as if we have known them for years.

When it comes to reading auras, there is no one right way. They all deal with psychic abilities and some people will be more naturally inclined to one or more and may choose to only pursue that which comes easier to them. The ways to read auras include seeing, feeling, and knowing them; they are all similar and even connected in some ways, but all are equally effective. So, when you decide which path to pursue, you might decide to choose the feeling because you are someone who already depends on your sense of intuition. Opting to further develop what is already a natural psychic gift will make the process easier since it is already something you have used and at least somewhat developed, even if you are not consciously aware of doing so.

Just like the human body, auras are complex. They are direct reflections of how we feel at any given time. Even if we are not aware of it, our auras can show those capable of reading them how we are feeling about our lives and how our past experiences have impacted us. As we grow and evolve, so will our aura, since it is basically a mirror of what we are feeling on the inside. This means that if you want a brighter aura, there are things you can do to make that happen.

Intuition

When it comes to developing intuition, the number one thing that would be debated would be the third eye. The third eye is the seat of intuition. It is the key to the power of clairvoyance, also known as clear seeing. The third eye, or Ajna chakra, is probably the most common chakra that many people are familiar with. It is what will allow you to see into the world of spirits. Remember that the exact location of the third eye is right between your eyebrows.

The good news is that everyone has a third eye. It is just a matter of developing it, and this is something that you can do. Once you develop your third eye, you will have powerful intuition, and you will even be able to access the Akashic records. It will depend on how you make use of it. Another interesting reason to develop the third eye is to be able to see prana more clearly. Many things can be associated with the third eye, but the most common of all is intuition.

Psychic Abilities Guide

Every person has some level of intuition. For example, have you experienced simply knowing who is calling your phone, even without looking at it? This is a classic example of the use of intuition. Of course, there are many other practical uses, such as being able to avoid danger or merely knowing the right course of action to take in a difficult situation. Indeed, developing intuition can be very helpful. Let us now look more into enhancing this natural and psychic ability.

The third eye is also the pineal gland. It is a small endocrine system that regulates the wake-sleep pattern. In spirituality, when you talk about the pineal gland, then you also refer to the third eye.

Activate and Decalcify Your Pineal Gland

The pineal gland or your third eye holds remarkable power. However, only a few people can tap into this power and use it effectively. Many people simply have an underdeveloped third eye. But the virtuous update is that there are exercises that you can do to strengthen your third eye so you can start using and enjoying its immense power. Let us converse them one by one:

Who Is It?

This is to some degree that you can do every time your phone rings or beeps. Simply ask yourself, "Who is it?" Pay attention to what you see in your mind's eye. Do you see any images or impressions? Be open to receiving messages. This is how you can connect to your intuition. You should also realize that you have a strong intuition and that you only have to learn to connect to it. Of course, this method is not limited to calls or texts on your phone. You can also adjust it a bit and use it in other ways. For example, if you hear a knock or any sound at night, you can ask, "What is it?" and pay attention to any messages that you get from your intuition. The important thing is to start connecting to your intuition once again.

Forehead Press

This technique is becoming popular these days. The forehead press, however, does not work on everyone, but it is still worth trying. This will allow you some specks of prana in the air. They usually appear as little dots or any form of white light. The steps are as follows:

Place your index finger in the part amid the eyebrows where the Ajna chakra is. Press it gently and maintain pressure for about 50 seconds. Slowly remove your finger, blink your eyes around five times, and look at a blank wall. Just focus lightly and try to see with your peripheral vision. Do you see little dots or any specks of white light? This is prana in the air.

To help you see the energy, you might want to do this in a dimly lit room. Look at a wall with a neutral background. This is an excellent way to use your third eye to see energy, but it is not a recommended method to strengthen the Ajna chakra. Still, this is worth trying, especially if you just want to see prana.

Visual Screen

The visual screen is an excellent technique to use for visualization exercises. To locate the visual screen, close your eyes and look slightly upward. With eyes shut, look at the area of the Ajna chakra. This is your visual screen. You can project anything that you like to this screen, especially images. You can consider this as some form of an internal magic mirror.

Psychic Abilities Guide

The main purpose of this visual screen is for your visualization exercises. Here is a simple exercise you can do to increase your concentration and willpower:

• Assume a meditative posture and relax. Now, look at your visual screen. Visualize an apple floating in front of you. Now, just focus on this apple and do not entertain any other thoughts. This exercise is just like breathing meditation. However, instead of focusing on your breath, focus on the apple on your visual screen.

• When you are ready to end this meditation, simply visualized the apple slowly fade away and gently open your eyes.

• You are also welcome to use any other object for this meditation. If you do not want to use an apple, you can visualize an orange or even an elephant. The important thing is to have a point of visual focus for this meditation.

Charging with the Fire Element

Remember that intuition is associated with the pineal gland, in the pineal gland is the third eye chakra. Now, this third eye chakra is associated with the fire element. Therefore, you can empower your third eye chakra by charging it with the element of fire. This is a powerful technique, so be sure to use it carefully. The steps are as follows:

• Assume a meditative posture and relax. Close your eyes. Now, visualize the brilliant and powerful sun above you. This powerful sun is full of the element of fire. As you inhale, see and feel that you are drawing the energy from the sun. Let the energy charge your third eye chakra and empower it.

- Do this with every inhalation. The more that you change your third eye, the more that it lights up and becomes more powerful. Have faith that with every inhalation, you become more and more intuitive.

Keep in mind that this is a powerful technique. If you are just starting, it is suggested that you only do up to 10 inhalations in the beginning. You can then add one or two more inhalations every week. You will know if you can execute this technique properly because you will feel pressure on your forehead in the area of your third eye chakra. Take note that you should not just visualize your third eye chakra getting stronger, but you should also be conscious that your intuition becomes more powerful the more that you change your third eye. The power of visualization should be accompanied by your intention.

Note

It should be noted that the Ajna chakra and crown chakra are closely connected. If you want to improve your intuition, it is only right that you also work on your crown chakra. Of course, this does not mean that you should ignore your other chakras. Again, the whole chakra system is vital to your spiritual development and the awakening of the kundalini.

Mythic Capability

As if being highly sensitive to the surrounding energy is not already a big responsibility, you will also have to resist a lot of misconceptions about yourself. As an empath, you really have a big calling on your hands and you need to understand that not everyone will understand this. You might be labeled as being too emotional or too dramatic. You might even be accused of being one of the energy vampires that you are so keen to eliminate from your life. Understanding the many misconceptions that people have concerning empaths is the first step towards gently educating those around you. Even if you do not feel like being the myth buster in your circle, you can still learn to differentiate the myths from the facts for your own sake. Knowledge is power, and knowing yourself is one of the most powerful things you can do for yourself.

Psychic Empaths Are Extremely Self-Absorbed and Only Worry about Themselves

Psychic Abilities Guide

Fact: Psychic empaths often care about others more than they care about themselves.

From the outside looking in, the moodiness and emotional nature of a psychic empath can come across as the disposition of a person who is only concerned with how they are feeling. The fact of the stuff is that a psychic empath is more likely to be moody because of the people around them, and not because of their own emotions. It is easy to be judgmental towards a psychic empath because of how they carry themselves. They are often quiet and reserved and will not want to come out to play too often. This might be interpreted to mean that they do not care about interacting with others and only worry about themselves. The truth is that while the empath might want to be a ray of sunshine to everyone else, they often find themselves incapable because of the overwhelming feelings they go through when dealing with different energies given out by others.

Psychic Empaths Are Just Mentally Ill

Fact: Being highly sensitive is not a mental illness.

Many empaths make for good listeners and confidants based on their ability to empathize and truly feel for others. Because of this, empaths often find themselves the designated dumping ground for all emotional baggage. When you are burdened with the emotional problems of others, it is easy to become depressed and anxious, which might cause others to assume you are mentally ill. Many times, empaths are just sad because of all the emotional burden that they have to shoulder. This immense sadness may mimic the signs of a person that is going through clinical depression. Yes, there are instances when an empath may be diagnosed with depression, but this is not simply because they are highly sensitive. There are frequent features that must be present for one to be diagnosed with depression. These factors are not exclusive to an empath. They can affect just about anyone, especially those who are genetically predisposed to the same.

Empaths Are Psychologically Weak

Fact: The moments of "weakness" that empaths exhibit are the result of all the negative energy they have to deal with.

What might be normal to a typical non-empath may be extremely difficult for the empath. Take, for instance, holding down an office job. For the person that is not highly sensitive to the energy of other people, an office job is just another opportunity to earn a paycheck and advance in their career. For the empath, an office job means being constantly bombarded by the negative energy from all sides. As such, an empath might struggle to hold down a normal 9 to 5 job, while this is just another workday for everyone else. When this happens, the empath might be accused of being weak, lazy, fussy, or just unwilling to try. This could not be further from the truth. Being an empath is hard work. Imagine walking through life everyday while someone carries a huge ball that they hit you with every time you take one step. This is how it feels to be an empath. You are constantly being hit by a big ball of negative energy and you must lift yourself up every time you fall from this hit. After a while, it can be easier to stay on the ground because you have run out of energy to lift yourself up. As an empath, it is important to remember that you are not psychologically frail. Being able to deal with other people's negative energy daily and showing up in the world even though you know what coming takes a lot of strength is.

Empaths Are Emotionally Volatile

Psychic Abilities Guide

Fact: Being exposed to varying emotional energy can make you more in control of your emotions.

People who believe that empaths are emotionally volatile base their arguments on the fact that empaths are often exposed to various energies, which might interfere with how emotionally stable they are. True, it is common for an empath to be moody, but this does not mean that they are always going to lash out when provoked. Many empaths are often moody when they retreat into themselves to introspect on the emotions that they have picked up. This does not make them a volatile person who is at the mercy of their emotions. An empath can be highly stable when it comes to their feelings and those of others. In fact, an empath can easily learn how to be calm and in control, regardless of those around them, by understanding how to process and shield the energy that surrounds them. Some of the calmest and collected people that exist in this world are actually empaths. They have learned to read people and so nothing really takes them by surprise.

Most Empaths Are Cold and Detached from Everyone Else

Fact: Detachment is a side effect of being emotionally drained.

Many empaths who come across as detached do not become so because they intended to. It is often a result of being emotionally abused by people around them. When they cannot take it anymore, an empath may become numb as a way of protecting themselves. It is not correct to assume that an empath is cold and unfeeling simply because they are an empath. Even the most outwardly detached empaths tend to have a light of empathy flickering deep inside of them. Empathy is not something you can switch on and off at will. If you care about other people, you will always care about them regardless of where you go or what you do.

Empaths Are Often Highly Dependent on Their Loved Ones

Fact: Empaths like for positive energy to flow both ways.

When an empath finds a source of positive energy, that source becomes an asset that they can draw their strength from. This is why empaths really thrive when they are deeply and genuinely loved. However, unlike energy vampires, empaths realize the need for the flow of positive energy to be two-sided. They love giving as much as they enjoy taking. You are not likely to find an empath that loves leeching on their loved ones. It is also important to note that empaths are not really dependent on positive energy from other people to survive. They are capable of doing it all on their own, as long as they learn how to protect themselves from the negative energy around them. If you are an empath, you do not have to worry about being a leech to others. As long as nobody is complaining, and as long as you can feel the good, positive energy flowing both ways, then it is safe to assume that the people in your life love you and the presence you bring.

Empaths Are Just Glorified Doormats

Fact: With the right boundaries, an empath can care about others without feeling used.

Sure enough, empaths struggle with saying no. Empaths often want to take care of others and struggle with the guilt of feeling as if they are not helpful. It is effortless for an empath to find them relegated to the role of a doormat if they have not set the limits and boundaries for other people. This; however, does not mean that all sensitive people are just pushovers that allow anyone and everything in their lives. Empaths who are conscious of their powers and abilities know that it is easy for others to take advantage of them. As such, they often have ways of managing the people in their lives and striking the balance between being helpful and being everyone's doormat.

Empaths Are All Good People

Fact: Being highly sensitive does not automatically qualify you for decency.

The question of whether a person is good or bad can only be answered after evaluating the choices that the person makes, and not as a factor of their genetic predisposition. Just because a person has been born as an empath does not mean they will always be a good person. An empath is a human being who is capable of hurting others and even making bad choices based on the prevailing circumstances in their life. While it is true that many empaths are often not manipulative people, it is also true that they are just humans and have the choice to be bad or good, just like everyone else.

Empaths Take to Narcissists like Moths to a Light

Fact: The relationship between empaths and narcissists is complex.

It has been said that opposites attract, and this could never be overstated in the case of narcissists and empaths. Empaths are the complete opposite of narcissists, and when these two categories of people meet, there are often fireworks. Why is this so? Is it because the empath is keen on healing the narcissist? In many cases, the empath is not even aware that they are dealing with a narcissist. This might seem like a contradiction because, after all, empaths are supposed to be intuitive and highly capable of reading other people's energy and intentions. Narcissism is a personality disorder that brings forth highly manipulative individuals. At the beginning of a relationship, the narcissist might make it seem as if they are the healer that the empath needs. As such, the empath will gravitate towards the narcissist because they seem kind and decent, and loving. The narcissist, on the other hand, will pursue the empath because they love the adoration that the empath can give so freely. The narcissist-empath relationship evolves to become a highly toxic relationship where the empath keeps on giving and forgiving, while the narcissist cannot stop taking and creating chaos because that is what they thrive in. There is often never a happy ending when a narcissist and an empath meet and fall in love.

Dreams

For example, I am very close with my cousin Diana. If we haven't spoken in a while I will have dreams about her life including new changes, current emotional state, or overall life concerns. We share a strong telepathic connection and will often communicate with each other in our dream states.

You may also pick up on information about someone's past with dreams. Have you ever met someone or started dating a new person and then a vivid dream about them? One client came in telling me about the same dream she kept having about a love interest, and the theme was secrecy and deception. Months later, she found out he was married and having an affair with her. Dreams can communicate positive and negative messages to us about ourselves, the people we know, and life.

Personally, I love to dream. It's one of the reasons I look

forward to falling asleep at night. At the beginning of my psychic development, my dreams were the doorway to my intuition and Spirit communication. They still are but differently. Usually in the beginning, when you start to become more aware you will have more vivid intuitive dreams about the past, present, or the future.

You are subconsciously working in your sleep to tap into your psychic ability. You may also communicate with passed loved ones or Spirit Guides in your dreams. I have many clients, including myself, who communicate with the deceased or a guide in the dream state.

Why would the deceased want to communicate with us after they pass? One reason is to let us know they are okay and around us. Another is to provide guidance or information on current issues or comfort us. A common dream I've noticed people have about passed loved ones is just seeing their faces and nothing else. This is usually a sign from them letting you know they are around you and sending you a little hello.

You may also receive symbols and numbers in your dreams. If you aren't able to interpret the meaning behind them, write it down for reference later. I would highly suggest keeping a dream journal or recording your dreams on your phone or an audio-recording device. A dream journal will help document specific dreams, messages you receive, or patterns of themes and symbols. If you are still perplexed by a symbol received in a dream, then I would recommend looking at some books on symbols and those meanings.

Dream Exercise

One common bedtime dream exercise to do is write down a question or concern you'd like guidance on. An example of this would be a question focused on a career such as "Is this job right for me?" Focus on that question and read it in your mind a few times, concentrating on receiving guidance about it. Then say in your mind, "When I wake up tomorrow I will remember all of my dreams."

This exercise may work immediately, or it may take a few times of practice to receive anything. If you don't receive an answer but just see something instead, write it down and keep practicing this every night. You can also buy a crystal specifically for dreams and try putting that under your pillow before bed.

Guided Meditation

Guided Meditation and Yoga

This really can be an absolute prerequisite on the off likelihood you have received a bustling mind with jelling personality gab and horrible musings because most empaths do. A bustling disordered style is un-establishing.

Reflection motivates one to handle debilitating conditions and provides you an even far more precise comprehension. There are quite a lot of sorts of contemplation. It's just a good example of finding what satisfies you personally.

Case in Point—Your Jaguar Protection Meditation

For those who require additional security studies to prescribe this manifestation to approach the high level of the puma to guarantee you, you ought to use it if there's an inordinate quantity of antagonism coming in you too quickly. The panther is just a barbarous and patient Gate Keeper who'll reduce the chances of dangerous energy as well as humans. In a calm, thoughtful condition, in the deepest soul, approach the spirit of this puma to protect you.

Feel the character input. Now, envision this perfect, incredible animal-watching your energy field, surrounding it, ensuring that you personally, keeping out interlopers or some other negative forces which have to acquire past. Picture what the puma looks like: its lovely, crazy, loving eyes; eloquent figure; the nimble, deliberate manner the panther moves. Have a feeling of safety from the area with the present puma's security. Give inward gratitude to the panther.

Yoga

Many people declare that yoga isn't for these, yet it's the most individuals who undergo some good space from yoga who're those who want it all. Yoga is beautifully establishing. It requires an attempt at the bodily and playful bodies also functions everyone, whatever era or capacity. Yoga should be basic in every person's life. There's really a yogic expression: 'We're equally as young as the backbone is more elastic.' Since yoga tries to earn a healthy spine, it might possibly be hailed as a blend of childhood. The most middle of yoga relies upon the breath. By carrying through stances, it stills and quiets the mind, making a sound, body. Meditation is similarly called a moving manifestation.

Nature

Becoming out in life features a recuperating and setting influence on every empath. Being an empath, about the off likelihood that you simply invest little energy in kind, you may struggle to stay afloat or detect balance. In case you work in a metropolis, without an entry into parkland, then make certain you obtain out at endings of this week out of autos and atmosphere pollution.

Stress

Since adults' individuals invest a great deal of energy being tomb and genuine, as well as in brief span with a whole lot of pleasure (especially from today's occasions). Would you recollect the last time you experienced a proper paunch snicker? Imprint that, 'that you don't quit playing as you grow old; you grow old as you stop playing!' You hear youths snicker always. They don't need any idea just how to look closely at life; it is all about fun and play, which can help keep them seated. Everyone needs to attempt to continue to be untainted. To observe the planet in surprise or maybe more all have a bunch of pleasure and chuckle. Whatever causes you to giggle is likely to create your spirits to shoot off. It genuinely is just therapy.

It is difficult for a non-empath to grasp the concept of feeling people's emotions. Imagine feeling happy, sad, anxious, and fearful. All at the same time. And these are just some emotions that could be going on through an empath at any given moment.

Meditation is recommended for anyone but highly recommended for empaths. Your ability to absorb foreign emotions and energies makes you susceptible to anxiety and stress, which makes your life difficult. Meditation aims to quiet the mind for a moment and give it a break from the dozen competing emotions seeking to occupy it.

Psychic Abilities Guide

Empathy is a gift that can make things easier at the workplace, but it can also make them difficult. If you cannot control the dozens of emotions you are dealing with, you will be overwhelmed, and your work performance will suffer.

The Meditation Processes

Can you train your mind to be quiet? Can you calm your mind enough to concentrate only on the present moment and nothing else? Can you block out your emotions? As an empath, you are probably so accustomed to multiple emotions that the idea of having a clear mind seems unattainable.

Think about it: how many things are on your mind at any given time? Let us say you are sitting at your desk at work editing a document, and you have multiple tabs open. The first one is your email, so you can check out any new one that comes in. Remember, they are also those you are yet to reply to. You are antagonizing over some sports rerun on a different tab, noticing how badly your team is doing. You are also half-listening to a conversation your colleagues were having about that finance meeting last week. Oh, you also have your eye on the clock. Is it lunchtime yet? You have to check out that restaurant in the new mall two blocks away. Oh, and there's a gym there too. You need to stay in shape.

All these items are fighting for space in your mind. How many are these? Like 7? Sounds like such a high number when you stop to count, yet this is nothing unusual. Our minds are constantly burdened with information going in and out. No wonder fatigue and anxiety have become the order of the day. Unfortunately, even with all this activity on your mind, you are hardly productive. You are like the proverbial rocking chair, an activity without much progress. Every person deals with such thoughts, but as an empath, you have to include emotions. As if yours are not enough, you have to deal with the emotions of those around you. They all exhaust you and drain your energy.

It may not feel relaxing at first. In fact, in the beginning, you may struggle with the entire concept. The mind takes about 20 minutes or so before it settles and longer for others. Do not dwell on the difficulty. Do not stop trying. Meditation is a skill; you get better with time.

Empath Journal

As an empath, a journal is going to be one of the most helpful tools that you can use to help better manage your emotions. A journal is a way for you to express your feelings without worrying about anything else in life. You can use this as an escape. You can share your deepest, darkest secrets without judgment. You can let even the worst thoughts come out.

Begin first by choosing how you want to journal. Do you want to use paper and pens, or would you prefer something digital? You can go out to the store and get the nicest Moleskine journal with calligraphy pens. You can also simply use the notes unit of your phone for the journal. You could even use a voice recording app and talk out loud to yourself, going back and reflecting on this later. You can use a transcription service like Otter.ai to help you keep track of your thoughts and feelings. You simply speak into your phone while recording, and it automatically transcribes this for you.

Once you write that down and read it back to yourself, you might discover that there's too much negativity within that, and that's not how you actually feel. When we keep our emotions trapped inside of us, they can fester like a big infected wound. Once you actually begin to get those thoughts out, it becomes easier to realize the reality and the truth behind them.

Some people hate writing altogether, so you can also use your journal more analytically. You can make charts and graphs to help track your emotions. Maybe you have daily check-ins at 8 am-noon, 4 pm, 8 pm, and right before bed. You write down a simple word or two to describe your emotions.

You can use this data to help pinpoint a period in time that made you feel that way. Perhaps you notice that your worst emotions are every day at 8 am. Maybe they get a little bit better throughout the week. This is a sign that you're just not a morning person, and there's something about waking up that is causing you emotional turmoil. Maybe you discover that you really hate your job, and that's completely ruining your day-to-day life.

Crystals and Nature

The adjusting strength of prized stones has for a while been understood in a variety of societies, from Atlantis to older Egypt. It's recognized that the individuals of yore had pricey stone barrels that they had to fix physical, deep, or playful infirmities. Precious stones might be utilized linked to these chakras to help balance them expel blockages. Discovering their usual adjusting vibration, so many empaths have been instinctually brought to prized jewels for their own establishment and defensive capabilities.

Water Cleansing

Your system is constituted of seventy-five percentage of plain water (individual cells have ninety-five percent). Therefore, it shouldn't surprise anybody this is much up there around oneself fixing scale. Quite a few people are aware of how dry they truly are. Lacking a source of water makes difficulties with all the working of their physical and enthusiastic bodies, affects overall wealth, and quickens the aging process. Water is an excellent guardian for the empath, plus so they want tons of it—both in and out of their own bodies. Most should drink, in just about any event, eight glasses of water that is drinkable to re-charge what your system generally wins through perspiring or urine. The heavier you're, the more water that you require. There's an outdated spiritual expression: "Neatness can be an underdog to righteousness." Water Spray something aside from earth off; it could rinse the revived human body and clear cynicism. If you're doubtful, whenever you get home from a tough day on the job, attempt this: in the place of pursuing your wine, then dip directly from the shower and also see exactly what an elevating and draining impact it's. Or, however, if setting really tired, drink a half-gallon of tepid to warm water and also comprehend the way that it interrupts the result.

Telepathy

Telepathy, clairvoyance, precognition, psychokinetic, telekinesis - it seems like there are a whole lot of psychic abilities that people claim to possess. But what does it all mean?

Telepathy has to do with the reception and transmission of thoughts. Clairvoyance is getting information about something that is going to happen or has already happened, often through dreams or visions. Precognition knows about something in advance without any normal sense of how you would know that information. Psychokinetic is the power to influence a physical system using only your mind. And telekinesis, also known as psychokinetic, is the power to move objects on a molecular level only through concentration and willpower alone.

All of these abilities are related, in some way or another. For example, psychic abilities often act as receptors for spiritual energy.

Psychic Abilities Guide

When a person with a psychic ability receives information from the spiritual world, they often experience a strong emotional reaction to it. When these people are in tune with the spiritual world, they can receive many details about an event, like themes and imagery that would otherwise be hard to predict.

Most commonly, some kind of psychic ability is thought to be an inherited trait that is passed down from generation to generation. But there are also theories that psychic abilities are a result of a birth-defect like something is wrong with the wiring of the brain. Still, others say that psychic abilities are simply out of the ordinary mental processes that most people can't access because their brains just don't work like that.

People who have psychic abilities often say they were born with them. When asked how they know they have these powers, one woman said that as far back as she can reminisce, she has always been able to remember her past lives. But the most famous psychic, Edgar Cayce, said that he didn't know why he was psychic in a book called The Story of Your Mind. He says that his answers to questions about what happens after death are completely correct, but he can't figure out why they are true.

For these people to have these amazing abilities, something needs to be wrong with their brains. However, they all have the same types of flaws as everyone else. They are often just as prone to emotional problems, and they can also be manipulated or tricked into giving false information.

One more thing about psychic abilities: when you ask them to do their psychic stuff, the most common way for them to get what you are asking is through another person's mind. This worth that they have to be really close for it to work. And if that other person is mentally healthy, they can block the psychic's ability.

A great book about psychics is called The Truth about Psychics, and it has everything you need to know about these kinds of people.

So, are psychics really good at getting information? Although some people seem to think so, most psychics would probably say no. Most of the time they get things wrong because they aren't as powerful as the spiritual world thinks they are.

Emotional

Clearing and Calming of the Mind

As with any practice which includes meditation, these practices will naturally clear your mind. When you allow yourself to meditate for at least 15 minutes a day, you will see that even if you had a racing mind, it would start to calm down. This is a benefit that most people will find beneficial, even when starting with the Kundalini awakening process.

Improvement in Memory

With the combination of the pranayama and yoga poses, you will be introducing more oxygen into your system. This, in turn, benefits the blood to flow more easily throughout the body, including the brain. More blood entering the brain improves the cognitive functions and the pituitary and pineal glands.

Psychic Abilities Guide

Physical Ailments Can Be Relieved or Cured

During the process of Kundalini awakening, you are working towards cleaning out your nadis and chakras to facilitate Kundalini Shakti's movement. This cleansing brings about an environment in your body that diseases cannot survive, so they will be greatly reduced or eradicated.

Increased Physical and Mental Strength

There is no doubt that the dutiful practice of yoga poses will get you into shape. Coupled with the other exercises in Kundalini, your mind will become sharper and focused, which in turn increases your mental fortitude. You will find that you will be able to control your emotions as well.

Proven Build Up of Willpower

There is no hesitation that certain of these Kundalini exercises are difficult. There are some that you will need to practice other exercises before you even think about graduating yourself. The need to continue to push yourself systematically strengthens your willpower and drives you to succeed.

Feeling One with the Universe

When you can connect with the higher energies within yourself, you will realize that we are all just from the same source. No matter what your background, education, upbringing, belief system, or marital status, we are based on the same energy of the Ultimate Consciousness.

Tap into Inner Intuition and Guides

As you dig deeper within yourself and can silence your thoughts, you will start to hear another voice that will never steer you wrong. This inner guide is your intuition, your gut feeling, which always has your higher interests at heart. Learn to trust this voice, and you will excel more quickly during the Kundalini awakening process.

Feeling Overall Bliss and Peace

When you go through the Kundalini awakening process, there certainly are low points. However, just as quickly, you can be sent up to soaring heights that blow your mind. You cannot even imagine this state at this point in your journey. Feeling these emotions certainly makes up for any hardships you will go through.

Psychic Abilities Are Enhanced

You will find that you will become more sensitive to the sounds, colors, and vibrations around you. This happens when you come more in tune with your body and then it radiates from there. When your intuition becomes more enhanced, you will start to know everything that you need at the moment that you need it.

Slower Aging Process

When you get to the higher levels of Kundalini yoga practice, you will see a glow that will start to show in your skin. This is partly because of the cleaning process. It is also because you are balancing out the elements within your body to function more efficiently. Your body will no longer need to work so hard in maintaining itself.

Psychic Abilities Guide

Connection with the Divine

This is the ultimate goal of Kundalini yoga and awakening. When you can be in direct connection with the creator, anything is possible. You lose all earthly bounds and can achieve the so-called unachievable. Going back to the Source is the perfect prize for all the hard work and dedication you have put into your practice.

Sacred Chant

Many of the chakras can be healed through a sacred chant. When you use a mantra, rhythm, and breath, it has been found to have beneficial effects on well-being and health. It can also bring joy to the heart and the soul. The sacred sound is known as Naad Yoga. The experience comes from how your voice's vibrations can have a positive effect on the body, the mind, and the spirit. In fact, sound can change the chemicals in your brain.

Inner Soul Guidance

Through Kundalini Awakening and Kundalini Yoga, you will learn all about the power of your intuitive mind. As we mentioned before, you need to learn how to listen to the voice inside your head. Each person has this voice, but it is up to you to choose to listen to it. As you clear your mind, especially your subconscious mind, you will learn how to listen to your thoughts without needing to rely on others. This way, you can always be present and sense your intuition. The more you rehearse, the sturdier your ability to face choices and decisions will come!

Karma

It is thought that it takes you out of the karma cycle when you practice Kundalini. As you begin to practice, your positive intention will grow; therefore, putting you into Kundalini Kriyas. These are exercises that help you burn off karma. As you practice more, you will become more intuitive to your decisions as well as your conscious. As you do this, you will begin to walk on a Dharma path instead of living according to karma.

Spiritual Chain

As you now know, Kundalini has been taught for thousands of years. Originally, it was taught by the Master to the student. In a Kundalini Yoga class, you will chant, "Ong Namo Guru Dev Namo." As you do this, you will be linked to spiritual masters from the times before your existence. The lineage is known as The Golden Chain. Through spiritual awareness, it will guarantee Kundalini's teachings to make sure you will remain unadulterated and pure.

Emotional Balance

What you may not distinguish is that by balancing your Kundalini, you will also be balancing your glands, purifying your blood, strengthening your nervous system, and cleaning out your subconscious. As you awaken your Kundalini, you will gain the strength to choose how you respond to your views and moods instead of just reacting. You will also have a greater awareness during your daily activities. As you practice more, you will also learn how to let your emotions go. No longer will you just react emotionally? By developing a neutral mind, you may find yourself living a more positive life. The key is to act instead of reacting.

Psychic Abilities Guide

No More Negativity

As you practice awakening your Kundalini, you will begin to expand your aura. This is the energy field that surrounds you. Its main job is to alert you of any positive or negative emotions around you. At this point, you probably have a weak aura. When it is weak, you can easily allow negative influences to affect you. As you strengthen your aura, it will keep you centered, and you will know your true identity.

New Lifestyle

In life, we make a lot of excuses that keep us unhappy. Luckily, Kundalini Yoga is meant for people with busy lives. That means that it can be done quickly and still work effectively. It is a yoga that can fit into many lifestyles. Whether you attend weekly or bi-weekly, there are many benefits to be found. There are also yoga teachings that can change other parts of your life. Whether you want to change your hygiene, child-rearing, or conscious communication, there is yoga for that!

Relax

As we mentioned earlier, Kundalini yoga will work to strengthen your nervous system. If your nervous system is weak at this point, you are probably susceptible to stress. Through yoga, you will learn how to relax as you have never felt before. You may find that you will reach a rejuvenating state through yoga to bring you to total relaxation. Through regular practice, it can help you build resilience to stress and give you some extra stamina.

Community

On your journey, you do not need to do this alone. Often, yoga brings people together who are like-minded. This can be a very powerful tool as you travel along your consciousness journey. If you weren't already aware, many Kundalini yoga centers and studios could help welcome you into a community. With other people, you will develop a community that can meditate and chant together. It also helps to have people to help you make positive changes in your life.

Befriending Your Soul

As you practice Kundalini, you may begin to get a grip on your ego. You will slowly be learned about your soul's depth so you can learn the truth of your connection to your soul and the Universe. Through more practice, you will learn how to unite yourself with the Infinite. Gaining the experience can help you forget your insecurities of knowing who you are. This way, you will let go of the past and healthily manifest your destiny.

Astral

Astral Travel

Astral travel is defined by some as the ability to have an out-of-body experience. This concept theorizes that the soul is capable of traveling around outside of one's physical body that the soul cannot be trapped within one's physical form and may be projected at will. Most people experience astral travel during near-death experiences or during times of great illness. With the enhancement of psychic abilities, it is entirely possible to perform astral travel at will. Astral projection usually only lasts for a few hours, though it may feel much longer (more like days or months) to the one who is experiencing astral projection.

Astral Travel is often described as "dreaming while awake," and many consider this concept to be like having an out-of-body experience. Astral travel is your mind's ability to experience your surroundings without being limited to your physical body. Astral travel allows your soul to be free from your physical body to travel the universe freely. While experiencing astral travel, you control the astral projection's length of time. During astral projection, you remain in control of your mind and are able to steer yourself away from any source of negativity that you may encounter. The ability to see and communicate with those who have passed away is not an uncommon experience during astral projection, and those who can achieve astral travel are also able to visit various countries, planets, and even other realms during their projections.

An individual's soul or astral body is said to be connected to the individual's physical body by an astral cord (also known as the silver cord) that can stretch to an almost infinite length. The silver cord cannot be severed, with the only exception being in the occurrences of death.

1.   Sitting in a quiet environment and in a relaxed position, perform meditation to relieve all tension and stress from your body.

2.   Remain relaxed until you hear or feel the vibrations often experienced during meditative exercises. Keeping your eyes closed; imagine your astral body rising out above the limits of your physical body.

Clairvoyance (Psychic Vision)

One of the most popular forms of psychic ability is clairvoyance, and (especially in books or television) it is often referred to as "the gift." The ability of clairvoyance originates within the sixth chakra (the Third Eye) in the areas of the brain biologically recognized as the pituitary and pineal glands. While everyone has the ability to possess some psychic ability, not everyone will have the same ability to be a clairvoyant individual. The majority of individuals are born with relatively strong clairvoyant abilities, but most people lose these abilities by a certain (often young) age. This can be demonstrated when children claim to see deceased relatives (even those whom they have never met).

When they have seemingly realistic "imaginary" friends, or when children seem to know intuitively when something is wrong with the adults surrounding them.

Clairvoyance is defined, simply, as the ability or skill of psychic vision. A more in-depth definition of this skill can be described as "perceiving things or events in the future or beyond normal sensory contact." Clairvoyance is sometimes referred to as "second sight" or "psychic sight" and translates to meaning "clear seeing." This skill is described by those who experience it as the reception of intuitive clues, often in the form of symbols, images, or visions. Some clairvoyants claim that certain tools can help them to connect easily with or strengthen their abilities: the more common tools for this purpose are tea leaves, tarot cards, runes, or even crystals. Precognition is a form of clairvoyance in which an individual can foresee events before they happen. Precognitive abilities usually present themselves as visions while one is asleep.

Spiritual

Have you ever met someone who bowls you over from the second you meet them? Is it a force of nature that fills you with joy, makes you grateful to be in their company, and does not need to be loud or in your face? Do they simply radiate goodness and love? If so, you know they are good people who aren't afraid of anything and are capable of whatever they put their minds to.

These people have a higher vibration than others. They are spiritually in tune with their inner selves, filled with positivity and love, and vibrate on a higher plane, which attracts people to them like moths to a flame. In the spiritual world, higher vibration is also the way you attract spirits.

A higher vibration tells the spirits you are ready to receive them, and you welcome their wisdom. Fear is the main cause of a low and short vibration, so it is important to dispel the things that make you fearful. You need to fill your life with joy and make your vibration sing!

Raising your vibration is not difficult, but it can take time. If you have lived your life ruled by fear, it will turn negativity into positivity. You will need to remind yourself constantly to stay on the path of positivity and be prepared to forgive yourself if you step off for a while. Everyone is human with human emotions, and the best thing you can be is kind to yourself.

How to Raise Your Vibrations and Find Your Spirituality

Count Your Blessings

Are you constantly worrying about what you don't have? Are you focused on what other people have rather than what you are grateful for? Change that mindset and create a list of things you should be grateful for. You can create a segment in your spiritual journal or dedicate a whole book to the subject.

Write Something Positive

• Your family: How do you feel when you think about your family? Are they the perfect support group, or are they a bunch of individuals with such different personalities they all have different qualities?

• Your friends: Do you have a best friend? Why do you love them so much? Which of your friends is always there for you when you are down?

• Your courage: You have lived your life with courage and have overcome many heartbreaks and pain.

- Your strength: Life isn't easy. You have survived it so far, so your strength is apparent. Use your strength to grow as a person and become stronger.

- Your mind: You are blessed with a complex mind that can transport you to places you have never been and help you solve the most difficult problems. Your mind is a major part of who you are, so be grateful for it.

- Your tears: Do you remember the last time you cried? Was it because you were sad, or were they tears of joy? Your tears are badges of honor to mark the best and worst times of your life. Contrary to some people's beliefs, tears do not signify weakness; they show emotional strength.

- Your mistakes: Yes, you can be grateful for your successes, but what about your mistakes? Own them and understand what you learned from them. This attitude will make you more determined to try new things and welcome change.

Create

Sometimes, life and work can be overwhelming. You work, you go home, and you look after your family and yourself. You then relax and sleep before another day on the treadmill of life. So, when do you find time to be creative, to let your talents flow, find new outlets, and learn new things? Find time to do something fun, like cooking new recipes, creating art pieces, or learning a new musical instrument. When you find things to stimulate your inner sense, your mood elevates. This raises your vibration and makes your outlook more optimistic.

Give Without Receiving

When you give something from the goodness of your heart, you don't just feel a warm glow; you also raise your spiritual vibration. You can financially donate to a charity, or you can give your time by volunteering. Maybe you know someone who has been having a rough time lately, and you can help them. Just giving without expecting a reward will help you feel more spiritual.

Use Your Words Wisely

Your words are possibly the most powerful weapon you have. When you speak ill of anyone or even yourself, you are setting yourself back on a negative energy path. Gossiping, complaining, and being unkind to others don't achieve anything, but it will lower your vibration. Use your words to raise your spirit and be kind to people. Compliments and encouragements are much better for your inner psyche.

Exercise and Movement

When your body feels sluggish, so does your soul. You need to incorporate plenty of movement into your daily routine. Take a brisk walk among nature to raise your vibes. Escalate the magnificence of your surroundings as you get your heartbeat rising. Feel the crispness of the air and the warmth of the sun. Nature and exercise should fill your soul with love and positivity and get that vibration rising!

Just Let It Go

If you consider yourself a victim whom others have maligned, that is how you will be treated. Nobody else has control over your life. They may have the power to influence certain aspects of your life, but ultimately you are in control. When you hand this power to others, you are always fearful about what they will do. Take rear the regulator and absorb how to let go of this fear. Forgive people for what they have done to you in the past and acknowledge the power shift.

Create a Rule for Life

Everyone needs a spiritual roadmap with a specific destination. This is your rule of life and a guide to connecting with your higher self, your true power, and your spirit guides. This isn't destined to be a firm plan, but it should be a fluid and changeable guide to inspire you when you feel a bit lost. Use a journal to note down prayers and mantras you can use to lift your spirits. You can also include meditation techniques you find especially helpful.

Change Your Diet

The foods you eat affect how you look and act. A healthy diet is important to keep your body active and fit for a purpose. Fresh, healthy ingredients mean you digest more nutrients and vitamins, so you function better. Can food affect spirituality, though? The simple answer is, "Yes, it can." As your vibration moves up a level, it can adversely affect your body. As frequencies are raised, you can feel unstable and shaky. Your dreams may become more vivid and disturbing while your emotions are heightened.

The foods listed below will help you nourish your body to support you through this process. The pineal gland in the human body is often referred to as the third eye, and it needs certain nutrients to help it function correctly.

• Healthy fats: When you add natural healthy fats to your foods, you establish contact with nature that helps ground you. Coconut, almond, and olive oils will all make your food taste amazing and support your nervous system.

• Cacao: This is a true superfood! It is from the purest part of the cocoa bean and can be taken as a supplement or used to create amazing food you will love. It contains a potent detoxifying agent that will help you clear your body and soul. It removes negative energy and dispels toxic energy. Cacao provides you with high energy levels without suffering the aftermath of a crash. Replace sugar with cacao wherever you can and benefit from its nutritional properties.

• Beets: These amazing vegetables will help you clean your system and repair any damage to the pituitary gland. They are filled with nutrients and cover antioxidants as well as anti-inflammatory properties. You can eat them raw or cooked, and they make a colorful addition to your dishes. The juice of beetroots can be a healthy alternative to fruit juice in your diet.

• Herbs: These easy-to-grow plants aren't just a quick way to make food taste better; they are key ingredients in your diet that will help you with ascension symptoms. You can add them to food or use the dried leaves to make herbal teas. Try rosemary, nettle, thyme, basil, and chamomile to help soothe you and move your vibration through higher levels of consciousness.

• Water: Staying hydrated is essential. Ascending can be tough on your body and cause uncomfortable side effects. When you drink water, you help your brain function, which supports your pituitary gland's health.

What you add to your diet is just as important as the things you leave out. Avoid fluoride, sugar, alcohol, processed foods, fast foods, fried food, and any products that have been treated with pesticides. Your body is your temple, and you must fill it with worshippers who will help you ascend rather than drag you down.

Spend Time with Loved Ones

The way you spend your leisure time is vital for your spiritual enhancement. Sometimes, people take their loved ones for granted, as they are constantly seeking new connections and experiences. While it is important to put yourself out there and meet new people, you must look after the people who love you. Spend quality time with them over a shared meal or just relax together and talk.

It may sound clichéd, but you can forget to keep romance and love alive with your partner. Children, work, housework, and other mundane chores can seem endless, and you both feel exhausted at the end of the day. Just take a minute to remember what dating was like. Counting down the minutes until you saw each other and then that uplifting feeling when you catch sight of your partner.

Recapturing that feeling is the perfect way to raise your inner vibration. Love makes souls soar, and people feel invincible when they are loved.

Take time once a month to have a date night. It sounds corny, but what's wrong with a bit of cheesiness? Choose to dress up, leave the house, and spend a few good hours talking over a chilled-out meal or just a drink.

Become Involved with Your Community

How well do you know your community? Remember when everybody seemed to know everyone else, and you felt connected to your neighbors? Well, they are still there, and it can be deeply satisfying to feel part of something wholesome.

Here are some key ways you can reconnect with your community:

• Shop locally: Even though it is more convenient to do all your shopping in one big outlet, you lose that sense of connection. Try sourcing your shopping with local stores and visit farmers' markets in your area. The food will be fresher, and you could find real bargains close by.

• Support your local teams: Are there any little league teams in your area? Do you have a school or college team playing nearby? You can gain a lot from attending these amateur events. Teams play with spirit and energy, and they will help you feel part of the experience.

Chanting

The term channeling is used to describe a form of communication between humans and non-physical beings such as the Higher Self, Angelic realm, Spirit Guides, Ascended Masters, and/or souls that have transitioned. Channeling is also done by artists, musicians, painters, writers, and yes, psychic mediums. I've been blessed with being on the receiving end as well as the giving end when a channeled message has transformed someone's life in a powerful, loving, and positive manner. The gifts channeling can provide for the receiver of the message are priceless if done ethically.

We all have channeled information, whether we are consciously aware of when it's happening or not. It is the stream of consciousness that flows to us and through us. The majority of us have randomly said things without knowing where the information came from. I can't strain sufficient the significance of taking the time to investigate where the information you are receiving is originating from. There are various ways to channel. With trance channeling, for example, the medium (person channeling) has no recollection of what is being said or taking place while they are in the channeling trance. Therefore, taking the necessary precautions to make sure only high vibrational beings are allowed to work through the channel is imperative for the well-being of the channel. Yes, I have strong opinions about channeling. I suggest being cautious when delving into channeling because I speak from experience. I've witnessed people channel lower frequencies. Faith me when I about a lot can go wrong when you channel a lower frequency entity. They can zap your energy, poke holes in your aura, and worst-case scenario takes residence within your body and refuse to leave.

To prove that you are super psychic or have been chosen by higher beings of light are absolutely not valid reasons to channel. These reasons satisfy the negative ego, the Lower Self. Yes, we are channels. However, not everyone has a soul contract to become a trance channel. And yes, I agree, trance channeling is intriguing; however, over time, it can take a toll on your physical body. Trance concentrating takes a toll on the physical body because your body was created for you, not another entity. I suggest if you are interested in trance channeling, proceed ahead with caution and consult with a trusted mentor.

Sometimes the channeled information is so powerful and thought-provoking that the individual who is channeling thinks they must be connecting with a Master Teacher or an evolved light being. Is it really a Master they are talking with? While yes, it is possible. However, around 90 percent, I have found they are usually channeling their Higher Self.

Remember, the Higher Self exists beyond time, space. Your Higher

Self IS an evolved light being, after all. Don't mistake me, there is nothing wrong with seeking to connect with an Ascended Master, but if the messages from your Higher Self are raising your consciousness, then please do continue as you were.

Suggestions and Tips for Conscious Channeling, Automatic Writing

• Create sacred space, sage, incense, crystals every time you plan to do any spiritual work.

• Don't forget your inner sacred space. Absolutely no mind-altering substances. Yes, some use psychedelics, but I strongly advise against using any mind-altering substances when planning to work in the psychic realm. Set your prayers of intention before going into a channeled space.

• Call in your protection, your Higher Self, Guides, and spiritual helpers.

• Check-in with your motives. What is the intention for your session?

• In order to have a productive channeling session, realize that it does take discipline. I am referring to all types of channelings, automatic writing, conscious channeling, etc.

• Repetition of the same rituals will create the conditioning that takes you into the channeling space quickly.

• Keep in mind that just because someone is a channel, it does not mean they are a highly evolved individual. I have witnessed some channels that are channeling questionable beings. Don't forget there are lower beings on the astral just as there are highly evolved beings on the astral as well.

• Some people experience more than one voice or presence trying to communicate with them. I suggest checking in with your Higher Self-filter with help to facilitate an orderly process. You can also ask the group to communicate as a collective or ask if there is a spokesperson.

Suggested Questions to Ask While Channeling

Here are a few sample questions to ask whether communicating with an Angel, your Higher Self, Guides, crossed over loved ones, Masters of Light, or a spiritual collective.

• Whom am I speaking with?

• What name do you go by?

• What is the message?

• How can I improve the quality of my life?

If channeling interests you, I highly, highly recommend that you do not rush into it. Take your time, find a reputable mentor, and make sure you are taking the proper precautions (mentioned in the guidelines). Carelessly opening yourself to etheric energies can be detrimental to your soul's well-being.

Learning how to channel unfiltered information can be quite an eye-opening, soul-expanding, karmic clearing, and enlightening experience.

Technique on Astral Travel

You Could Learn to Astral Travel

People who completely access the third eye sometimes learn to astral travel. As you realize that there are limitless possibilities and that your spiritual self is not necessarily connected to your physical body, it will become apparent that you do not have to be limited by your existence in the physical world. Time and space are not definite, fixed elements in your life unless you allow them to consume you. Some people experience this as the ability of their soul to leave their body, traveling to any time and place in the universe.

You Will Gain a Deeper Intuition

Some people experience an extreme sense of intuition after opening the third eye, which is often referred to as a sixth sense. Some people have natural psychic powers that are buried deep within them. These powers come from tapping into the instinctual signals that are being sent from the world around them. This speaks a lot to the proverbial saying that "all you need to know is already contained within." You can learn the secrets of the world by expanding your consciousness and turning your focus inward.

You Will Develop a Deeper Sense of What You Want

It is incredibly easy to be distracted by the material pull of the world around us. Advertisements are everywhere, telling us the things that we "need" to be happy. The idea of success is often pushed as making as much money as possible, even more money than you could ever need in a lifetime. The problem with this is that it leaves a lot of people unhappy, unsure of what goals they should be striving for to achieve that "dream" that has been promised to many.

Upon opening your third eye, you will notice that the desires and material gains of the world around you do not seem quite as important. You'll gain a deeper insight into what you want in life that will make you happy, as well as the path that you must take to get there.

You'll Experience Heightened Creativity

People who are limited by their physical existence in the world often hold themselves back because of the guidelines and judgments from the world around them. It is easy for people to feel as if others are critical of their creative work, since creativity cannot be mandated or regulated. When you open the third eye, you are no longer bound to the strict lines of the world around you. You gain the confidence to take on your creative projects and bring them into reality.

Stress Will Melt Away

Awakening the third eye shifts your feeling of consciousness inward, so the things going on in the world around you are not as significant. This reduced level of stress and anxiety may realize that the small occurrences in the world mean less in the grand scheme of things. When you are connected to everything around you, it gives you greater control over the things that are stressing you out, and you develop the ability to make a greater, more positive impact in your own life.

The third eye also gives your insight into how you can make stresses melt away. Instead of focusing on the stress and anxiety, you will find your mind is open to solutions and that each day, you wake up determined to work toward your goals and remove the stressors from your life.

Improved Overall Life

The bottom line is when the third eye is awakened, you are inviting the things that you need for success into your life. You gain a deeper insight into your goals, achieving happiness, and stress reduction. Your quality of relationships with yourself and others will improve, and you will experience better sleep, heightened creativity, and possibly even experience certain powers, like foresight, astral projection, or seeing auras. All these things will come together to help you achieve a better quality of life so that you can start living in the way you were intended to.

Out of Body

In the last few pieces, I mentioned something called the "energy field." Well, this part is all about this field and the spiritual body. In spiritual settings, an energy field is called an aura.

Every individual and object in the universe emits energy. An aura is an electromagnetic field through which you channel spiritual energy, surrounding every living and non-living thing. Your aura is an invisible projection of your life force. Contrary to what many people think, it is not a single entity.

The aura comprises seven separate layers, all of which are interconnected. Together, these layers form a somewhat cohesive body. Thus, it might look like a less refined form of their physical body when you see the aura around someone. Each layer reflects one aspect of a person's life.

Psychic Abilities Guide

A person's aura is a sign of his/her energy. It has a lot of impact on their ability to connect with others. Typically, it extends about two to three feet from the body, but those who have experienced tragedy and trauma often have much broader auras, meaning that theirs may extend over three feet from their body.

The energy field is invisible, so most people don't see it around others. But those with the gift of clairvoyance can see, read, and interpret the aura. Being clairvoyant means you can see people's energy patterns, scenes, and blockages when looking at his/her aura.

When you meet a person and you sense his/her "vibe," it is the emission of his/her personal energy you perceive. The aura is the channel through which you get specific information about people you don't know. It is the reason you can tell if someone is trustworthy or not. How you react to someone depends on the energy they radiate around you.

At this point, you are likely wondering what this has to do with your journey to mediumship. As I said, an aura is a projection or manifestation of a person's spiritual energy. You can tell a person's mental, emotional, spiritual, and even physical standing by reading their aura's colors. From the shape to the color and color shade, all aspects of the life force energy field are there for you to understand a person better.

As a medium, when you clairvoyantly see a ghost, you can also see its aura. Through this, you can detect valuable information about the spirit.

One of the auric field layers is the astral layer, which you may call the spiritual layer. This layer is home to your celestial body, or if you prefer, your spiritual body. You cannot go to spiritual dimensions in your physical form because it is made of entirely different elements. To visit nonphysical dimensions, you need your astral body. Some people also call the astral form the soul.

When you start developing your mediumship ability, there will be plenty of situations when you need to go into a spiritual dimension yourself. It might be because you need to talk to a spirit, your spirit guide, or another higher-dimensional being. Regardless of the reason, you can only astral travel in your spiritual form. Therefore, understanding the aura's operations and the spiritual body can make all the difference for you.

Back to the layers of the aura. There are seven, as I said. Each layer has one solid color, which carries a lot of meaning, but it goes beyond that. Every layer is also connected to your seven energy centers, which are also known as the Chakras.

Individually, the auric layers vary in size and depth, and this is determined by an individual and the point they are in life. In a healthy individual, the aura usually has very bright colors. In contrast, dull colors are found in an unhealthy and weak aura. The size may also become small or large, depending on a person's quality of health. This means that no two people have the same auras.

The seven layers of your aura pulsate from your body. The first layer is the closest to your material form, while the 7th layer is the furthest. In retrospect, the seventh layer is the closest to your higher awareness. It has the highest vibrations because the further away a layer is from the physical body, the more vibration increases.

Psychic Abilities Guide

Some layers can be odd-numbered, while others are even-numbered. The odd-numbered layers have a defined structure, and they carry yang energy. In contrast, the even-numbered layers are more fluid, and they carry yin energy. Together, they culminate in a balanced and harmonization of your energy field.

The Seven Auric Layers

1.   Etheric layer: This layer is the closest to your material body. It is directly connected to the root chakra. With a bluish-grey color, you can easily see the etheric layer with your physical eyes.

2.   Emotional layer: After the subtle etheric body, the next is the emotional layer. It is the home of emotions and feelings. It is directly connected to the sacral chakra. In most people, this layer has all the colors of the rainbow. When you go through emotional stress, the colors turn murky and dark. You can tell someone's emotional state from reading this layer. It can also provide information on the state of the chakras.

3.   Mental layer: The mental layer is the third subtle energy body of the aura. It is linked to your solar plexus chakra. It indicates your cognitive processes and mental state, which makes it the seat of your thoughts. The standard color of this layer is bright yellow.

4.   Astral layer: When you hear of a spiritual cord connected to everything in the universe, the astral layer is the first thing that should come to mind. It is where you form the thread that connects you with every other being. This subtle body usually is bright pink with a rosy tint. And is connected to your heart chakra. You can get information about interpersonal relationships by reading the astral layer colors.

5.　　　Etheric template: An etheric template is a nonphysical form of your body. It contains the blueprint of your material body on the physical plane. Everything that happens on the physical level is recorded in your etheric template. The color may vary from person to person. The throat chakra is associated with this layer.

6.　　　Celestial layer: This is the sixth layer away from your physical body. It is linked to the third eye chakra. The celestial layer carries powerful vibrations, so the third eye is the seat of intuition. It is your connection to the Divine and all other higher-dimensional beings. This layer typically has a pearly white color.

7.　　　Ketheric template: The Ketheric template is about 3 feet from the body. It is the layer where you can become one with the universe. It contains every information about your foregoing lifetimes. Of all the auric layers, this one has the most potent and most powerful vibrations. It is connected to the crown chakra, with a golden color.

Your aura can change, depending on the events of your life. Still, most people always have two primary colors around them. Sometimes, an inauthentic color may even appear around a person's aura. That happens because of environmental issues or programming. For instance, being in a stressful relationship can add another color to your aura for the relationship duration.

Also, your emotional and physical experiences impact the colors in your aura. Suppose you have a severe case of acute pain. There, your aura's colors may change to reflect that. Having a hangover can also change your auric colors.

Despite all these, some colors usually are part of everyone's aura. These colors represent different things in different people, particularly when they appear with other colors. Interestingly, their meanings also change based on their tone and shade. The bright orange color in the auric field has a different interpretation from a dark orange color.

You must keep this information in mind when reading your aura or that of another person. Here are the most common colors in the aura and their respective meanings. Note these colors aren't in order, and they can appear in any of the seven subtle energy bodies.

• Yellow: Yellow means creativity, friendliness, and relaxation. You can find this in the aura of an individual who is curious and highly interesting. A yellow aura represents a busy mind. Someone with this aura color always has something going on in their head. To deal with this, you will find them immersing themselves in things such as baking, sewing, interior design, painting, and other practical forms of art. This color concentrates strongly on joy and is typically found around intelligent people.

• Green: Green in a person's aura indicates compassion, healing energy, divine wisdom, and a natural connection to Mother Earth. It is the color you find around the auras of energy healers. People of this color are innovative, logical, and visionary. They tend to live in their reality. They have a knack for solo activities due to their lone-wolf nature. A green aura means that the person is nurturing, social, and a great communicator.

• Red: Red in an aura symbolizes materialism. It is a color centered upon the material realm. Individuals with red in their auras like to think and do. They are strong and assertive, making them suitable for leadership positions. They are also risk-takers and are intrinsically motivated in life. They love to win, which is why this color is common among professional athletes and CEOs. Red-aura people also love intense activities.

• Purple: Conversely, auric purple represents intuition, creativity, and emotions. That explains why purple is the color of the third eye chakra, the intuition seat in the energy system. If you find purple in your aura, it means you take spiritual evolution seriously. It also indicates that you are gentle and spiritually enlightened.

• Blue: A blue aura can be called the complete opposite of a red aura. Just like red, blue represents compassion. But it also represents a tendency to shy away from the spotlight. People with this color in their aura are selfless by nature, which explains why it is common among teachers, nurses, caregivers, etc. Empaths typically have blue auras.

The above are the most common colors you would typically find in people's auras. Some people have more peachy colors, such as pink, orange, peach, in their field. Colors like these symbolize a sort of creativity quite peculiar. They also focus significantly on relationships, fun, and companionship. To people with peachy auras, family and friends are everything.

Knowing the meanings of the aura colors is not quite as important as seeing the aura itself. To read your aura, you need to learn how to see it first. Now, you can either perceive the aura through your clairvoyance or intuition.

For you or anyone else to sense or perceive the aura, some level of self-awareness is necessary. You must be perceptive enough to understand the end of the self and the beginning of another.

Otherwise, your perception and interpretation of someone's aura may be your perception of them.

Put simply; you must develop the ability to see through yourself to see someone else's energy field. You have your energy field, meaning you perceive yours first before seeing other people's. If you don't learn to make a discernment, you may read your aura as that of another person.

Intuition Ability

When Keysha's niece, Sierra, had a child, Keysha was thrilled. Finally, she got to be a great auntie! Keysha lived a hefty seven hours away, but when she visited her family in Galveston, she was always ready to babysit. She adored her grand-niece, Faith, but was in full disbelief when, one day, she found out that Faith, now five, had just been diagnosed with a rare form of leukemia.

Because of her job, Keysha wasn't able to get back to Texas in the early days of Faith's treatments. She kept in contact with her girls, who helped, but her heart was always with both Faith and Sierra. Often, Keysha would find herself staring into space or at a blank wall, and even at the back of a work partner's head. She lost time this way. Once, when asked if she was all right, it took her a few moments to be able to answer.

In her mind, Keysha had been in the hospital room with Faith and

Sierra. She could have told you detail about the place: the way the room's trim didn't quite get along with the wall color, the layout of the furniture and the machines—the way the window sill was cluttered with flowers and stuffed animals, the view from the window. She even had a feeling of where different things were located concerning the room: the common waiting area on the floor, the women's bathroom, the vending machines, and even the nurse's station.

Keysha realized she'd been doing this for weeks. She could even envision the nurses. A part of her had been there with the girls the whole time, and it was exhausting.

What Keysha was experiencing was called a soul tie. Soul ties can cause you to have unconscious reactions. In Keysha's case, it had become physical, too. She had begun clenching her teeth so hard in the night that a tooth abscessed and eventually had to be pulled out.

As soon as she was able, she visited her family in Galveston. She was surprised to find the details of the hospital were very close, if not dead on, to what she'd envisioned in those bouts of lost time. Even more, Keysha found out that her other niece, with whom she'd been close, too, had to have a tooth pulled because—yes— she'd been grinding her teeth so much that it had abscessed at the root.

In most of the phases, people don't mean to create soul ties with intuition. It's not an intentional, malicious thing, even though it can have negative effects on their partner. It's up to the intuitive to recognize the signs and take steps to free themselves from the aspects of the relationship that are unhealthy. Letting go of a soul tie to a person doesn't mean you must disappear from her life; it means that when you are present; you are your whole thriving self.

Signs You Might Be Intuitive

• As an adult, you catch yourself losing time. You may not immediately know what you were thinking about, as you weren't actually daydreaming. When you try to access what you'd been thinking about, it's real people and situations, feelings and places, not fiction or fantasy.

• You are often struck by the beauty of things that go unseen by most people and can easily access stories about their origins.

• Patterns of abstract things, like emotions and events, emerge easily for you.

• When talking a friend through a problem, you know the right questions to help them untangle their emotions and thoughts.

• You are unintentionally aware of others' schedules.

• You sometimes forget to look at a person's appearance when you're interacting with them. It's usually a secondary thought, as your primary attention was on something else about them. Sometimes, you have no idea what they were wearing or carrying after they were gone, even though you had a face-to-face conversation with them that lasted ten minutes.

• Words can be hard to come by. If somebody asks you a meek question like, "Where did you put the tape?" Out of the blue and you weren't expecting it; you sometimes have great difficulty remembering words like "mud room" and "drawer."

Psychic Abilities Guide

- You experience setbacks, like traffic detours, long lines, or a store is closed, and you're able to let it go when other people might get mad. You figure you're not supposed to be where you thought you should be quite yet, and that it will all work out.

- You suddenly develop a new habit, like nail-biting or tapping your foot, and then see someone else doing it shortly after.

- You can find your way around a new town or building without much effort.

- Intuition can be a pleasant and useful gift, but keep aware of what belongs to you and what does not. Don't allow people to connect to you on a spiritual level without your consent and don't feel obligated to share your insights or your energy with just anyone.

Most Common Symbols and Meanings

There are signs and symbols to just about everything in life, such as the heart for love, flags for countries, dove for peace, and the superstitious black cat for caution. Symbols are used to represent an idea, belief, or action for something.

Your intuition will also receive communication symbols in psychic impressions about a place, person, object, or yourself. For example, sometimes when you dream at night you will receive a symbol to communicate an overall theme or aspect of your life such as dreaming you are caught in a spider web, which could mean you are feeling trapped or stuck.

As you develop your psychic ability, you will receive symbols clairvoyantly or clairaudient. You may see an image in your mind but aren't sure what the meaning is or how to interpret it. Other times you will just know what the symbol means. The symbols we receive psychically are rarely literal. Usually, symbols are 10% literal and 90% symbolic.

Symbols represent different meanings for each person so when you receive a symbol in a psychic impression, it's subjective and based on your own personal interpretation. Each psychic's interpretation of a symbol is very different and based on the person's background, belief system, and values. Also, one symbol may have many meanings and will change based on the person you read for.

For example, a student of mine was practicing giving a reading to her partner when all she could see was a red telephone booth on the corner of a sidewalk. Immediately her logic thought "London!" and thought her partner may have a connection to London. This would be a literal interpretation. However, as we broke it apart, we saw three symbols in this one image.

The color red which she interpreted as love; the telephone booth represented communication, and the placement of the telephone booth on the corner meant a crossroads. After she put all her interpretations together, she felt this symbol was a representation that her partner was at a crossroads, with an intimate relationship and communication concerns.

If someone else received this symbol of a red telephone booth at a crossroad, they may have a completely different interpretation. How would you interpret it? You may see colors, images, and symbols when you first meet someone, visit a place in meditation, or in your dreams. For example, you attend a business meeting and the symbol of an engagement ring pops into your mind when your boss addresses everyone. This could mean literally she is engaged or it could represent a new commitment in her life.

When you receive a symbol, there may be strong emotion with it. Pay attention to any feelings or emotions you may sense when you interpret the symbol. I once saw the symbol of a woman hidden behind a keyhole and felt a strong sense of loneliness and isolation. My partner confirmed her aunt was married to a controlling man who isolated her from the world.

As you work more with your intuition, write down common symbols you receive and create a symbols dictionary. Your subconscious mind will create a database for these symbols along with emotions, colors, and feelings associated with them, which will become easily accessible to you with time and practice.

There is no right or wrong interpretation of a symbol as this is personal and subjective. You can receive a ton of information in a symbol such as a timeframe, personal relationships with family/ friends/significant other, personality, interests, job, characteristics, location, age, and personal messages.

I remember my teacher telling me everything is contained in a symbol. Remember, the symbol may not always have the same feelings attached to it as it will change with who you are reading for but may relate to a general aspect of life.

Partner Symbols Reading Exercise

You should practice this exercise with a partner. Without saying anything, sit with your partner and feel free to close your eyes, and take a few deep breaths. Clear your mind and shift your awareness to your partner. As you begin to tune into your partner's energy, focus on any symbols or colors that may appear.

Notice any physical sensations that arise when you see the symbol, subtle feelings, or emotions. When you are ready, open your eyes and share with your partner what you received. Write down in your journal what symbols or colors appeared.

Tarot Card Exercise

For this exercise, you can either have a physical deck of tarot cards or you can search online for images of tarot cards. Pick one tarot card and put it in front of you. Don't look for the meaning of the card in the book or online just yet. Get into a meditative state by focusing on your breath and clearing your mind. Take a couple of deep breaths to ground you and feel free to surround yourself with the universal white light. Once you feel relaxed and open, focus your energy on the card and notice what sensations, feelings, or symbols appear intuitively.

Write down your impressions and then feel free to compare your impressions with the actual card meaning. Remember, even if the card has a specific meaning, you can include your own interpretation to it as well.

Symbols Exercise

Concentrate on the following symbols and write down both your literal and subjective interpretation of each.

1.   Ocean waves.

2.   Golden retriever dog.

3.   Rose.

4.   A gold watch.

5.   The color green.

Add your interpretations of these symbols to your symbols dictionary and use them for reference when necessary.

Reading Symbol/Psychic Readers

Signs and Symbols can serve as a wonderful tool when connecting on either a psychic or medium level. Many psychics and mediums use signs and symbols to help in their communication and interpretation of the information they are receiving. A sign or symbol has a representation, a meaning attached to it. As a lightworker, you would catalog your signs and your symbols and set a particular meaning to them. Perhaps you are shown a rose and a rose would either represent a relationship of a family member, such as a grandmother. Perhaps it represents someone's name. It could have a literal meaning of an actual rose or raised garden. It may simply be a symbol for a token of affection or love. The meaning behind the rose is unique to the psychic or medium. As you cross paths with signs and symbols, you can develop your personal encyclopedia of their meanings. Each time you receive a sign, or a symbol asks yourself "

What does this mean to me?" The important aspect is not to go with what everybody else thinks it means, but to be true to what meaning it represents for you. This is important so when Spirit or your higher self is trying to connect and communicate, they will use those signs and symbols to create a form of dialogue to convey those messages to you.

Another example would be a key. Many people feel that a key represents opportunity or a new car, perhaps a new home. Others would see a key as representing success. A key could symbolize a new beginning, letting go, or a need for safety and security. As you can see, a simple key has many possible explanations as to its potential meaning. This is why understanding what this means to you will help you connect it to the recipient as it becomes a form of language. Many psychics and mediums will use these signs and symbols to validate to a sitter that their loved ones in spirit are connecting with them and giving them those signs and symbols as a way to show them they are present.

When connecting on either a psychic or medium level, always go with the literal meaning of a sign or symbol first. You would be surprised at how often there is a literal meaning rather than a figurative one attached to that sign or symbol. A lot of readers will immediately jump to a symbolic meaning first out of fear that their logical mind has played a cruel trick on them by giving them something unique. They tell themselves "that can't be real, it must be a symbol." Perhaps you see an eagle and you think that it's not possible for the sitter has an eagle or any connection to one, so you immediately change the reference to "I see an eagle and for me, that's my symbol for a new sense of freedom." Take a chance and FIRST say. "I am seeing an eagle." "Would you understand the connection to an eagle?" Internally and simultaneously ask your compass, "Do they have a pet eagle?" "Did they save one?" and "Are they an eagle scout?" "Are they an Eagles football fan?" By having the courage and willingness to put it out there directly, you are learning to trust your connection and that literal meaning may just be something like " Oh my goodness, we saved an eagle we found last week and felt such joy when we were able to help it fly away." Perhaps there is a loved one in spirit that was showing you the eagle to let you know that they are aware of this random act of kindness that their family did, and they wanted to make sure they knew they were still among them.

Options are endless with signs and symbols and what they could mean, but with practice and attunement, you will be able to discern if that sign or symbol is literal or figurative. You will also learn how to determine if it's from someone in spirit or connected to the sitter in a more psychic capacity. Each time you see something that catches your eye; think about what that means to you. Lock and load that internal response and catalog the meaning as you move forward. Establish as many signs and symbols as you can to help you convey the messages of those loved ones and the higher self. Below are a few exercises to help you create your symbol encyclopedia; however, it's important to remember to always go literal first when conveying the image you are being shown!

Symbol Journal

Keep a journal and start to log if you have symbols that pop up for you and write the symbol and the meaning. Start to build a catalog of any symbols that you see. Keep this with you during the day.

Psychic Abilities Guide

Common Signs of Awakening

The period of psychic awakening can be an exciting and magical time in your life. But, it can also become uncomfortable and confusing. If you know what is going on, the process becomes less worrisome and more magical, as it should be. That said, below are some of the mutual signs that help you to tell if you have the gift.

A Strange Tingling in Between Your Eyebrows

If you feel a strange tingling sensation, it may be because your third eye is starting to develop. The third eye area is found between your eyebrows. You may feel the tingling sensation in this area, near your chakras, or at the crown of your head.

The tingling may occur for two reasons. First, it could be a sign that you are beginning to pick up energetic signals. Second, it is also possible that your chakras are starting to open up.

Psychic Abilities Guide

It will feel strange, especially at the early stages of development. The sensation can be very strong, but know that it will eventually subside. There is nothing to fear, as this is completely harmless.

A Stronger Connection with the Spirit World

Another sign that you may have a gift is that you possess a stronger sensitivity to the spirit. This simply means it may become much easier for you to sense the presence of someone from the other side, such as a loved one who has already passed away. It is also possible for you to sense the presence of other spirits. If it is not your loved one, it could be someone else. It is quite natural for people who have experienced a psychic awakening to progress into becoming mediums.

A Growing Desire to Move Away from Negativity

When your psychic powers start to manifest, you may also become a little more sensitive to other people's emotions. You may pick up on what they are feeling, as if you were experiencing your own emotions. This ability is simply known as "empathic."

As your sensitivity becomes much more pronounced, it will be easy for you to feel drained. This experience may make you feel hesitant in terms of being around other people, especially those who seem too dramatic or negative. In such a case, it would be clever for you to respect what you are feeling. Regardless of your psychic ability, it is smart to steer clear of drama as much as possible.

A Growing Desire to Eat Healthily

You may suddenly feel health conscious. It could be that you are starting to realize that eating junk has taken a toll on your physical health. Or, it is also possible that you are feeling the need to eat healthier foods because of the changes that you feel as a result of your manifesting psychic power.

Intuitive work uses a higher frequency. When your intuition becomes more pronounced, you tend to vibrate at a high frequency, or at least, higher than normal. This will prompt you to crave foods that are also higher in vibration, which includes vegetables and the like. Such healthier sorts of foods can help ease the strain caused by the higher vibrations and prevent you from becoming weighed down. In fact, there is what is called a psychic diet specifically designed for this purpose.

An Increasing Appetite for Learning

People who experience a psychic awakening may also feel an increasing desire to learn. It is not just knowledge that you crave; you may also experience a growing desire for spiritual growth. This may mean that you will have a growing interest in books and everything that can help you learn about the things you still do not understand. Awakening can also make you want to take a more spiritual path.

More Frequent Dreams

Everyone dreams and people often dream about the people they are familiar with or people who they have seen in their everyday lives. You may have a dream or two that suddenly becomes manifested in real life. That is normal. However, if it starts to occur more frequently, it is a clear sign of psychic awakening and one that should not be ignored.

Psychic Abilities Guide

There is also a big alteration between normal dreams and the prophetic kind. Prophetic dreams tend to be more vivid, detailed, lucid, and compelling. When you understanding these kinds of dreams, it is recommended that you write about them. Keep track of these dreams so that you won't forget them. Take note of those dreams that actually manifested in real life after you dreamed about them.

Dreaming more often than usual is a symptom of psychic awakening. This is since while sleeping, you have no resistance. Logic usually stops your mind from exploring what defies it. However, while dreaming, your mind does not get in the way. You can receive messages, visions, and sensations intuitively.

When you are awake and receive one of these messages, you tend to consult logic. In the state of sleep, however, that kind of resistance is absent. This does not mean that all of your dreams are premonitions. It simply means that you are more receptive, such that it allows you to access different levels of consciousness.

An Increasing Physical Sensitivity

Another symptom of awakening is a heightened sensitivity of the senses. You may feel that your hearing ability has improved or that you have greater attention to detail. Becoming more sensitive is a clear sign that your senses are becoming stronger. This is a normal process that everyone goes through at the beginning phase of awakening.

Becoming More Intuitive

Seeing visions is not something that everyone can get used to easily.

It can be scary, especially if you are not yet prepared for it. That being said, it is actually a common sign of awakening.

For some people, intuitive hits are limited to the ability to sense when certain things are about to happen. This can cause anxiety, especially if the intuitive sense concerns a loved one. There is a good way to address this kind of situation. It is a matter of setting the intention that you are not to receive these kinds of intuitive hits for the things or events that you cannot alter. Spirit guides are actually considerate. In this case, the guides may honor your request.

More Frequent Headaches

Now, don't misunderstand. Some people get headaches due to medical reasons. In the case of frequent headaches, seeking medical attention is recommended to rule out other possible underlying causes. However, headaches are also a sign of awakening.

In the case of psychic awakening, headaches are experienced as the result of an influx of energy. This does not unpleasant that there is no remedy for this kind of headache. Simply soak your feet in warm water. This remedy will help lower your energy to the feet and away from the head. You can also add essential oils or Epsom salts to the warm water, as they are proven to increase relaxation.

A Developing Ability to Know Something before Anyone Else

Some people have the habit of informing their family and friends about certain experiences they are going to have. This may include information about specific circumstances and dangers. Do you have this habit? Are your hints of warning more often true than not? If you responded yes to these questions, then you are definitely going through the awakening process.

The habit could make logical sense, since you may know your family and friends well enough to be able to predict some of the things that happen to them, both the good and the bad. Because you know their plans, habits, and personalities, it is only logical to assume that you are quite capable of making reasonable guesses. However, psychic awakening is more than that.

The type of knowledge that comes with a psychic awakening is indicated by a strong feeling that usually comes out of the blue. This knowledge is not merely based on whatever you know about the person or what is bound to happen to them. In the phase of awakening, these feelings are so strong that you feel compelled to share them with others.

Knowing Things Before They Happen or As They Happen

It can be something as simple as knowing the phone is going to ring before it actually does, or knowing who is on the other end before you even pick it up. People usually refer to this as mere coincidence. This can also occur when a certain call is expected. When you can sense a totally unexpected call from a random person, however, then you cannot dismiss your intuition with a logical explanation.

Rather than a simple coincidence, it could be precognition—and you are possibly a psychic!

The Déjà Vu Experience

Have you ever gone to a friend's house for the first time, but felt a sense of familiarity with the place? This is called the "déjà vu" experience. It happens when you know you have not been in that place before and yet you know tiny details about it. This is usually a fleeting feeling, but if you can catch it, it may be enough to convince you of your gift.

A Heightened Perception

Some people are naturally perceptive to people and things. It does not take much for such people to figure out information about a certain object or a specific person. All it takes is a few minutes, or a simple touch or look. This is completely natural.

However, if it feels like you know a lot of accurate details about a certain object or person at first glance or first contact, then it is a clear sign. This may mean you have extrasensory perception, also referred to as "psychometric." Not all people have it. It is limited to psychics.

When you experience some of these things, as well as a feeling of growth from within, then you should start acknowledging your gift. The process of awakening is usually accompanied by a feeling of tremendous change. Some things you used to feel were important may no longer seem as significant. When this happens, you are encouraged to go with it. It is the universe's way of putting you in your rightful place. All you need to do is trust.

The Prophecy

After 40 days of fasting and prayer, I asked the spirit to speak through me and to deliver a message for everyone that would read this book; I included. This channeled message is a form of automatic writing.

There is no time coming. The time is now. Your heart seeks for the end of suffering, an end of what you see and feel does not belong. The spirit knows the cycle and rhythms of the Divine, but the ego lacks understanding. What you see as oppression is the Divine strengthening you for battle. What you see as torture is the Divine sharpening your spirit. No change will come if you have convinced yourself that all things are good. War is not pretty, but at times necessary. Your oppressors are powerful only because you see yourself as weak. You do not get to love and light without destruction. The flowers don't bloom until the season of death passes. How long will you extend this season? When will you stand

and fight back? You have the tools to be warriors, and yet you use these tools for excuses to be weak. The light cannot shine on the path of victory if it hides behind the enemy.

If you genuinely sought a connection with the creator, you would see and feel your power. Reciting empty prayers and dressing for meetings in broken temples does not constitute a relationship with the creator. If the creator had a phone, would you call? What would you say? Would you be proud to speak of the way you perform and degrade yourself when you think you are unseen? How about your mission? Are you any closer to bringing change into this world, or have you gotten distracted with all the pretty deception laid before you by the enemy?

Those that carry the light, where have you gone? Where are your lanterns that are supposed to light the path for those sent to follow? Where are the signs that you have destroyed the systems and temples of the enemy? You should have the rubble of their buildings underneath your footsteps. Why are your sisters and brothers starving? Why are the children being taught to fight on the side of evil? Where are those that carry the light, are they no longer alive? Divinity is in this world. Divinity is within, but you have allowed the ego to shut down the works of God and work for the likes of the darkness. Do not pray to God to show up. God has shown up. God is inside the belly; you feed poison. God is inside the body that you hate and filled with chemicals to impress the enemy. God is inside the womb that you corrupt. God is inside of the mind you feed filth. God is in the lungs that you use to breathe death. God is inside of the men that you degrade. God is inside the women that you strike. God is inside the child you abandoned. Why do you cry out for God but work to destroy its presence when it shows up?

Where is your courage? Did you lose sight of your limited time on earth? Do you believe you will have a vessel forever, even though truth shows up every season to prove otherwise? The enemy is increasing in numbers because you're too busy looking through someone else's window. You have filled your time with distractions, complaining, and things that do not matter. Your enemy is powerful because you fall for the traps set before you. You have inherited the land, but yet you choose not to use it. Food lies at your feet, but you decide to slave for coins to buy what is not free. Do you not know how soil works? Water falls from the sky so that you may fill your cups, but you choose to slave for bottles that pollute your land. Trees were created to give you fresh air, but you choose to cut them down and suffocate. Do you not see that you are sick? Do you not see the error of your ways?

The enemy is powerful because you practice division. God gave colors for creativity, and yet you use them as a source of hate. Separation due to the amount of paper in your pocket makes no sense. Money is paper, and yet you have been easily convinced it does not grow on trees. You should separate well from evil, not paper from paper. Do you not see the ill mind behind this? You separate yourselves because of religion. God did not create religion. Any religion that carries a date of origin was never here at the beginning of creation. Creation has no age. Let nature be your religion. Let Love be your bible. You pray and worship to man, and your ways of life validate that. You give power to the enemy, and that is why it roams with strength. You fear truth and sleep with lies but somehow are left confused with the lack of honesty in the world.

You Cry for Change When You Are the One Chosen to Bring It

- Know that God is inside. When you accept this truth,

things will change. When you feel the warrior inside, you will be empowered to fight this war and win. When you know who you are, you will respect others because they also carry another piece of God within them. When you know who you are, you will stop poisoning your bodies. When you know who you are, you will break free from oppression. When you know who you are, you will join forces with one another and knock the enemy off its throne.

- You have come to this place many times before. Nothing here is new. This has all happened in another lifetime. Chance after chance to get it right and yet you still choose the path of darkness. To see the light, you must break the pattern, or the cycle will repeat. This is the bad dream where you keep running from the boogeyman. Now is the time you stop and face what keeps chasing you. Do not look for someone to save you; you must rescue yourself. The division does not work. Feeding the system leaves you weak. Following the blind will leave you lost. Until you rise, you will be a victim of what the enemy has built. You will drown in the sea of sorrow. You will burn in the fires set by man. You will cry out in hunger from the famine that the enemy has set in place to control you. There is no end down the path of darkness. If you choose to see peace, you must create it.

- The power you seek to bring change is within. When you ignite your strength, all things will open to a new phase. What will be destroyed will allow growth. Doesn't fear destruction, for it brings a new beginning? Celebrate when you see the system of the enemy failing and use it as a doorway to create something new. There is no more time left. The time of destruction that has been prophesied is now. Those that choose to be buried under the bricks of the enemy leave them be. Focus on your spirit. Feed the Spirit, starve the ego.

Protect your prophets, healers, and warriors, for they will lead, heal and fight for the light. Keep the children safe. Lead simple lives, for the earth, will soon be reset back to its original state. She is in her last trimester, and when the water breaks, all will be wiped out as new life is ushered in. If you don't learn the ways of the land, leave your egos behind, and return to nature, you will not survive the next wave that will hit.

What is soon to come is more potent than any virus, hotter than any fire, and more powerful than any earthquake ever felt. Those that carry the light will lead a new generation to tend to the land and the God within. Do not lead them astray for if so, the pattern will repeat. We must break the pattern and to do so, we must start within.

Psychic Power and Astrology

According to some experts, astrology influences the psychic abilities innate in a person. As each person is unique, astrology helps the person to identify which power may work well to his skills, personality, and tendencies. It comes to a point where we get confused over the things that we need to focus on in our lives. Astrology guides us to the right path so we can focus on things that will be beneficial to us in the long run.

Once you have accredited that you have a certain psychic power (all humans have) tapping on that power becomes easier when you know your astrological sign.

Here are the details to help you decide which psychic power you are most good at:

- Aries: You are naturally good at discovery. You tend to

always be at the right place and at the right moment. Your psychic ability should be related to discovering something that should be of significant value tomorrow. For example, you pass by an alley and you found a bar where an indie band is playing a beautiful song. Your discovery of this band will most likely bring forth success to your industry tomorrow.

- Taurus: Invisible boundaries never escape a Taurus. Their psychic power lies in the deep and profound understanding of relationship borders. This is exactly the reason why Taurus people normally enjoy a life without conflicts. Taurus knows it right away when someone is trying to break into their own borders and when their peace is disturbed; they confront the person boldly before damage is created. The psychic ability of the Taurus lies in their ability to see these invisible barriers which most people fail to see and so when these people cross these boundaries, conflicts arise save for the Taurus.

- Gemini: Gemini knows what to say and when to say the words. Their senses are acute and powerful that a sixth sense becomes insignificant to them. They are good speakers. Words just come out of their mouth and people will be left dumbfounded by how accurately they can express the words. Gemini just knew what they have to say.

- Cancer: The psychic powers of a Cancer lie in their strong gut. They can feel what is going to happen. Their strong senses are able to feel what others are feeling. They are very emphatic. They can say when a person is about to explode because of anger and so even before that happens, Cancer has created a countermeasure.

- Leo: Leos believe that there is time for everything. Their psychic ability is in their perception of time. Whenever they do something, it is just the perfect timing. If they arrive late in a meeting it is because they are meant to arrive late. Leos have a strong perception of time. They know when to make their move, plan something, speak, and they know when to arrive at a scene.

• Virgo: Disaster prediction is the specialty of the Virgos. They sense danger even before it starts. Doctors who are intuitive under the sign of Virgo can very well identify and give an accurate prognosis on a disease even before a complete diagnosis. Virgos are naturally clairvoyant. They can sense which place will boom next and will be more likely good for their future family. They can invest in something that will be useful later. They can predict what a building will look like in the future.

• Libra: People born under this sign can read the other person and understand them better than they understand themselves. They read people very accurately. They can predict what the other person is about to do, as well as the motives of that person. Unfortunately, people born under the sign of Libra tend to focus outward and fail to see themselves. Their sense of self is blinded by their power to perceive other people correctly. This is why these people tend to lose their self-worth when they enter into serious relationships.

• Scorpio: Scorpios have the psychic ability to detect false and malicious intentions from those that are pure. They can detect who are flirts and those who are on the lookout for real affection and love. Their longing for deep affection fuels this ability. They can easily spot genuine people and those who are only after their own satisfaction.

• Sagittarius: People born under the sign of the hunter

429

know where to hunt for opportunities. They are natural positive thinkers. They easily find the right place where they can gamble without major risks. While other people gamble and risk away everything, Sagittarius people enjoy comfort in their own choice of opportunities. Whether it is love or business, they tend to pick the right choice most of the time.

• Capricorn: The psychic ability of the Capricorn is in their strong sense and innate understanding of the pace of life. While others start to feel bored, lose their momentum, quit their job, stop what they are doing and move out to someplace else, Capricorns maintain a steady pace in life. They know when to move, they know right away when to do a radical change in their life. Their growth is perfectly synchronized with that of life.

• Aquarius: Mindreading is certainly a psychic ability perfect for Aquarius people. Their ability to read the minds of people gives them the best advantage to get what they want in life. While other people demand to be told what other people really want, Aquarians know what you want right away. They also know exactly how to make you give in to their desires without them uttering the obvious words to you.

• Pisces: Among all zodiac signs, Pisces is the most psychic of all. They can see the real and broader picture. They know where all the puzzle pieces should be placed together. They can normally travel from one dimension to another and they can extract truths from their visions.

Protecting Your Energy

The most unsafe thing in the world to empathy is toxic people. Toxic people and toxic relationships drain empathy of their positive energy without offering anything but negative energy in return. To avoid or escape toxic relationships, you first need to learn to recognize them.

In this stage, we will discover the traits of the various types of toxic relationships: the codependent relationship, the abusive relationship, and the parasitic relationship. Then, we will look at how to carefully and kindly remove you from such relationships and discover some tips for avoiding such relationships in the future.

Codependent Relationships

The codependent relationship is a relationship in which you define yourself by your relationship with the other person. You might be a spouse, mother, sister, brother, father, son, or friend. Whatever you are, you see that as your primary identity, and should that person for some reason leave or pass on, you feel you would have nothing and no identity.

Again, this goes beyond the normal amount of grief one would feel at the loss of the other person. Instead, you feel hopeless at the thought of losing this person.

This type of relationship is marked by a few signs, which are as follows. First, you feel at ease only around this other person, and if he/she leaves the area where you are, you begin to feel incredibly uncomfortable. Second, you feel happiest in life when you are helping this other person, so much so that you prefer to be helping him/her than doing anything else in the world, even taking care of yourself. Third, you would do anything for this person, especially if threatened with him/her leaving the relationship.

As you might have fathomed, this is a toxic relationship because it gives you no time or energy for caring for yourself. You are constantly thinking about the other person in the friendship or relationship. You forego self-care for this person's sake and, as a result, you begin to wither. This makes you desperate for purpose, which you take to mean you need to invest more in this relationship, which drains you more. It is an endless and vicious cycle.

Abusive Relationships

Abusive relationships can manifest in various ways: emotional, physical, verbal, sexual, neglectful, etc. These types of relationships are characterized by the putting down of one of the individuals in the relationship, likely the empathy. This can be done through calling the empathy names, forcing sexual intimacy with the empathy, hitting or kicking the empathy, or implying a lack of worth in the empathy.

The emotionally abusive relationship is the type of abusive relationship that is the hardest to define but also is the one in which most empathy finds themselves. In many ways, this is a relationship of manipulation. It might be as overt as the other person saying something like, "If you can't _____ for me then you are nothing to me!" or it might be as sly as the other person asking, "Don't you love me? Why won't you _____ then?"

Abusive relationships confuse the empath, especially with their general sense of responsibility, whenever something goes wrong in a relationship. You might begin to doubt your self-worth because of emotional or verbal abuse, or you will berate yourself for not wanting to be intimate with your partner in cases of sexual abuse. You may think, "Surely, he/she is just expressing love for me, and I cannot accept it," right? This is not the case, I assure you.

Your worth is not wrapped up in what the other person communicates or thinks about you. You are far worthier of affection than the manipulating standards that have been set by your partner. You are far more precious than the measure of your acts of kindness toward your best friend. You are far more capable of love than just the care you can show in one relationship. You are an empath: you feel deeply and express emotion in ways that many people could not hope to do in their entire lives.

If you are in an abusive relationship, it is important to get help from trusted friends or family, or even law enforcement.

Parasitic Relationships

Psychic Abilities Guide

Parasitic relationships are another form of toxic relationships. Remember, first of all, that being in a parasitic relationship and being in an abusive relationship or a codependent relationship are not mutually exclusive. The parasitic relationship, however, has different signs for which you can watch.

First, parasitic people never ask about your well-being, nor do they show any signs of interest in your life. Your conversations are always about their lives and concerns, and should the conversation turn to your life, they will quickly interject how something from their own lives relates and use that as a platform to continue speaking about them. You know instinctively never to call these people when you need help or someone to listen to your struggles.

Second, in parasitic relationships, you always feel drained. You, the empath, feel like the other person is sucking the energy and life out of you, which, in fact, is the case. The parasitic person exchanges his/her negative energy for your positive energy and thereby replaces any spiritual positivity you might have had with despondency, fear, anxiety, depression, and despair.

Third, the parasitic person often does not have any other friends, or if he/she does, the other friends are also empathetic. This is because most parasitic people latch onto those of whom they can take advantage. Other than empathy, most people will not put up with the one-way nature of the relationship with these parasitic individuals for long. Thus, if you are someone's only or best friend despite the fact that he/she knows next to nothing about you, you can be sure that you are in a parasitic relationship.

Avoiding and Exiting Toxic Relationships

Most empathy, as you might suspect, can spot a parasitic, abusive, or codependent person a mile away. The reason they become blinded is that they are caught up in problem-solving and the desire to heal and do not remember to guard themselves and protect their energy.

The first line of protection when facing a potential codependent, abuser, or parasite is to take a moment to evaluate the spiritual energy that you are receiving from this person. Is the energy of a codependent, abusive, or parasitic personality? Are they overly needy, jealous, possessive, or manipulative? If so, take a moment to decide to hold back. Use the few seconds before entering a conversation with them to decide whether to withhold your full energy from the interaction. Refrain from engaging at all if possible, but if not, keep the conversation at the level of small talk, and do not offer more of your energy than is necessary.

A second line of defense is to keep your life filled with positive people. That is, fill your time and your schedule with positive relationships and kind people so that you will literally have no time for the codependents, abusers, and parasites that seek to eat up your energy and your life. Empaths have a very difficult time lying or misrepresenting the truth, so you will need a legitimate excuse if you want to get out of a potential commitment to a toxic relationship. What better way to excuse yourself than to fill your life with good energy and positivity?

One thing you need to keep at the forefront of your mind in these toxic interactions is that "helping" these people actually hurts them. It allows them to unload without consequences to themselves. Codependents will never develop a true sense of self, and should you ever need to leave for some reason or another without warning, you would leave the codependent feeling debilitated and disabled. Ignoring the warning signs of an abusive person reinforces his/her idea that his worth far outweighs your own and allows him/her to carry those ideas to the rest of his/her interactions. Allowing a parasitic person to use you tells him/her that other people do not matter, keeping them from the type of intimacy that we all desire deep-down because they cannot recognize the two-way flow of a good relationship. You must realize that your "helping" these types of people is truly only hurting them, and this will help remove the blinders that your desire to heal puts on you. Healing comes through tough love sometimes, and you need to know when that is the case.

Of course, even the most vigilant empath may fall into a toxic relationship. It is important to remember that it is not your fault. In the case that you need to leave a toxic relationship, however, the best option is gracious honesty. To the parasite, you might say something like, "I feel like this relationship is very one-sided." To the abuser, you might tell, "I love you, but your actions and words hurt me, so I need some space to rebuild myself." To the codependent, you might say, "It seems like we have gotten our identities all mixed up together, and I think it would be good for both of us to find our own selves for a little while." Being honest while maintaining a sense of kindness and respect will keep you from feeling the guilt you would if you gave a reason that was false or misconstrued. Honesty is the only way to free you from these relationships.

A psychic guide eliminates the confusion and frustration that arises when trying to contact a psychic. It stretches you the gears you need to make sense of your own thoughts, emotions, and feelings

CONCLUSION

through a variety of methods such as meditation, picking up on vibes, astrology readings, or tarot cards. You can also get in trace with your intuition by using things you already have in your possession such as tea leaves or coffee grounds.

Psychic ability is one of the most important abilities you can have. It can increase your confidence, reduce anxiety to give you a more in-depth understanding of yourself. It will also help you to achieve enlightenment and answer real questions from deep inside yourself by interpreting your dreams or visions, as well as direct communication with a spirit, which gives even greater insight into the meaning behind things.

But psychic ability may be difficult to acquire easily because we've been trained not to trust our senses, especially our thoughts and feelings. We're told not to listen to our inner voice.

Psychic Abilities Guide

But if you don't believe in psychic ability, it will remain hidden, perhaps even forever. And even if you believe in your "insane" intuitive talents, you will never be able to see their manifestation. If you want the full effect of psychic ability, how can it be given to you? The answer is as follows: psychic ability can be achieved by using the techniques mentioned below as a guide which are absolutely step-by-step instructions used to achieve your goals.

The first thing to do is to start with meditation because this technique helps you to relax and open up your mind. It's important that you pay attention and concentrate on what's happening around you. Do not push your concentration, let it come naturally. Usually, after an hour or two of meditation, your head will feel clearer than ever before. You will also be able to discern things you have never been able to sense before and this is where psychic abilities begin. So sort sure you put pen to the paper down entirety that pops into your head while meditating so that later on you can interpret it correctly by using an astrology chart or tarot cards (you can find a lot of free online tarot card readings).

Now you have to pay attention to the way you feel. The easiest way of undertaking this is by concentrating on your dreams and visions. A lot of us already do this whether we realize it or not, so no need to force ourselves. Simply get a pen and paper and write down everything that comes to mind about your dreams. If you don't remember everything, no worries! Just take the parts that appear in your mind's eye most clearly and use them as a springboard for other areas of your life that are unclear to you.

Understanding these dreams will give you a greater understanding of yourself as well as help you when interpreting future ones. You should also read tarot cards and do some research on things that you are unsure of, like past life memories, etc. One way of getting a good grasp on these is to ask a loved one to ask you about them while you are having a conversation. This will put your thoughts into words as well as give you more profound insights into the meaning behind situations in your life.

These steps will really help to clear up your mind and get rid of any confusion or self-doubt which can block intuition from manifesting fully.

CPSIA information can be obtained
at www.ICGtesting.com
Printed in the USA
BVHW031704090922
646658BV00008B/411